# REVIEW OF MEDICAL NURSING

Norma H. Ercolano
R.N., B.S., M.S.
Associate Professor of Nursing
Nassau Community College

# Review of
# MEDICAL NURSING

**McGRAW-HILL BOOK COMPANY**

New York  St. Louis  San Francisco  Auckland  Bogotá  Düsseldorf
Johannesburg  London  Madrid  Mexico  Montreal  New Delhi  Panama
Paris  São Paulo  Singapore  Sydney  Tokyo  Toronto

**Library of Congress Cataloging in Publication Data**

Ercolano, Norma H.
    Review of medical nursing.

    Bibliography: p.
    1. Nursing—Examinations, questions, etc. I. Title. [DNLM: 1. Nursing—Examination questions. WY18.3 E65r]
RT55.E7      610.73'076      78-15051
ISBN 0-07-019541-2

**NOTICE**

Medicine is an ever-changing science. As new research and clinical experience broaden our knowledge, changes in treatment and drug therapy are required. The editors and the publisher of this work have made every effort to ensure that the drug dosage schedules herein are accurate and in accord with the standards accepted at the time of publication. Readers are advised, however, to check the product information sheet included in the package of each drug they plan to administer to be certain that changes have not been made in the recommended dose or in the contraindications for administration. This recommendation is of particular importance in regard to new or infrequently used drugs.

**REVIEW OF MEDICAL NURSING**

Copyright © 1979 by McGraw-Hill, Inc. All rights reserved. Printed in the United States of America. No part of this publication may be reproduced, stored in a retrieval system, or transmitted, in any form or by any means, electronic, mechanical, photocopying, recording, or otherwise, without the prior written permission of the publisher.

1 2 3 4 5 6 7 8 9 0 K P K P 7 8 3 2 1 0 9 8

This book was set in Helvetica by Offset Composition Services, Inc. The editors were Laura A. Dysart and Sally J. Barhydt; the designer was Anne Canevari Green; the production supervisor was Robert C. Pedersen.
Kingsport Press, Inc., was printer and binder.

# Contents

Preface vii

Instructions to the reader xi

| | | |
|---|---|---|
| **UNIT 1** | Stress and adaptation and the nursing process | 1 |
| **UNIT 2** | Nursing care of the patient with terminal cancer | 15 |
| **UNIT 3** | Nursing care of the patient with an infectious disease | 33 |
| **UNIT 4** | Nursing care of the patient with fluid and electrolyte imbalance | 53 |
| **UNIT 5** | Nursing care of the patient with a skin disorder | 77 |
| **UNIT 6** | Nursing care of the patient with a disorder of the blood | 89 |
| **UNIT 7** | Nursing care of the patient with a disorder of cerebral function | 113 |
| **UNIT 8** | Nursing care of the patient with a disorder of body movement | 137 |

| UNIT 9 | Nursing care of the patient with an endocrine disorder | 161 |
| UNIT 10 | Nursing care of the patient with a gastrointestinal disorder | 187 |
| UNIT 11 | Nursing care of the patient with a hepato-pancreatic disorder | 207 |
| UNIT 12 | Nursing care of the patient with a cardiovascular disorder | 225 |
| UNIT 13 | Nursing care of the patient with a respiratory disorder | 249 |
| UNIT 14 | Nursing care of the patient with a renal disorder | 263 |

Bibliography 283

# Preface

This *Review of Medical Nursing*, one of a series of four books, contains over 645 multiple-choice questions and the answer, rationale, and related reference(s) for each question. Every unit is preceded by cognitive objectives from which the questions are derived. Although some questions relate to anatomy and physiology and to the pathophysiology of select medical disorders, the bulk of the questions relate to nursing care. Highlights of the book thus include questions relating to the role of the nurse in preparing and caring for patients having specific diagnostic tests, in identifying pertinent signs and symptoms, in administering medications, and in performing various nursing skills. Questions that relate to dietary teaching, preparing the patient for discharge, and caring for the terminally ill patient have also been included in this review book.

Theoretical content and study guides have been omitted since the reader should have acquired the basic knowledge in medical nursing before attempting to answer the questions. However, to assist the student in organizing study habits, unit headings designate the broad category of information to be tested. Each unit consists of cognitive objectives followed by a series of related questions. For each question the correct answer, the rationale for selecting it, and reference(s) are given. This combination of objectives, multiple-choice questions, rationale, and references is the prime advantage of this series.

The objective test has become a tool for determining upward mobility in today's society. Nursing has long used objective tests as a means of evaluating graduates of nursing programs for licensure. The objective test has been expanded to include evaluation of candidates for the Regents External Degree, for advanced standing in various educational programs, and for credit for continuing education. On the basis of these trends, proficiency in objective-test taking is mandatory. This series of reviews contains a battery of over 2500 objective questions in the four basic areas of nursing: medical, surgical, maternal-child, and mental health. The number and variety of questions will provide the student ample opportunity to gain this proficiency.

The authors believe that the objective test is an excellent diagnostic tool for self-evaluation. It enables the learner to identify specific areas of knowledge requiring further study. The learner is then required to utilize other resources. In addition, this series of reviews will be especially valuable to those who have mastered classroom content but cannot apply their knowledge in a testing situation.

The experience of the authors teaching in all types of basic nursing programs and in continuing education, plus their association with the New York State External Degree Program, enables them to identify and assess those aspects of nursing that are vital for the learner to have mastered. This series should be most beneficial to those nurses wanting to become more knowledgeable in their profession.

We wish to acknowledge our appreciation to Dr. Dolores Saxton, who recommended that we write this series. We are most grateful to Irene Elber for proofreading and typing our manuscripts in record time with a tender loving care that was far beyond what could be expected and to our families, whose patience and understanding made these books possible.

**Anna Desharnais**
**Norma Ercolano**
**Judith Green**
**Phyllis Haring**

My very special thanks to my mother, whose patience and concern for me have been endless, and to my sister, Irene, whose understanding and confidence in me have been immeasurable.

**Norma Ercolano**

# Instructions to the reader

Carefully read the objectives at the beginning of each unit before attempting to answer the questions. If you believe that you have achieved the objectives, you should be able to answer the related questions. If there are any objectives that raise doubts about your knowledge, refer to the appropriate text to refresh your memory.

Now you are ready to answer the questions. Each question is multiple-choice and consists of a stem and four possible answers, one of which is the correct answer. First you should recognize the critical element that is being tested in the stem of the question. Next you should evaluate the specific item (*a, b, c,* or *d*) that *best* represents the answer to the critical element. Please note that there is only *one* correct answer for each question.

The following are helpful hints for taking objective tests:

1. Know the terminology.
2. Read *each* word carefully.
3. Stick to the situation outlined. (Do *not* read into it.)
4. After reading the stem, answer the question in your own words, then select the one answer closest to yours.

5 Remember, the correct answer may be partially right but *never* partially wrong.
6 Unless stated, each question stands alone and should *not* influence the following questions.

At the end of each unit you will find the correct answer for each question, the rationale for that answer, and the appropriate reference(s) for further study.

**Good Luck!**

REVIEW OF MEDICAL NURSING

# UNIT 1
# Stress and adaptation and the nursing process

**OBJECTIVES**

To answer the questions in this unit, the reader should be able to
1. Identify the major categories of stressors;
2. Describe those factors that influence the individual's ability to adapt to stress;
3. Describe the defensive responses triggered by stress;
4. Describe the interrelationship of the physiological and psychological adaptations to stress;
5. Identify the components of patient assessment;
6. Formulate a nursing-care plan;
7. Identify nursing action to assist patients to resolve their problems;
8. Evaluate patients' responses to nursing care.

## QUESTIONS RELATED TO OBJECTIVES

*Instructions*: Choose the *one best* answer to the following questions.

1. An example of a universal experience shared by all humans is
   a Stress.
   b Sex.
   c Self-actualization.
   d Sibling rivalry.

2. Prolonged exposure to cold that results in frostbite is classified as which kind of stressful factor?
   a Chemical.
   b Physical.
   c Developmental.
   d Psychological.

3. Which of the following statements relating to stressors is true?
   a An individual can successfully cope with only one stressor at any given time.
   b Prolonged exposure to a stressor can eventually deplete the individual's energy resources.
   c Individuals respond alike when exposed to the same stressor.
   d Previous learnings and experiences have no significant effect on the individual's ability to adapt.

4. Which of the following statements relating to stress is true?
   a "Health" can be defined as an absence of stress.
   b An individual's adaptive potential is determined by the external environment.
   c Stress serves as a motivating factor to increase functioning and productivity.
   d Stress is present only when the individual must cope with an overt danger or threat.

**5** "Critical time" refers to that period in the life cycle in which an individual is unable to adapt to a stress. The factor that influences the critical time of an individual is
 **a** The developmental level of the individual.
 **b** The nature of the stressor.
 **c** Whether the stress is localized or generalized.
 **d** The effect of the immune reaction.

**6** Which of the following persons will probably make the best adaptation to stress?
 **a** 3-month-old infant.
 **b** 4-year-old child.
 **c** 29-year-old construction worker.
 **d** 63-year-old business executive.

**7** The inflammatory process is
 **a** Initiated only as a specific response to bacterial irritants.
 **b** An irreversible process that causes damage or injury to cells.
 **c** The body's most important defensive response to injury at a local level.
 **d** Antagonistic to tissue repair and the healing process.

**8** The substance that is initially liberated during the local inflammatory response is
 **a** Aldosterone.
 **b** Histamine.
 **c** Cortisol.
 **d** Norepinephrine.

**9** The exudate that is formed during the inflammatory response
 **a** Causes vasoconstriction and impairment of blood flow.
 **b** Brings to the area of injury the nutrients necessary for tissue repair.
 **c** Causes further damage to the injured cells.
 **d** Is high in bacterial toxins and low in white blood cells.

**10** The cells of the reticuloendothelial system that are responsible for providing the body with resistance to infection are the

   **a** Erythrocytes.
   **b** Megakaryocytes.
   **c** Basophils.
   **d** Reticulum cells.

**11** Which of the following hormones is decreased during the body's general systemic response to intense stress?

   **a** Insulin.
   **b** Growth hormone.
   **c** Antidiuretic hormone.
   **d** Aldosterone.

**12** Which of the following statements best describes the general adaptation syndrome?

   **a** The response is produced immediately by a minor chemical change that alters the pH of the blood.
   **b** The stage of exhaustion occurs after the individual has adapted to the stressors and has reestablished equilibrium.
   **c** The adrenocortical response decreases the blood levels of the adrenocortical hormones.
   **d** During the stage of resistance, the capacity to resist rises considerably above normal.

**13** One of the main functions of cortisol, which is released when the body is exposed to severe stress, is to *decrease*

   **a** Peripheral resistance.
   **b** Protein catabolism.
   **c** The inflammatory response.
   **d** Blood-sugar levels.

**14** The function of the mineralocorticoids during the general systemic response to intense stress is to
- **a** Convert glucose to glycogen.
- **b** Increase renal reabsorption of sodium.
- **c** Inhibit the inflammatory process.
- **d** Stimulate the vagus nerve.

**15** A common physiological effect produced during an acute stress response is increased
- **a** Peristalsis.
- **b** Blood sugar.
- **c** Gastric secretions.
- **d** Urinary output.

**16** Identify the true statement.
- **a** Functional illnesses are characterized by organic pathological changes.
- **b** Persons with psychophysiological disorders can consciously control the occurrence of symptoms.
- **c** Physical treatment of psychophysiological illnesses produce permanent alleviation of symptoms.
- **d** The autonomic nervous system plays a role in producing organic changes in psychophysiological illnesses.

**17** During acute anxiety states, the heart rate is increased and the blood pressure is elevated. These symptoms are caused by the effects of
- **a** Acetylcholine.
- **b** Cortisol.
- **c** Epinephrine.
- **d** Insulin.

**18** Which of the following statements relating to anxiety is true?
  **a** Moderate anxiety decreases an individual's capacity to learn.
  **b** Mental defense mechanisms inhibit the individual's capacity to adapt to psychological stress.
  **c** Sustained anxiety increases an individual's tolerance to pain.
  **d** Denial is a harmful mechanism if it is used as an immediate reaction to loss of a loved one.

**19** Mr. T. is a cardiac patient who refuses to take his medications or to adhere to a low-sodium diet. The defense mechanism he is using to cope is
  **a** Projection.
  **b** Rationalization.
  **c** Denial.
  **d** Reaction formation.

**20** The primary source of data collection in the assessment phase of the nursing process is the
  **a** Patient.
  **b** Family.
  **c** Physician.
  **d** Patient's chart.

**21** While interviewing Mr. K., the nurse states: "I understand that you are having problems voiding. Can you tell me more about it?" This is an example of
  **a** Paraphrasing.
  **b** Inference.
  **c** Open-ended statement.
  **d** Direct questioning.

**22** While taking a nursing history on Mrs. L., the patient states: "I feel so nervous today! I don't think I'll be able to cope with being in the hospital." The nurse responds by saying, "You're nervous about being admitted to the hospital." The nurse's response is an example of
- **a** Open-ended statement.
- **b** Reportorial response.
- **c** Summarizing.
- **d** Reflection.

**23** Mr. Jones is admitted to the Emergency Room complaining of shortness of breath and chest pain. The first action initiated by the nurses would be to
- **a** Interview the patient for a nursing history.
- **b** Assess his breathing and circulation.
- **c** Send to the Record Room for his old chart.
- **d** Consult the supervisor.

**24** An explicit statement that describes the patient's unmet needs or problems is referred to as a
- **a** "Patient assessment."
- **b** "Nursing diagnosis."
- **c** "Hypothesis."
- **d** "Nursing process."

**25** During the planning phase of the nursing process, the nurse would
- **a** Test the proposed nursing action and reassess the patient's problems.
- **b** Compare the data collected with acceptable standards or norms.
- **c** Select nursing action that will best achieve the objectives of care.
- **d** Modify the nursing-care plan as the patient's problems change.

**26** Which of the following actions by the nurse has the highest priority?
  **a** Changing a soiled colostomy dressing.
  **b** Suctioning an unconscious patient.
  **c** Restarting an IV that has infiltrated.
  **d** Measuring hourly output.

**27** During the implementing phase of the nursing process, the nurse would
  **a** Take a nursing history from the patient.
  **b** Define goals and objectives of care.
  **c** Share the plan of care with other members of the health team.
  **d** Determine what progress has been made toward the stated objectives.

**28** Teaching Mr. O. how to care for his arteriovenous shunt is an example of a nursing action performed during which phase of the nursing process?
  **a** Assessment.
  **b** Planning.
  **c** Implementation.
  **d** Evaluation.

**29** During the evaluation phase of the nursing process, the nurse would
  **a** Assess the patient's response to care and adjust the nursing-care plan as needed.
  **b** Collect baseline data and identify the patient's problems.
  **c** Identify the goals and objectives of care and predict possible outcomes.
  **d** Make a nursing diagnosis and establish priorities of care.

**30** Reviewing the patient's charts to determine the quality of patient care received is called a nursing
   a  "Audit."
   b  "Process."
   c  "Care plan."
   d  "Diagnosis."

## ANSWERS, EXPLANATIONS, AND REFERENCES

**1 a** Stress is a factor that is always present during an individual's life cycle. Each person, young or old, rich or poor, man or woman, black or white, is exposed to and responds to stress throughout the entire life cycle. (*Luckmann and Sorensen, p. 10.*)

**2 b** Extremes in temperature are a physical factor or stressor that strains people's capacity to adapt successfully. Prolonged exposure to cold elicits an alarm reaction by the body and triggers an activation of the adaptive processes. (*Luckmann and Sorensen, pp. 42, 43. Saxton and Hyland, p. 3.*)

**3 b** If a person is exposed to severe stress for a continued or a prolonged period of time, the body's ability to resist the stressor during the first and second stages of the general adaptation syndrome fails. The individual then enters the third stage (stage of exhaustion), which decreases the body's capacity to resist the stressor and depletes the energy reserves of the body. Death can result if the stressor continues to be unresolved. (*Selye, p. 64. Byrne and Thompson, p. 51.*)

**4 c** During the life cycle, stress is a powerful teaching tool. Stress is essential for life, is part of our daily living, and serves as a motivating factor to increase functioning and productivity. (*Saxton and Hyland, p. 6.*)

**5 a** According to Saxton and Hyland, "critical time" refers to that period during the life cycle when an individual is unable to adapt to a stress not because of the nature of the stress, but because of the developmental level of the individual. During this period of time, the normal tasks to be accomplished and the development process create stress and increases the individual's vulnerability to stress. (*Saxton and Hyland, p. 14.*)

**6 c** According to Beland, adaptability is generally greatest in youth and young middle life and least at the extremes of life. Infants and young children have a limited capacity to adapt because not all organs and systems are fully mature. In later years, the capacity to adapt declines. (*Beland and Passos, p. 66.*)

**7 c** Some of the responses utilized by the body to protect it from injury and damage include the immune response, the shift of fluids and electrolytes from one compartment to another, and the inflammatory response. The inflammatory response is the body's major and most important physiologic response to damage and injury at the local level. (*Luckmann and Sorensen, p. 150.*)

**8 b** Histamine is a substance released immediately upon tissue damage or injury. Its main function is to produce an increased blood flow and increased capillary permeability at the site of the injury. (*Vander, Sherman, and Luciano, p. 481.*)

**9 b** During the inflammatory response, there is increased capillary permeability, causing an increased passage of fluid called the "inflammatory exudate." This fluid dilutes bacterial toxins. It contains nutrients necessary for repair of damaged tissues and certain phagocytic cells. (*Luckmann and Sorensen, p. 152.*)

**10 d** The reticulum cells of the reticuloendothelial system are found in the spleen, liver, bone marrow, lymph channels, and lining of the blood vessels. These cells are the precursors of plasma cells that ultimately form the antibodies and phagocytic cells necessary to engulf bacteria. (*Luckmann and Sorensen, p. 144.*)

**11 a** Hormones that are increased during periods of severe stress include aldosterone, antidiuretic hormone, cortisol, and growth hormone. Recent studies indicate that insulin and the sex hormones are decreased. Insulin could possibly be antagonistic to the glucocorticoids. (*Vander, Sherman, and Luciano, p. 502.*)

**12 d** The general adaptation syndrome is characterized by a triphasic course. The phases are referred to as the "alarm phase," the "resistance phase," and the "exhaustive phase." In the alarm phase, resistance to the stressor falls below normal. The capacity to resist climbs above normal in the resistance phase. Resistance drops below normal in the exhaustive stage and irreversible damage or death can occur. (*Selye, p. 14.*)

**13 c** The general adaptation syndrome is the body's response to physical, chemical, microbiological, and psychological stressors. The high level of cortisol that is released during this response has an antiinflammatory effect on damaged tissue. (*Langley, Telford, and Christensen, p. 736.*)

**14 b** During overwhelming stress, the body reacts by triggering a systemic response. There is an increase of the adrenocortical hormones. The mineralocorticoids work specifically on the renal tubules and increase the reabsorption of sodium. (*Byrne and Thompson, p. 54. Vander, Sherman, and Luciano, p. 502.*)

**15 b** During periods of acute stress, there is an increase in the glucocorticoids, namely, cortisol. One of the effects of increased cortisol is an increased blood-sugar level. (*Moidel, Giblin, and Wagner, p. 282.*)

**16 d** Those organs innervated by the autonomic nervous system are usually the sites associated with psychophysiological illnesses. This relationship supports the belief that the autonomic nervous system is involved in producing organic changes in psychophysiological illnesses. (*Luckmann and Sorensen, p. 122.*)

**17 c** Epinephrine and norepinephrine are responsible for the stimulation of the effector organ sites of the sympathetic nervous system. The signs and symptoms of this stimulation include increased heart rate and increased blood pressure. (*Moidel, Giblin, and Wagner, p. 282.*)

**18 a** Mild anxiety increases an individual's ability to learn. However, during periods of moderate or severe anxiety, perception is decreased and learning ability is decreased. Attempts at patient teaching during this time can be ineffective. (*Mitchell, p. 222.*)

**19 c** Denial is a defense mechanism commonly used by persons who unconsciously refuse to acknowledge the existence of a severe illness. One way these persons learn to cope with the anxiety is to unconsciously refuse to adhere to the prescribed medical therapy. (*Mitchell, p. 224.*)

**20 a** The primary source of data collection needed for a systematic assessment of the patient can be obtained from the patient. The exception to this would be if the patient is unconscious, is aphasic, or is an infant or toddler. (*Mitchell, p. 84.*)

**21 c** An open-ended statement is a question that encourages elaboration by the patient. This is in contrast to a closed question, which elicits a yes-no response or a one-word response. An example of a closed question is, "Do you feel ill today?" The open-ended statement states, "Tell me how you are feeling today." (*Mitchell, p. 94.*)

**22 d** Reflection is a response that paraphrases what has been said by the patient. This response to elicit information allows the patient to elaborate without feeling threatened by the interviewer. (*Mitchell, p. 94.*)

**23 b** Chest pain and shortness of breath could be symptoms of an acute myocardial infarction. Since a myocardial infarction could be death-producing, examination and observation take precedence over all other methods of data collection. (*Mitchell, pp. 85, 104.*)

**24 b** A nursing diagnosis is an exact statement that describes the patient's unmet needs or problems and requires nursing assistance to resolve the problem. The statement usually is made after the data has been collected, analyzed, and interpreted by the nurse. (*Beland and Passos, p. 18.*)

**25 c** During the planning phase of the nursing process, the nurse formulates a written plan of care. The written plan includes realistic goals and objectives and describes what nursing action should be utilized to achieve the objectives. (*Shafer et al., p. 7.*)

**26 b** Maintaining a patent airway has the highest priority. If the brain is deprived of oxygen for more than 4 to 6 minutes, irreversible brain damage can occur. Seconds, not minutes, count. Not suctioning the patient immediately could be life-threatening. (*Mitchell, p. 143.*)

**27 c** Once the nursing-care plan has been written, it is essential that the plan be shared with all persons involved in the care of the patient. The use of written and verbal communications is part of the implementing phase of the nursing process. (*Beland and Passos, p. 18.*)

**28 c** Carrying out the proposed plan of care is part of the implementation phase of the nursing process. The nurse can administer direct patient care, or it can be delegated to other members of the health team. In many instances, the patient or the family can be taught how to administer the necessary care. (*Shafer et al., p.18.*)

**29 a** The final phase of the nursing process is evaluation. During this phase, it is important to assess how the patient responded to care, determine if the goals and objectives were achieved, and then modify the plan as needed. Members of the health team should then be notified of the change. (*Byrne and Thompson, p. 74.*)

**30 a** The nursing audit is currently being used by nursing service to measure the quality of patient care being given. A review of patients' charts is done to determine if the care given was adequate, safe, and appropriate for the problems identified. (*Shafer et al., p. 10.*)

# UNIT 2
# Nursing care of the patient with terminal cancer

**OBJECTIVES**

To answer the questions in this unit, the reader should be able to

1. List the characteristics of benign tumors;
2. Identify specific diagnostic tests used to detect cancer;
3. Identify the five stages of the grieving process;
4. Describe the nursing care of the patient receiving radiation therapy;
5. Describe the nursing care of the patient receiving antineoplastic chemotherapy.

## QUESTIONS RELATED TO OBJECTIVES

*Instructions*: Choose the *one best* answer to the following questions.

1. The term used to describe the process leading to the development of a tumor mass is
   a "Metaplasia."
   b "Neoplasia."
   c "Hyperplasia."
   d "Anaplasia."

2. The loss of cellular differentiation seen in some neoplasms is called
   a "Anaplasia."
   b "Metaplasia."
   c "Hyperplasia."
   d "Dysplasia."

3. When malignant cells leave the primary site and spread to other tissues via the blood and lymph nodes, the cancer is thus classified as a (an)
   a Premalignant lesion.
   b Cancer in situ.
   c Invasive cancer.
   d Metastatic cancer.

4. Which of the following statements *best* applies to benign tumors? They
   a Invade surrounding tissues.
   b Recur after removal.
   c Are encapsulated.
   d Grow rapidly.

5. Malignant tumors have the following characteristics: Cells
   a Are well differentiated and resemble the original cell.
   b Travel to distant organs to set up new tumors.
   c Grow by expansion in an orderly, restricted manner.
   d Tend to be encapsulated by a band of normal tissue.

**6** An example of a benign tumor is a
   **a** Glioblastoma.
   **b** Teratoma.
   **c** Melanoma.
   **d** Lipoma.

**7** A malignant tumor that originates from epithelial tissue is called a
   **a** "Papilloma."
   **b** "Sarcoma."
   **c** "Teratoma."
   **d** "Carcinoma."

**8** The term used to describe a malignant tumor of connective tissue is
   **a** "Osteoma."
   **b** "Sarcoma."
   **c** "Teratoma."
   **d** "Carcinoma."

**9** Which of the following statements is true?
   **a** Different individuals respond in a similar manner to the same carcinogens.
   **b** Dark-skinned individuals have a higher incidence of skin cancer than fair-skinned persons.
   **c** The incidence of cancer is highest in older persons.
   **d** Research has proven that human cancer is genetically transmitted.

**10** Which of the following carcinogens is also classified as a physical stressor?
   **a** Radiation.
   **b** Cigarette smoke.
   **c** Hormones.
   **d** Viruses.

**11** Which of the following practices is linked to the incidence of cancer?
   **a** Breast-feeding.
   **b** Circumcision.
   **c** Sunbathing.
   **d** Smoking of marijuana.

**12** Which of the following situations is most suggestive of cancer?
   **a** A sore in the mouth for 3 weeks.
   **b** Vomiting and diarrhea for 3 days.
   **c** Painful breasts prior to the onset of menses.
   **d** Hoarseness for 5 days.

**13** A diagnostic test that provides histologic information about the kind of lesion is a (an)
   **a** Biopsy.
   **b** Scanning procedure.
   **c** Endoscopic examination.
   **d** Ultrasonic echogram.

**14** Another name for the Papanicolau (Pap) smear is
   **a** Needle biopsy.
   **b** Frozen section.
   **c** Exfoliative cytology.
   **d** Culture and sensitivity.

**15** In preparing Mr. J. for a brain scan the nurse would
   **a** Administer the radioactive mercury by mouth $1\frac{1}{2}$ hours prior to the exam.
   **b** Assure the patient that the procedure is painless.
   **c** Isolate the patient for 24 hours after the examination.
   **d** Avoid using soap and water on the face.

**16** Patients who have received tracer doses of radioisotopes for diagnostic purposes
   **a** Require no special precautions in their care.
   **b** Are isolated for at least 1 hour following the test.
   **c** Should postpone bathing for 24 hours following the test.
   **d** Should discard urine in a special lead container.

**17** The most penetrating and the most damaging type of radiation emitted from radioisotopes is
   **a** Alpha.
   **b** Beta.
   **c** Gamma.
   **d** Infrared.

**18** Rapidly proliferating cells are particularly vulnerable to the effects of radiation. Examples of rapidly proliferating cells are cancer cells and cells of the
   **a** Muscles.
   **b** Kidneys.
   **c** Pancreas.
   **d** Intestinal mucosa.

**19** A toxic effect of excessive radiation exposure is
   **a** Impotency.
   **b** Polychythemia vera.
   **c** Renal failure.
   **d** Leukemia.

**20** Which of the following statements relates to the care of the patient receiving external radiation therapy?
   **a** Rubber gloves should be worn when emptying the bedpan.
   **b** Local applications of moist heat will soothe the irritated skin.
   **c** The patient should be instructed to avoid washing the skin in the area being treated.
   **d** Visitors will be allowed to visit for 1 hour at a time.

**21** Ms. F. is receiving cobalt teletherapy for carcinoma of the bladder. Ms. F. should be told
   **a** To use small amounts of talcum powder on the area being radiated.
   **b** That her husband may be with her while she is being radiated if he wears a lead apron.
   **c** To avoid contact with persons who have an upper respiratory infection.
   **d** That smoking is not permitted by visitors because radiation particles can be inhaled.

**22** An example of a sealed source of internal radiation is radioactive
   **a** Gold.
   **b** Phosphorus.
   **c** Radium.
   **d** Iodine.

**23** Mr. L. is being treated with radioactive gold for terminal lung cancer with pleural effusion. The half-life of radioactive gold is 2.7 days. The nurse should
   **a** Transfer urine into a lead container.
   **b** Use long-handled forceps when removing soiled linen from the bed.
   **c** Enforce the principles of time, distance, and shielding.
   **d** Use no special precautions when disposing soiled dressings from the puncture wound.

**24** In caring for a patient who is receiving therapeutic doses of radioactive phosphorus intravenously, the nurse would use
   **a** Special precautions if the patient vomits.
   **b** No special radiation precautions.
   **c** Paper eating utensils for the first 24 hours.
   **d** A metal can lined with plastic bags to collect soiled linen.

**25** The major source of radioactive contamination during care for a patient receiving therapeutic doses of radioactive iodine is
   a Urine.
   b Sputum.
   c Sweat.
   d Feces.

**26** Mr. B. vomited about 3 hours after receiving an oral therapeutic dose of radioactive iodine. Some of the vomitus spilled on the bed linen. The nurse should
   a Use rubber gloves to handle the soiled linen, place it in a plastic bag, and discard into a metal container.
   b Use no special precautions except meticulous hand washing because the radioactive iodine has been absorbed.
   c Use metal forceps to pick up the soiled linen and then send the linen to the laundry in a separate laundry bag.
   d Wear a lead apron and lead gloves to clean up the vomitus and discard the soiled linen into the laundry chute.

**27** An example of an antiemetic used to alleviate the nausea and vomiting associated with antineoplastic chemotherapy and radiation therapy is
   a Sodium Luminal.
   b Compazine.
   c Lomotil.
   d Atropine.

**28** Karen is a 21-year-old woman who has been told that she has inoperable cervical carcinoma. She avoids any mention of her illness, reassures the staff that she is feeling fine, and speaks openly about plans for her marriage. Karen is coping with her terminal illness by using
   a Conversion.
   b Denial.
   c Repression.
   d Transference.

**29** The nurses expressed concern about Karen's denial of her illness. They should
  **a** Allow Karen to use these defenses.
  **b** Encourage Karen to face reality.
  **c** Realize that Karen has an immature attitude.
  **d** Insist that the doctor speak to Karen again.

**30** While caring for Karen, who has had radium inserted vaginally for inoperable carcinoma, the nurse should be aware that
  **a** Perineal care should be given once a day.
  **b** Special precautions are needed for disposal of the patient's dishes and linens.
  **c** Urine must be collected in a special lead container.
  **d** Priorities of care should be established and administered as quickly as possible.

**31** One day Karen states: "I don't want Dr. L. caring for me anymore. He doesn't know what he's doing . . . he's not ordering the right medications and won't let me eat what I want." The nurse should realize that Karen is probably entering which stage of the grieving process?
  **a** Acceptance.
  **b** Depression.
  **c** Anger.
  **d** Denial.

**32** Which of the following statements relating to the grieving process is true?
  **a** During the bargaining stage, the dying person expresses anger and hostility.
  **b** Persons who are depressed and detached will have difficulty moving into the acceptance stage.
  **c** During the stage of acceptance, communications are predominantly verbal.
  **d** Once the patient states that he or she has no hope, death is usually imminent.

**33** Methotrexate is a folic acid antagonist that causes severe toxic effects on the hematopoietic system. The antidote used to combat these toxic effects is
   a  Calcium leucovorin.
   b  Allopurinol.
   c  Cyanocobalamin.
   d  Wyamine sulfate.

**34** The alkylating agent that can cause the most severe tissue reaction when it comes in contact with the skin is
   a  Cytoxan.
   b  Chlorambucil.
   c  Triethylenemelamine.
   d  Nitrogen mustard.

**35** Alkylating agents have as their main effect damaging the DNA found within the nucleus of the cell. An example of an alkylating agent is
   a  Methotrexate.
   b  5-fluorouracil.
   c  Vincristine.
   d  Cytoxan.

**36** Which of the following statements relating to cyanophosphamide (Cytoxan) is true? Cytoxan
   a  Is a potent antimetabolite.
   b  Cannot be given by mouth.
   c  Causes severe bladder irritation.
   d  Has a vesicant action on subcutaneous tissue.

**37** "Antimetabolites" are chemical substances that interfere with the synthesis of nucleic acids necessary for cell growth. An example of an antimetabolite is
   a  Chlorambucil.
   b  5-fluorouracil.
   c  Uracil mustard.
   d  Propylthiouracil.

**38** Bone marrow depression is one of the toxic effects of antineoplastic chemotherapy. Early signs of bone marrow depression can be identified by frequent
  a  Complete blood counts.
  b  Prothrombin time.
  c  Bleeding and coagulation time.
  d  Electrophoresis.

**39** The major indication for reverse isolation for the patient receiving antineoplastic chemotherapy is
  a  Anemia.
  b  Leukopenia.
  c  Thrombocytopenia.
  d  Polycythemia.

**40** The physician has ordered reverse isolation on a patient who is receiving large doses of antineoplastic chemotherapy. The nurse should
  a  Double-bag soiled linen when removing it from the room.
  b  Use disposable dishes for all meals.
  c  Wear a gown, gloves, and mask when caring for the patient.
  d  Use rubber gloves when handling urine.

**41** Studies have indicated that patients in isolation may suffer from sensory
  a  Stimulation.
  b  Overload.
  c  Deprivation.
  d  Hypesthesia.

**42** Hyperuricemia often develops as a side effect of antineoplastic agents. The medication used to counteract this effect is
  a  Cyanocobalamin.
  b  Folinic acid.
  c  Allopurinol.
  d  Compazine.

**43** Annette Lohse is receiving doxorubicin hydrochloride (Adriamycin) intravenously for terminal pancreatic carcinoma. Doxorubicin causes
  **a** Complete alopecia.
  **b** Minimal toxic effects.
  **c** Severe local tissue reactions.
  **d** Severe hemorrhagic cystitis.

**44** While caring for Ms. Lohse, who has stomatitis secondary to antineoplastic chemotherapy, the nurse would tell the patient to
  **a** Take Maalox after meals and at bedtime.
  **b** Use an electric toothbrush to cleanse the teeth, then rinse the mouth with Cepacol.
  **c** Avoid eating spicy foods, smoking, and drinking alcoholic beverages.
  **d** Take an antiemetic before meals and at bedtime.

## ANSWERS, EXPLANATIONS, AND REFERENCES

**1 b** "Neoplasia" refers to uncontrolled cell proliferation that leads to the development of a tumor mass. (*Snively and Beshear, p. 109.*)

**2 a** "Anaplasia" refers to a cellular process in which the new or malignant cells are unlike the parent cells. (*Shafer et al., p. 285.*)

**3 c** Metastasis occurs when cancer cells leave their site of origin, travel via blood and lymph nodes to other tissues, and set up new tissues. (*Luckmann and Sorensen, p. 349.*)

**4 c** Benign tumors tend to grow slowly within a capsule, are not invasive, and do not recur after removal. (*Shafer et al., p. 286.*)

**5 b** Malignant tumors are anaplastic, tend to invade surrounding tissue, and metastasize via the blood and lymph to distant organs. (*Shafer et al., p. 285.*)

**6 d** A lipoma is a benign tumor that originates from adipose tissue. (*Luckmann and Sorensen, p. 357.*)

**7 d** "Carcinoma" refers to a malignant tumor originating from epithelial cells. (*Shafer et al., p. 286.*)

**8 b** "Sarcoma" refers to a malignant tumor originating from connective tissue. (*Shafer et al., p. 286.*)

**9 c** Although cancer occurs at all ages, statistics indicate that the highest incidence occurs in persons over 65. (*Luckmann and Sorensen, pp. 360–361.*)

**10 a** Radiation is a physical stressor and is also a carcinogen linked to leukemia and skin cancer. (*Luckmann and Sorensen, pp. 359–360.*)

**11 c** Prolonged exposure to the sun and sunbathing are linked to skin cancer (*Luckmann and Sorensen, p. 360. Shafer et al., p. 287.*)

**12 a** One of the seven warning signs of cancer is a sore or lesion in the mouth which does not heal within 2 weeks. (*Shafer et al., p. 289.*)

**13 a** The "biopsy" is the histologic examination of a small piece of tissue used to rule out or confirm a diagnosis of a malignancy. (*Luckmann and Sorensen, p. 365.*)

**14 c** "Exfoliative cytology" is the technique used to analyze the Pap smear. (*Luckmann and Sorensen, p. 365.*)

**15 b** Organ scans are painless procedures (*Luckmann and Sorensen, p. 374.*)

**16 a** Patients who have received a tracer dose of a radioactive isotope need to take no special precautions following the test. Since the tracer dose is so minimal (1 mCi or less), no precautions are necessary. (*Massachusetts General Hospital, p. 86.*)

**17 c** Three types of radiation emitted from radioisotopes are alpha particles, beta particles, and gamma rays. Of these, gamma rays are the most penetrating and the most damaging to living tissue. Concrete can be penetrated by gamma rays. (*Luckmann and Sorensen, p. 372.*)

**18 d** Rapidly proliferating cells are characterized by rapid cell multiplication and the presence of many cells in mitosis. Examples of this type of cell are cancer cells, bone marrow cells, and epithelial cells of the stomach and intestines, skin, and hair follicles. (*Moidel, p. 153.*)

**19 d** Leukemia is a toxic effect that can occur from excessive exposure to radiation. The incidence of leukemia is higher among radiologists than it is in other types of physicians. (*Shafer et al., p. 293.*)

**20 c** If a patient is receiving external radiation, nothing should be used to cleanse the skin in the area being treated. Soap is particularly irritating. The markings that were made on the skin by the radiologist should not be removed since they serve as guides. (*Shafer et al., p. 296.*)

**21 c** One of the side effects of radiation therapy is bone marrow depression. Since the patient can develop leukopenia, she becomes more prone to develop serious infections if exposed to persons with upper respiratory infections. (*Luckmann and Sorensen, p. 378.*)

**22 c** Radioactive substances that have a long half-life must be administered in a sealed container so that the radioactive substance can be removed when therapy is terminated. Examples of radioactive substances used for internal radiation in a sealed container are cobalt and radium. The half-life of radium is 1620 years; that of cobalt is 5 years. (*Luckmann and Sorensen, p. 372.*)

**23 c** In caring for patients receiving therapeutic doses of radioactive gold, the nurse should limit the amount of time spent with them and avoid close approximation to them. Shielding should also be enforced to protect the nurse. The principles of time, distance, and shielding should be enforced. The nurse should become familiar with the hospital's policy for caring for patients receiving radiation. (*Massachusetts General Hospital, pp. 86, 92. Luckmann and Sorensen, p. 381.*)

**24 b** Since radioactive phosphorus emits no gamma rays, special radiation precautions are not required when caring for these patients. However, it is recommended that rubber gloves be worn when handling urine. (*Massachusetts General Hospital, p. 94.*)

**25 a** Urine is the major source of contamination if a patient is receiving radioactive iodine. Urine should be collected in a lead container to be disposed of by the radiology department. Rubber gloves should be worn to empty the bedpan and when handling linen soiled with urine. (*Luckmann and Sorensen, p. 381.*)

**26 a** If there is a spill of vomitus on the bed linen, rubber gloves should be worn to handle the soiled linen. It should be placed in a plastic bag and then placed into a metal container used to collect soiled linen. (*Massachusetts General Hospital, p. 88.*)

**27 b** Compazine is a phenothiazine that can be used to relieve the nausea and vomiting associated with antineoplastic chemotherapy and irradiation. It is believed that the phenothiazines work by blocking stimulation to the chemoreceptor trigger zone in the brain. The CTZ is especially sensitive to certain circulating chemicals that cause emesis. (*Rodman and Smith, p. 593. Beland, p. 127.*)

**28 b** Denial is a defensive mechanism used during the first stage of the grieving process as a means of coping with the hopelessness of a terminal illness. Denial is used during the first stage of the grieving process and also used by some patients throughout all stages. (*Kübler-Ross, pp. 35, 37.*)

**29 a** Denial is Karen's way of coping with the shock of her terminal illness. Since this is an attempt to avoid reality, it is unwise to probe or encourage Karen to face reality. The nurses' role is to visit Karen frequently, allow her to speak when she is ready, and listen attentively without attempting to contradict her when she uses denial. (*Carter, p. 194. Kübler-Ross, pp. 37, 40.*)

**30 d** The less time the nurse spends in contact with the patient receiving radium therapy, the less the exposure will be. Although care of the patient should not be omitted, priorities of care should be established ahead of time and the care should be administered as quickly as possible. Nurses caring for the patient receiving radium should be rotated so that no one nurse will be overexposed. (*Massachusetts General Hospital, pp. 90–91.*)

**31 c** Anger is the second stage of the grieving process. Once the individual realizes that the illness can no longer be denied, the stage of anger begins. The patient finds fault with everything being done by the staff and by family members. Furthermore, the patient can become rude and demanding to the staff and to family members. (*Kübler-Ross, p. 44.*)

**32 d** The stage of depression prepares the dying person for the final stage, acceptance. During the acceptance stage, communications are predominantly nonverbal. Patients seem to hang on to hope throughout the entire dying process. It is hope that helps them to endure the long suffering. All patients, even the most accepting and the most realistic, express some hope, no matter how small. Once the patient loses hope, this usually signifies that death is imminent. (*Kübler-Ross, p. 123.*)

**33 a** Calcium leucovorin (folinic acid) is an antidote used to neutralize the effects of methotrexate toxicity. To be most effective, it should be administered promptly after the patient has received a toxic dose. (*Rodman and Smith, p. 639.*)

**34 d** Nitrogen mustard (mechlorethamine hydrochloride) is an alkylating agent with potent vesicant action. All personnel preparing the medication for intravenous use should wear rubber gloves. Caution should also be exercised when administering the medication, since it can cause severe tissue reaction at the injection site of the IV infiltrates. (*Bergersen, p. 537.*)

**35 d** Cytoxan (cyclophosphamide) is an alkylating agent used to treat some forms of cancer. (*Rodman and Smith, p. 638.*)

**36 c** Cytoxan is an alkylating agent chemically related to nitrogen mustard. Administration of Cytoxan can cause severe hemorrhagic cystitis. Forcing fluids can dilute the harmful urinary drug metabolites and thus lessen the incidence of bladder irritation. (*Rodman and Smith, p. 638.*)

**37 b** 5-fluorouracil is an antimetabolite that interferes with pyrimidine metabolism. Pyrimidines play an essential role in the synthesis of deoxyribonucleic acid (DNA) necessary for cell proliferation. (*Bergersen, p. 542.*)

**38 a** Antineoplastic agents can cause severe bone marrow depression. As a result, the physician usually orders weekly complete blood counts to identify early signs of bone marrow depression. (*Bergersen, p. 546.*)

**39 b** Since severe leukopenia decreases the patient's ability to combat infection, the patient becomes more vulnerable to developing life-threatening infections. Reverse isolation is a means of protecting the patient from being exposed to potentially harmful microorganisms. (*Asperheim and Eisenhauer, p. 476.*)

**40 c** The purpose of reverse isolation is to protect the patient whose normal resistance to infection is severely impaired. Patients on antineoplastic chemotherapy can develop severe leukopenia that makes them particularly vulnerable to developing overwhelming or life-threatening infections. Anyone entering the room should wear a gown, mask, and rubber gloves. Linen, dish, urine, and stool precautions are not necessary. (*Massachusetts General Hospital, p. 118.*)

**41 c** Sensory deprivation can occur in patients on isolation, patients wearing eye patches, patients with dysphasia, and dying patients. Patients on isolation should be permitted to have a radio, television, telephone, and visits from family and the nursing staff. In some cases, for example, radiation, frequent visits at the patient's bedside are contraindicated. The nurse could talk to the patient from the doorway if necessary. (*Moidel, p. 294.*)

**42 c** Neoplastic chemotherapy can cause an excess production of uric acid as the neoplastic cells are rapidly destroyed. This hyperuricemia can be particularly harmful to the kidneys. Allopurinol can be given to counteract the harmful effects of excessive uric acid. (*Bergersen, p. 542.*)

**43 a** Doxorubicin hydrochloride (Adriamycin) is an antibiotic that has potent antineoplastic properties. The medication, which is given intravenously, causes complete alopecia and severe bone marrow depression. (*Bergersen, p. 544.*)

**44 c** Stomatitis is an inflammation of the mucous lining of the mouth which can occur as a side effect of antineoplastic chemotherapy. The patient should avoid eating spicy foods, smoking, and drinking alcoholic beverages. Rinsing the mouth with an anesthetic mouthwash (Xylocaine) also relieves the discomfort. (*Luckmann and Sorensen, p. 371.*)

# UNIT 3
# Nursing care of the patient with an infectious disease

**OBJECTIVES**

To answer the questions in this unit, the reader should be able to

1. Identify the multiplicity of factors that influence an individual's susceptibility to an infectious disease;
2. Recognize the mode of transmission of select infectious diseases;
3. List the various stages in the course of infectious diseases;
4. Describe the role of the nurse in caring for patients with infectious diseases;
5. Recognize how to protect oneself and others from contracting an infectious disease.

## QUESTIONS RELATED TO OBJECTIVES

*Instructions*: Choose the *one best* answer to the following questions.

1. Characteristics of a microorganism that influence its behavior within the susceptible individual include
   a. Infectivity, pathogenicity, and virulence.
   b. Genetic influences, specific immunity, and nutrition.
   c. Hormone balance, previous exposure, and exogenous chemicals.
   d. Commensalism, symbiosis, and ecological equilibrium.

2. Which of the following statements concerning factors relating to host susceptibility to infectious diseases is true?
   a. There is increased resistance to infection among the elderly.
   b. Persons with increased levels of glucocorticoids are more susceptible to infections.
   c. Antibody formation is not significantly altered by protein depletion.
   d. Stress has no appreciable relation to infectious diseases.

3. When a disease is transmitted to an individual, the susceptible individual is referred to as the
   a. "Vector."
   b. "Host."
   c. "Agent."
   d. "Vehicle."

4. Vectors are a mode of transmission for infectious diseases. An example of a vector is
   a. Nasal secretions.
   b. Urine.
   c. Blood.
   d. Insects.

**5** A person who harbors and disseminates the infectious agent but manifests no signs or symptoms of the disease is called a
   **a** "Carrier."
   **b** "Contact."
   **c** "Vector."
   **d** "Host."

**6** The period of time between the entry of the causative microorganisms into the body and the appearance of the signs and symptoms of the disease is referred to as the
   **a** "Incubation period."
   **b** "Prodromal stage."
   **c** "Fastigium."
   **d** "Period of illness."

**7** Which of the following statements relating to the course of infectious diseases is true?
   **a** The period of communicability terminates with the onset of prodromal symptoms.
   **b** During the period of illness, most patients have an elevated temperature.
   **c** During the period of convalescence, the patient is not communicable.
   **d** The patient has no signs and symptoms during the prodromal period.

**8** Which of the following actions by the nurse is the *best* precaution in preventing cross-contamination between patients?
   **a** Using rubber gloves when emptying bedpans.
   **b** Cleaning washbasins after use.
   **c** Hand washing before and after patient care.
   **d** Keeping food trays covered.

**9** While caring for the patient with infectious mononucleosis, the nurse should be aware that the mode of transmission is
   **a** Oral and nasal secretions.
   **b** Contaminated hypodermic needle.
   **c** Blood.
   **d** Feces.

**10** The incidence of tuberculosis is more common in
   **a** Whites.
   **b** Rural areas.
   **c** Diabetics.
   **d** Women.

**11** Which of the following statements *best* relates to the characteristics of the tubercle bacillus?
   **a** It is a rapidly producing, gram-negative, aerobic bacillus.
   **b** Within the body, it can remain alive but dormant for many years.
   **c** It is difficult to destroy by heat and chemical disinfectants.
   **d** It is not capable of living outside the body.

**12** The most *common* mode of transmission for tuberculosis is by
   **a** Ingestion.
   **b** The placenta.
   **c** Inhalation.
   **d** A break in the intact skin.

**13** The first time an individual is infected with tuberculosis, the individual is said to have
   **a** Primary tuberculosis infection.
   **b** Progressive primary tuberculosis.
   **c** Miliary tuberculosis.
   **d** Active pulmonary tuberculosis.

**14** A negative tuberculosis skin test occurs if the person has been
   **a** Exposed to tuberculosis but is not infected.
   **b** Infected with tuberculosis but has been treated with antituberculosis medications for 1 year.
   **c** Infected with tuberculosis but has no clinical evidence of disease.
   **d** Exposed to tuberculosis and has active pulmonary tuberculosis.

**15** Primary tuberculosis infections will cause a positive reaction to tuberculin skin tests within what time span after exposure?
   **a** 24 to 48 hours.
   **b** 3 to 5 days.
   **c** 7 to 14 days.
   **d** 3 to 10 weeks.

**16** The most effective way to destroy the tubercle bacillus present in moist sputum is
   **a** Burning.
   **b** Chemical disinfection.
   **c** Boiling.
   **d** Exposure to direct sunlight.

**17** Which of the following statements relating to tuberculosis chemotherapy is true?
   **a** The medications are administered singly to slow the rate of producing drug-resistant strains.
   **b** Even after therapy has been discontinued, the sputum culture remains positive.
   **c** The medications currently being used completely destroy the tubercle bacillus.
   **d** Chemotherapy for tuberculosis is continued long after all clinical and bacteriologic evidence of the disease has disappeared.

**18** Which of the following antituberculosis drugs are considered primary or "first-line"?
   **a** Pyrizanamide.
   **b** Viomycin.
   **c** Isoniazid.
   **d** Kanamycin.

**19** One of the side effects of isoniazid (INH) is peripheral neuritis. To combat this, the doctor may order
   **a** Cyanocobalamin.
   **b** Folic acid.
   **c** Thiamine.
   **d** Pyridoxine.

**20** Ethambutol, an antituberculosis medication, is
   **a** A second-line tuberculocidal drug.
   **b** Better tolerated than para-aminosalicylic acid (PAS).
   **c** Given intramuscularly.
   **d** Most effective when used alone.

**21** Although Ethambutol is less toxic than other primary antituberculosis medications, the nurse should observe the patient for
   **a** Tremors.
   **b** Convulsions.
   **c** Disturbed vision.
   **d** Psychotic reactions.

**22** Which of the following medications is usually contraindicated in patients with active tuberculosis?
   **a** Corticosterioids.
   **b** Acetylsalicylic acid.
   **c** Penicillin.
   **d** Aminophyllin.

23 Mrs. R. is a 25-year-old woman who is being treated for active pulmonary tuberculosis. Since she has small children at home, she is anxious to participate in her care. Mrs. R. is on respiratory precautions. The nurse should
   a Wear a gown and mask when caring for Mrs. R.
   b Double-bag all soiled linen before disposal.
   c Wear rubber gloves when administering direct care to Mrs. R.
   d Teach Mrs. R. how to care for her own secretions and their disposal.

24 Para-aminosalicylic acid is often used in combination with isoniazid. Side effects of PAS include
   a Nausea, vomiting, and diarrhea.
   b Blurred vision, peripheral neuritis, and headache.
   c Ringing in the ears, skin rash, and arthralgia.
   d Convulsions, tremors, and urinary retention.

25 In preparing Mrs. R. for discharge, the nurse should tell her that when she takes PAS she should take it
   a With food.
   b Immediately upon arising.
   c At bedtime.
   d One-half hour before lunch.

26 One of the responsibilities the community health nurse will have in Mrs. R.'s care will be to identify those persons who have had direct contact with Mrs. R. This function is referred to as
   a "Nurse auditing."
   b "Terminating the case."
   c "Referral."
   d "Case finding."

27 The vector for Rocky Mountain spotted fever is the
   a Flea.
   b Fly.
   c Mosquito.
   d Tick.

**28** Jane is 22 years old and has been told that her fiancé, John, has infectious hepatitis. Which of the following preparations will provide immunity for Jane?
   **a** Hepatitis toxoid.
   **b** Gamma globulin.
   **c** Serum albumin.
   **d** Hepatitis vaccine.

**29** Jane's fiancé was placed on hepatitis precautions. The nurse should
   **a** Ask John to wear a mask while caring for him.
   **b** Wear gloves when in direct contact with soiled linen.
   **c** Treat feces with a chemical disinfectant before flushing down the toilet.
   **d** Use no special dish precautions.

**30** Which of the following persons runs the greatest risk of developing tetanus? The man who
   **a** Cut his finger while slicing meat.
   **b** Punctured his hand with a rusty nail while gardening.
   **c** Was bitten by a pet hamster while feeding it.
   **d** Was scratched by a cat while playing with it.

**31** The most common mode of transmission for infectious hepatitis is
   **a** The oral-fecal route.
   **b** Blood transfusion.
   **c** Insect bites.
   **d** Urine.

**32** The incubation period of infectious hepatitis is approximately how many days?
   **a** 2 to 7.
   **b** 5 to 14.
   **c** 10 to 40.
   **d** 60 to 90.

**33** The hepatitis virus can be destroyed by
  **a** Chemical disenfection.
  **b** Boiling for 15 minutes.
  **c** Exposure to sunlight.
  **d** Autoclaving.

**34** The presence of hepatitis B-antigen (HB-ag) is found in the blood
  **a** During the incubation period of infectious hepatitis.
  **b** During the acute phase of serum hepatitis.
  **c** In carriers of infectious hepatitis and serum hepatitis.
  **d** During the recovery phase of both serum and infectious hepatitis.

**35** The groups of persons who run a high risk of developing serum hepatitis are those
  **a** Over 65 years of age.
  **b** On hemodialysis.
  **c** Who have had myocardial infarcts.
  **d** Living in crowded places.

**36** A mode of transmission for serum hepatitis is contaminated
  **a** Venipuncture equipment.
  **b** Nasopharyngeal secretions.
  **c** Urine collection receptacles.
  **d** Shellfish.

**37** The incubation period for serum hepatitis is
  **a** 2 to 7 days.
  **b** 5 to 15 days.
  **c** 3 to 6 weeks.
  **d** 2 to 6 months.

**38** Arlene is an airline stewardess who travels back and forth to India. She was admitted to the hospital with a diagnosis of amebiasis. The mode of transmission is most probably
   **a** Droplet infection.
   **b** Contaminated water.
   **c** An insect bite.
   **d** Sexual intercourse.

**39** Enteric precautions were ordered for Arlene. The nurse should
   **a** Wear a gown, gloves, and a mask when caring for Arlene.
   **b** Instruct Arlene to wash her hands before eating and before and after elimination.
   **c** Use no special dish precautions for Arlene.
   **d** Use no special precautions for soiled linen disposal.

**40** The doctor ordered a stool specimen for examination of amoeba. Immediately after the patient's defecation, the nurse should
   **a** Test the stool for occult blood before sending it to the laboratory.
   **b** Send a warm specimen to the laboratory.
   **c** Place the specimen in the refrigerator in the laboratory.
   **d** Add a preservative to the specimen before sending it to the laboratory.

**41** Hospital-associated infections are referred to as
   **a** "Communicable."
   **b** "Sporadic."
   **c** "Contagious."
   **d** "Nosocomial."

**42** To control the incidence of nosocomial respiratory infections
  **a** Respiratory equipment such as breathing circuits and reservoirs should be changed daily.
  **b** Sterile rubber gloves should be worn while administering therapy.
  **c** Sputum cultures and sensitivity tests should be done on all hospital admissions.
  **d** Equipment should be sterilized daily by chemical disinfectants.

**43** Gram-negative microorganisms are being identified as a primary source of nosocomial respiratory infectious. Which of the following is gram-negative?
  **a** *Pneumococcus*.
  **b** *Staphylococcus*.
  **c** *Pseudomonas*.
  **d** *Streptococcus*.

**44** Which of the following nursing actions can be used to decrease the incidence of nosocomial urinary tract infections?
  **a** When cleansing the perineal area, the area around the urinary meatus should be cleansed first, then each inner labia, using a downward stroke.
  **b** When collecting urine for a culture, disconnect the catheter from the drainage apparatus, allow a few drops of urine to flow into the basin, then collect urine into a sterile test tube.
  **c** Irrigate the bladder four times a day with normal saline via a three-way Foley catheter.
  **d** Urine specimens should be collected by aseptically aspirating the urine from the catheter, using a small-gauge needle and a syringe.

**45** Intravenous therapy is another source of nosocomial infections. Which of the following statements is true?
   **a** If an antibiotic has been added to the intravenous fluid, the bottle can be used for more than 24 hours after the seal is broken.
   **b** Intracaths should be changed every 48 to 72 hours.
   **c** Since cannulae cause local irritation at the site of insertion, it is not necessary to remove the in-dwelling cannula if the site is red and swollen.
   **d** Rubber gloves should be worn by personnel doing the venipuncture.

**46** Which of the following infectious diseases are reportable to the state and/or local health department?
   **a** Rocky Mountain spotted fever, serum hepatitis, and staphylococcal infections.
   **b** Pneumococcal pneumonia, rabies, and amebiasis.
   **c** Tuberculosis, meningitis, and botulism.
   **d** Herpes zoster, streptococcal infection, and food poisoning.

## ANSWERS, EXPLANATIONS, AND REFERENCES

**1 a** Infectivity, pathogenicity, and virulence are host-related characteristics that relate specifically to their behavior within the host. "Infectivity" refers to the ability of the microorganism to enter, lodge, and multiply within the host. "Pathogenicity" refers to the capacity of the microorganisms to produce disease, and "virulence" refers to the severity of the disease produced. (*Fox, Hall, and Elveback, pp. 54–56. Beland, p. 156.*)

**2 b** Some of the factors influencing host susceptibility to infection include heredity, nutrition, sex, hormonal balance, and ability of the host's defensive mechanism to function adequately. The glucocorticoids counteract the effects of the inflammatory process, thus making the host who has increased blood levels of glucocorticoids more susceptible to infections. (*Beland, p. 153.*)

**3 b** The "host" is the susceptible person to whom the pathogenic microorganism is transmitted. (*Shafer et al., p. 308.*)

**4 d** A vector is the mode of conveyance by which an infectious agent is transferred from an infected host to a susceptible host. The vector is usually a living intermediate host that merely serves as a vehicle for the transmission of the disease agent, for example, rats, insects, etc. (*Fox, Hall, and Elveback, p. 29.*)

**5 a** A "carrier" is a healthy person who harbors and disseminates the infectious agent. The microorganisms grow and multiply; however, the person has no signs and symptoms of the disease. Examples of diseases that have carriers are typhoid fever, streptococcal infections, poliomyelitis, and diphtheria. (*Beland, p. 144.*)

**6 a** The "incubation period" refers to the period of time between the entry of the causative microorganisms into the body and the appearance of the signs and symptoms of the disease. The length of the incubation period is characteristic for each disease and varies from one disease to another. (*Beland, p. 163.*)

**7 b** The second stage of an infectious disease is the period of illness. In some diseases, this period begins with prodromal symptoms, which are the early manifestations of diseases and are often misdiagnosed as an upper respiratory infection. Fever is the one symptom characteristic of most infectious diseases. During this period of illness, most patients have an elevated temperature. (*Beland, p. 162.*)

**8 c** Careful and frequent hand washing is the best precaution in preventing cross-contamination between patients. Hand washing should be done before and after each patient contact and when the hands become contaminated with urine, feces, vomitus, saliva, sputum, and wound drainage. (*Moidel, p. 413.*)

**9 a** Infectious mononucleosis, sometimes referred to as "glandular fever" or the "kissing disease," is transmitted from one person to another via oral and nasal secretions. (*Shafer et al., p. 421.*)

**10 c**  Pulmonary tuberculosis is an infectious disease of the lungs which is more common in nonwhites, in crowded slum areas of large cities, in men, and in persons with diabetes. Persons with diabetes are twice as prone to tuberculosis as are nondiabetics. (*Luckmann and Sorensen, p. 965.*)

**11 b**  The tubercle bacillus is an acid-fast, gram-positive, aerobic bacillus that reproduces very slowly. The bacillus is readily destroyed by heat and can survive outside the body for months in dried sputum or dust. Within the body it can remain alive but dormant for many years. As a result, reactivation of the primary infection can occur years later. (*Luckmann and Sorensen, p. 960.*)

**12 c**  Inhalation is the *most* common mode of transmission. Coughing, sneezing, laughing, and expectorating produce infected droplets in the surrounding air from the patient with tuberculosis. These infected droplets can thus be inhaled by the uninfected person. (*Shafer et al., p. 559. Luckmann and Sorensen, p. 960.*)

**13 a**  The first time the tubercle bacillus gains access to the lung and is implanted in living tissue, the person is said to have a primary tuberculosis infection. (*Luckmann and Sorensen, p. 961.*)

**14 a**  A person can be exposed to tuberculosis and not be infected with the tubercle bacillus. In this case the skin test would be negative. However, it should be noted that if the individual has been exposed to tuberculosis, it takes 3 to 10 weeks after the primary infection for tuberculin sensitivity to occur. (*Shafer et al., p. 561.*)

**15 d**  Primary tuberculosis infections cause a positive reaction to tuberculin skin tests. However, it takes about 3 to 10 weeks after the initial infection for the skin test to become positive. (*Luckmann and Sorensen, p. 961.*)

**16 a**  Soiled tissues containing moist sputum are best destroyed by burning. The patient should be taught how to control the secretions and their disposal. If burning is not feasible, they can be flushed down the toilet. (*Shafer et al., p. 562.*)

**17 d** The nurse should stress to the patient the importance of uninterrupted therapy long after x-rays and bacterial studies are completed and clinical evidence of the disease has disappeared. The healing process of tuberculosis is very slow, and even though the patient feels well, he or she must continue taking medications to prevent a relapse. (*Luckmann and Sorensen, p. 970.*)

**18 c** Not only is INH a first-line antituberculosis medication, but it is also the safest, most effective, and least expensive of all the primary drugs. (*Rodman and Smith, p. 533.*)

**19 d** Pyridoxine (vitamin $B_6$) is sometimes used with isoniazid to prevent the peripheral neuritis that can be caused by continued use of it. (*Shafer et al., p. 562. Rodman and Smith, p. 661.*)

**20 b** Ethambutol is an antituberculosis medication that is being used as a primary drug in the treatment of tuberculosis. The medication is better tolerated than PAS and has less toxicity. Like PAS, it is used most frequently in conjunction with isoniazid. (*Bergersen, p. 482.*)

**21 c** The main toxic symptom of Ethambutol is optic neuritis. This can result in loss of visual acuity and decreased ability to discriminate colors. (*Bergersen, p. 482.*)

**22 a** Since the corticosteroids suppress the inflammatory process and inhibit wound healing, they are contraindicated. The exception would be if the patient sustains a life-threatening situation. In that event, the patient must also be maintained on antitubercular medications. (*Luckmann and Sorensen, p. 970.*)

**23 d** If the patient who has been placed on respiratory precautions can be taught how to control and properly dispose of secretions, gowns, gloves, linens, and dish precautions are not required. (*Massachusetts General Hospital, p. 108.*)

**24 a** Side effects of PAS include nausea, vomiting, diarrhea, and anorexia. Because of the gastrointestinal upset, PAS should not be used in patients with peptic ulcers or an irritable bowel. (*Luckmann and Sorensen, p. 971.*)

**25 a** Because of the gastrointestinal upset associated with PAS, the patient should be encouraged to take the medication with food or antacids. (*Bergersen, p. 483.*)

**26 d** Case finding is an important function of the community health nurse in prevention and control of tuberculosis. Persons who have had direct contact with Mrs. R. can be identified, they can be referred to their private physician or community agency, and prompt and effective treatment can be initiated if indicated. (*Beland, p. 166.*)

**27 d** The vector for Rocky Mountain spotted fever is the tick. Since this infectious disease is endemic in certain areas, if a person is bitten by a tick medical advice is suggested. (*Shafer et al., p. 267.*)

**28 b** If gamma globulin is given within two weeks of exposure to infectious hepatitis, immunity resulting from the gamma globulin will protect the individual from developing symptoms. Standard gamma globulin has no effect on serum hepatitis. (*Luckmann and Sorensen, p. 1131.*)

**29 b** Hepatitis precautions include wearing gloves when coming in contact with soiled linen, feces, or serosanguineous drainage coming from wounds or any body orifices. (*Massachusetts General Hospital, p. 112.*)

**30 b** The tetanus bacillus is a common inhabitant of the intestines of herbivorous animals and humans. It leaves the body via the feces and forms resistant spores that can live in the soil for years. Since the spore is anaerobic, puncture wounds that penetrate the deep tissue are especially vulnerable to developing tetanus. (*Shafer et al., p. 87.*)

**31 a** The most common mode of transmission for infectious hepatitis is the oral-fecal route. The nurse should exercise the greatest care in handling anything contaminated with oral secretions or with feces. (*Moidel, p. 705. Shafer et al., pp. 713–714.*)

**32 c** The incubation period for infectious hepatitis is approximately 10 to 40 days. (*Shafer et al., p. 713.*)

## NURSING CARE OF THE PATIENT WITH AN INFECTIOUS DISEASE

**33 d**  The virus for infectious hepatitis and serum hepatitis is very resistant to the usual methods of sterilization. Autoclaving for at least 20 minutes at 15 to 20 lb of pressure is the most effective method available. (*Shafer et al., p. 713.*)

**34 b**  Hepatitis B-antigen (HB-ag) is found in the blood during the incubation period and the acute phase of serum hepatitis. It has been found among carriers of serum hepatitis. The antigen for infectious hepatitis has not yet been isolated. (*Shafer et al., p. 714.*)

**35 b**  Patients on hemodialysis run a high risk of developing serum hepatitis. In addition, those physicians and nurses caring for patients in a hemodialysis unit also run a high risk of developing serum hepatitis. (*Luckmann and Sorensen, p. 1132.*)

**36 a**  The mode of transmission for serum hepatitis is through contaminated venipuncture equipment or equipment used for parenteral administration. Accidentally breaking the skin with this contaminated equipment can lead to serum hepatitis. Nurses, physicians, persons working in hospital laboratories, and drug users are particularly prone. (*Shafer et al., p. 713.*)

**37 d**  The incubation period for serum hepatitis is 2 to 6 months. (*Shafer et al., p. 713.*)

**38 b**  Amebiasis is a protozoal infection caused by the *Endamoeba histolytica*. Although the disease occurs in some parts of the United States, it is most prevalent in tropical countries that have poor sanitation. The mode of transmission is contaminated water, food, and milk. Since feces of carriers and convalescent patients contain the cysts of the amoeba, food that has been handled by these individuals is the greatest source of infection. (*Shafer et al., p. 682.*)

**39 b**  Feces are a great source of contamination, especially in the convalescent patient with amebiasis and in the carrier. Because of this, it is imperative to instruct Arlene to wash her hands before eating and before and after elimination. (*Shafer et al., p. 682. Massachusetts General Hospital, pp. 109–111.*)

**40 b** If a stool is to be examined for amoebae, it is necessary to keep the specimen warm and it should be sent immediately to the laboratory. In some instances, it may be necessary to keep the specimen warm by placing it in a pan of hot water while it is being transported. (*Shafer et al., p. 682.*)

**41 d** "Nosocomial infections" is a term used to describe infections that occur in a hospital setting. The infectious agent is usually highly resistant to antibiotics and to the usual methods of disinfection. The patient exposed to these infectious agents is usually more susceptible to nosocomial infections because of the debilitating effect of the underlying disease process for which the patient was admitted. (*Beland, p. 144.*)

**42 a** Respiratory therapy equipment has been identified as a source of nosocomial respiratory infection. Although the respiratory therapist is responsible for the maintenance of equipment, the nurse should be aware of the importance of changing the breathing circuits and reservoirs daily as a means of preventing infection. Chemical disinfectants are not effective in sterilizing equipment. (*Moidel, p. 414.*)

**43 c** *Pseudomonas*, a gram-negative bacillus, has been identified as a primary source of nosocomial respiratory infections. Other gram-negative bacilli causing respiratory infections are *Proteus*, *Serratia*, and *Klebsiella*. (*Bushnell, p. 215.*)

**44 d** By keeping the drainage-collection setup a closed system, the chance of contamination is decreased and the likelihood of urinary tract infections is decreased. Therefore, by collecting urine specimens aseptically with a small-gauge needle and a syringe, one maintains the integrity of the closed drainage system and decreases the incidence of urinary tract infections. (*Moidel, p. 413. Shafer et al., p. 458.*)

**45 b** It is estimated that more than 25 percent of all hospitalized patients receive intravenous therapy. Intravenous therapy thus becomes a great source of nosocomial infections. Intracaths or in-dwelling cannulae should be changed every 48 to 72 hours to decrease the incidence of infection. (*Moidel, p. 414.*)

**46 c** Tuberculosis, meningitis, and botulism are reportable to the state and/or local health departments. Staphylococcal infections, pneumococcal pneumonia, and herpes zoster are not reportable. (*Massachusetts General Hospital, pp. 120–125.*)

# UNIT 4

# Nursing care of the patient with fluid and electrolyte imbalance

**OBJECTIVES**

To answer the questions in this unit, the reader should be able to
1. Describe the composition and distribution of the body fluids in the extracellular and intracellular fluid compartments;
2. Describe how the body adapts to alterations in fluids and electrolytes;
3. List those stressors contributing to fluid and electrolyte imbalance;
4. Identify the major signs and symptoms of the more common fluid and electrolyte imbalances;
5. Describe the nursing management of patients with fluid and electrolyte imbalance.

## QUESTIONS RELATED TO OBJECTIVES

*Instructions*: Choose the *one best* answer to the following questions.

1. Intracellular fluid contains large amounts of
   a. Potassium, phosphates, and magnesium.
   b. Phosphates, magnesium, and sodium.
   c. Magnesium, potassium, and bicarbonates.
   d. Chlorides, bicarbonate, and sodium.

2. The cation that is responsible for exerting osmotic pressure in the intracellular fluid is
   a. Calcium.
   b. Potassium.
   c. Sodium.
   d. Magnesium.

3. The most abundant buffer found in the intracellular fluid is
   a. Hemoglobin.
   b. Bicarbonate.
   c. Ammonium.
   d. Amino acids.

4. The extracellular-fluid compartment is made up of two main divisions, namely,
   a. Interstitial fluid and cellular fluid.
   b. Intravascular fluid and interstitial fluid.
   c. Cellular fluid and secretions and excretions.
   d. Intravascular fluid and secretions and excretions.

5. Extracellular fluid contains large amounts of
   a. Sodium, calcium, chlorides, and bicarbonates.
   b. Calcium, potassium, chlorides, and bicarbonates.
   c. Chlorides, sodium, phosphates, and calcium.
   d. Bicarbonates, sodium, phosphates, and chlorides.

**6** The cation responsible for exerting osmotic pressure within the extracellular fluid is
  **a** Magnesium.
  **b** Sodium.
  **c** Potassium.
  **d** Calcium.

**7** The major buffer system of the extracellular fluid is
  **a** Ammonia.
  **b** Hemoglobin.
  **c** Phosphates.
  **d** Carbonic acid/bicarbonate.

**8** The hormone that regulates the level of sodium and potassium ions in the extracellular fluid is
  **a** Parathyroid hormone.
  **b** Antidiuretic hormone (ADH).
  **c** Aldosterone.
  **d** Cortisol.

**9** The hormone that controls the renal reabsorption of water is called
  **a** Angiotensin.
  **b** ADH.
  **c** Cortisol.
  **d** Norepinephrine.

**10** The major urinary buffers are
  **a** Carbonic acid and sulfates.
  **b** Ammonia and phosphates.
  **c** Proteinates and phosphates.
  **d** Ammonia and bicarbonates.

**11** Gastric secretions have a high concentration of
  **a** Bicarbonates.
  **b** Hydrogen.
  **c** Phosphates.
  **d** Magnesium.

**12** Pancreatic juices contain large amounts of
  **a** Chlorides.
  **b** Bicarbonates.
  **c** Proteins.
  **d** Phosphates.

**13** The function of the plasma proteins is to exert a
  **a** Colloidal osmotic pressure that draws fluid out of the capillaries into the tissue spaces.
  **b** Colloidal osmotic pressure that draws fluid from the tissue spaces into the blood.
  **c** Hydrostatic pressure that draws fluid from the tissue spaces into the blood.
  **d** Hydrostatic pressure that draws fluid out of the capillaries and into the tissue spaces.

**14** The plasma protein that exerts the greatest osmotic pressure in the intravascular compartment is
  **a** Fibrinogen.
  **b** Gamma globulin.
  **c** Albumin.
  **d** Amino acid.

**15** Parathyroid hormone regulates the active transport of
  **a** Calcium and bicarbonates.
  **b** Calcium and phosphates.
  **c** Potassium and phosphates.
  **d** Potassium and bicarbonates.

**16** The most abundant cation found in the body is
  **a** Calcium.
  **b** Sodium.
  **c** Potassium.
  **d** Magnesium.

**17** The hormone, secreted by the thyroid gland, which lowers serum calcium by inhibiting demineralization of the bones is
  **a** Thyroxin.
  **b** Triiodothyronine.
  **c** Calcitonin.
  **d** Parathyroid hormone.

**18** The normal serum calcium is how many milliequivalents per liter?
  **a** 4.5 to 5.8 meq.
  **b** 10.5 to 11.0 meq.
  **c** 15.5 to 16.4 meq.
  **d** 18.5 to 20.5 meq.

**19** Early signs of calcium deficit include
  **a** Numbness and tingling of the fingers and toes.
  **b** Tetany.
  **c** Crowing respirations.
  **d** Convulsions.

**20** Mr. Z. was admitted with hypocalcemia. While assessing the patient during his admission, the nurse checked for hypocalcemia by placing a blood pressure cuff on his arm and inflating it. After about 3 minutes he developed carpopedal spasm. The nurse recorded this finding as a positive
  **a** Chvostek's sign.
  **b** Trousseau's sign.
  **c** Babinski reflex.
  **d** Romberg's sign.

**21** The nurse tapped Mr. Z.'s facial nerve just below the temple. The side of his face began to twitch. This twitching indicates a positive
  **a** Chvostek's sign.
  **b** Romberg's sign.
  **c** Homan's sign.
  **d** Trousseau's sign.

**22** The doctor ordered 10 mL of a 10% solution of calcium gluconate intravenously for severe hypocalcemia. The nurse should know that calcium gluconate
  **a** Can be administered orally and intramuscularly.
  **b** Is nonirritating to surrounding tissues when given IV.
  **c** Is compatible with all IV solutions.
  **d** Potentiates the action of digitalis preparations.

**23** Each of the following foods has been measured in 1-cup portions. Which combination has the highest calcium content?
  **a** Broccoli and spinach.
  **b** Mashed potatoes and cauliflower.
  **c** Turnips and cooked peas.
  **d** Canned corn and mushrooms.

**24** Physiological stressors contributing to hypercalcemia include
  **a** Malabsorption syndrome.
  **b** Prolonged immobilization.
  **c** Vitamin D deficiency.
  **d** Hypoparathyroidism.

**25** A diagnostic test used to determine the amount of calcium being excreted in the urine is the
  **a** Clinitest.
  **b** Addis count.
  **c** Sulkowitch test.
  **d** Bence-Jones protein.

26 Patients with hypercalcemia are very prone to develop
   a  Decubitus ulcer.
   b  Renal stones.
   c  Metabolic alkalosis.
   d  Tetany.

27 In caring for a patient with hypercalcemia, the nurse should
   a  Maintain the patient on bed rest.
   b  Massage all bony prominences.
   c  Force fluids.
   d  Observe for muscle twitching.

28 The normal serum sodium level is approximately how many milliequivalents per liter?
   a  5 meq.
   b  35 meq.
   c  70 meq.
   d  140 meq.

29 Stressors contributing to sodium deficit in the extracellular fluid include all of the following *except*
   a  Diuretic therapy.
   b  Gastrointestinal suction.
   c  Corticosteroid therapy.
   d  Diarrhea.

30 The osmolarity of the intracellular fluid can be indirectly measured by determining the
   a  pH of the blood.
   b  Specific gravity of urine.
   c  Serum sodium level.
   d  Arterial-blood gas levels.

**31** The patient with hyperosmolarity will be
  **a** Dehydrated and oliguric.
  **b** Dehydrated and polyuric.
  **c** Edematous and oliguric.
  **d** Edematous and polyuric.

**32** Mrs. L. is an 84-year-old woman who has been admitted to the hospital with dehydration secondary to impaired fluid intake. The nurse should recognize that the urinary output will be
  **a** Increased.
  **b** Positive for sugar and acetone.
  **c** Dark and concentrated.
  **d** High in hydrogen-ion concentration.

**33** In caring for a patient with fluid and electrolyte imbalance who is on intake and output, the nurse
  **a** Notified the physician and the urinary output was 30 mL per hour.
  **b** Speeded up the rate of the infusion when the patient's hourly rate fell behind schedule.
  **c** Recorded ice chips taken by mouth as fluid intake.
  **d** Did not have to record fluid used for the bladder irrigation.

**34** Replacement therapy is one means used to correct fluid and electrolyte imbalance. Which of the following statements is true?
  **a** Electrolyte solutions should be given rapidly to assure maximum use by the body.
  **b** The nurse determines how much fluid should be administered in 24 hours.
  **c** Hypertonic solutions of glucose should be given slowly by IV to prevent hyperinsulinism.
  **d** Replacement fluid is given at a rate of at least 5 mL per minute.

**35** Which of the following physiological substances would be used to correct edema associated with hypoproteinemia?
 a  Dextran.
 b  Amino acids.
 c  Salt-poor serum albumin.
 d  Packed red cells.

**36** Protein hydrolysates (amino acid solutions) can be given intravenously to correct negative nitrogen balance. The nurse should be aware that
 a  Supplemental medications can be added to the IV solution.
 b  Amino acids are indicated for patients with impaired kidney function.
 c  The solution becomes cloudy if refrigerated.
 d  Rapid administration can cause nausea, vomiting, and flushing of the face.

**37** The normal serum potassium level is
 a  5 meq/L.
 b  24 meq/L.
 c  102 meq/L.
 d  140 meq/L.

**38** Which of the following diuretics can lead to excessive loss of potassium?
 a  Spironolactone.
 b  Urevert.
 c  Hydrochlorothiazide.
 d  Triameterene.

**39** When caring for a patient receiving potassium chloride intravenously, the nurse should be aware that
   a  Rapid administration reduces burning at the infusion site.
   b  In severe potassium deficit, it can be given IV push.
   c  The average IV dosage should not exceed 40 meq. in one hour.
   d  Oliguria is an indication for withholding intravenous potassium chloride.

**40** All the following foods are in 100-g portions. Which group has the highest potassium content?
   a  Cream of wheat and salt-free butter.
   b  Cooked rice and orange sherbert.
   c  Egg noodles and cheddar cheese.
   d  Lima beans and potatoes.

**41** Potassium excess in the extracellular fluids can be caused by which of the following physiological stressors?
   a  Decreased secretion of aldosterone.
   b  Prolonged gastrointestinal suction.
   c  Diarrhea.
   d  Damage to the renal tubules.

**42** Patients with hyperkalemia show changes on the electrocardiogram. This can be determined by
   a  Prominent U wave.
   b  Prolonged QT interval.
   c  Inverted P wave.
   d  Tall, peaked T wave.

**43** The normal pH of the blood is approximately
   a  7.0.
   b  7.2.
   c  7.4.
   d  7.6.

**44** The body is able to regulate hydrogen-ion concentration by excreting excess hydrogen ions via the
   a  Kidneys.
   b  Lungs.
   c  Intestines.
   d  Skin.

**45** The partial pressure of carbon dioxide in arterial blood (arterial $P_{CO_2}$) is
   a  12 to 15 mmHg.
   b  35 to 38 mmHg.
   c  50 to 53 mmHg.
   d  95 to 100 mmHg.

**46** The partial pressure of oxygen in arterial blood (arterial $P_{O_2}$) is
   a  35 to 40 mmHg.
   b  60 to 65 mmHg.
   c  80 to 85 mmHg.
   d  95 to 100 mmHg.

**47** When it is stated that the blood has an increased hydrogen-ion concentration, it means that the blood has a
   a  Decreased pH and is more acid.
   b  Decreased pH and is more alkaline.
   c  Increased pH and is more alkaline.
   d  Increased pH and is more acid.

**48** A physiological stressor that stimulates the respiratory center in the medulla is a
   a  Decreased blood pH.
   b  Decreased plasma $P_{CO_2}$.
   c  Increased arterial $P_{O_2}$.
   d  Decreased serum $H_2CO_3$.

**49** Carbonic acid excess is associated with
  **a** Metabolic acidosis.
  **b** Metabolic alkalosis.
  **c** Respiratory acidosis.
  **d** Respiratory alkalosis.

**50** Some of the physiological stressors that would stimulate the respiratory center in the medulla to increase respirations would be
  **a** Increased plasma pH and increased carbon dioxide levels in the blood.
  **b** Increased plasma pH and decreased carbon dioxide levels in the blood.
  **c** Decreased plasma pH and increased carbon dioxide levels in the blood.
  **d** Decreased plasma pH and decreased carbon dioxide levels in the blood.

**51** As the hydrogen-ion concentration of the blood decreases, the pH of the blood increases. When this happens the patient develops
  **a** Acidosis, depression of the central nervous system, and coma.
  **b** Acidosis, stimulation of the central nervous system, and convulsions.
  **c** Alkalosis, stimulation of the central nervous system, and convulsions.
  **d** Alkalosis, depression of the central nervous system, and coma.

**52** Ms. F. is receiving nasogastric suction for prolonged vomiting. Gastric suction can lead to
  **a** Bicarbonate excess.
  **b** Carbonic acid deficit.
  **c** Potassium excess.
  **d** Calcium deficit.

**53** In caring for Ms. F., who has a nasogastric tube hooked up to gastric suction, the nurse should
   **a** Encourage Ms. F. to take ice chips by mouth.
   **b** Irrigate the nasogastric tube with sterile distilled water.
   **c** Weigh the patient daily to detect early signs of fluid imbalance.
   **d** Clamp the tube every hour for 5 minutes.

**54** When irrigating a nasogastric tube for a patient on gastric suction, the nurse should use
   **a** Distilled water.
   **b** Hypotonic saline.
   **c** Normal saline.
   **d** Hypertonic saline.

**55** Ms. F. is receiving 3000 mL of intravenous fluid over a 24-hour period. The drop factor of the infusion set is 10 gtt/mL. The IV should be set to run at how many drops per minute?
   **a** 12.
   **b** 21.
   **c** 30.
   **d** 40.

**56** Mrs. M. has been admitted to the hospital with a diagnosis of metabolic acidosis. In metabolic acidosis
   **a** The pH of the blood is increased.
   **b** The respiratory center in the medulla is depressed.
   **c** The plasma bicarbonates are increased.
   **d** Excess hydrogen ions are excreted in the urine.

**57** A physiological stressor leading to metabolic acidosis is
   **a** Renal insufficiency.
   **b** Loss of gastric secretions.
   **c** Damage to the respiratory center in the brain.
   **d** Hyperventilation.

**58** Signs and symptoms of metabolic acidosis include
   a   Air hunger, disorientation, and coma.
   b   Cheyne-Stokes respiration, dulling of the sensorium, and restlessness.
   c   Hyperventilation, twitching, and convulsions.
   d   Depression of respirations, mental confusion, and tetany.

**59** To correct metabolic acidosis the doctor may order IV administration of
   a   Potassium chloride.
   b   50% glucose.
   c   Sodium bicarbonate.
   d   Calcium gluconate.

**60** Mr. M. is receiving $\frac{1}{6}$ sodium lactate to correct severe metabolic acidosis. The doctor wrote an order for the IV to run at 75 mL per hour. The infusion set has a drop factor of 15 gtt/mL. The nurse regulates the infusion to run at how many drops per minute?
   a   13.
   b   19.
   c   24.
   d   75.

**61** To determine Mr. M.'s hydration status, the nurse pinched his skin, then quickly released both fingers. Mr. M.'s skin remained in the pinched position for a few seconds. The nurse made an assessment that Mr. M. had
   a   Poor skin turgor and was dehydrated.
   b   Pitting edema and was overhydrated.
   c   Normal skin turgor and was adequately hydrated.
   d   Anasarca and was dehydrated.

## ANSWERS, EXPLANATIONS, AND REFERENCES

**1 a** Although all body fluids in the intracellular and extracellular compartment contain water and electrolytes, their main difference occurs in the amount of electrolytes found in solution. Intracellular fluid contains large amounts of potassium, phosphates, and magnesium and relatively small amounts of sodium, bicarbonate, calcium, and chlorides. (*Metheny and Snively, p. 4.*)

**2 b** Potassium, the cation found in the intracellular fluid, plays an important role in maintaining water and electrolyte balance within the cell. (*Metheny and Snively, p. 26.*)

**3 a** The protein buffer system is the most abundant and the most powerful buffer found within the body. Hemoglobin, which provides nearly three-fourths of the buffering activity of body fluids, is an intracellular protein buffer. (*Luckmann and Sorensen, p. 221.*)

**4 b** The human body is made up of two fluid compartments, the extracellular and the intracellular compartments. The intracellular, or cellular-fluid, compartment contains the fluid found within the cell. The extracellular-fluid compartment is made up of the intravascular fluid (liquid component of blood) and the interstitial fluid that is found in the spaces between the blood vessels and the surrounding cells. (*Beland and Passos, p. 482. Shafer et al., p. 109.*).

**5 a** Extracellular fluid contains large amounts of sodium, calcium, chloride, and bicarbonates. Potassium, magnesium, and phosphates are found in smaller amounts. (*Metheny and Snively, p. 4.*)

**6 b** Sodium, which is the cation found in high concentrations in the extracellular fluid, is responsible for exerting osmotic pressure in the extracellular fluid. (*Metheny and Snively, p. 22.*)

**7 d** The main buffer system of the extracellular fluid is the carbonic acid/bicarbonate system. It is this buffering action that binds hydrogen ions, thus minimizing the hydrogen-ion concentration of the extracellular fluid. (*Luckmann and Sorensen, p. 220.*)

**8 c** Aldosterone is a mineralocorticoid that works directly on the kidney tubules to aid in the reabsorption of sodium and the excretion of potassium. (*Beland and Passos, p. 490. Langley, Telford, and Christensen, p. 686.*)

**9 b** ADH, a hormone released from the posterior lobe of the pituitary gland, works directly on the kidney tubules to aid in the reabsorption of water. (*Langley, Telford, and Christensen, p. 685.*)

**10 b** The kidney plays a major role in maintaining pH by excreting excess hydrogen ions. This role is dependent upon buffers in the urine. The major urinary buffers are the phosphates ($HPO_4$) and ammonia ($NH_3$). (*Langley, Telford, and Christensen, p. 353.*)

**11 b** Gastric secretions have a high concentration of hydrogen ions. It is this loss of hydrogen ions that occurs with vomiting or gastric suction which leads to metabolic alkalosis. (*Metheny and Snively, pp. 58–59.*)

**12 b** The primary anion found in pancreatic juices is bicarbonate, which neutralizes the acids entering the intestine from the stomach. This neutralization of acid prevents damage to the intestinal wall. (*Vander, Sherman, and Luciano, pp. 374–376.*)

**13 b** The plasma proteins play an important role in the distribution of body fluids by exerting a colloidal osmotic pressure in the intravascular compartment. The colloidal osmotic pressure draws fluids from the tissue spaces into the blood. A balance is achieved by the hydrostatic pressure of the blood, which pushes fluid out of the capillaries and into the tissue spaces. (*Langley, Telford, and Christensen, p. 385.*)

**14 c** Albumin is the plasma protein that exerts the greatest colloidal osmotic pressure in the intravascular compartment. As a result albumin plays a major role in drawing fluid into the intravascular compartment. (*Langley, Telford, and Christensen, p. 385.*)

**15 b** The renal reabsorption of calcium and the excretion of phosphates is regulated by the action of parthyroid hormone. (*Langley, Telford, and Christensen, p. 686.*)

**16 a**  Calcium is the most abundant cation found in the body. The greatest portion of it is found in the bones and teeth. Some is found in the blood serum and the body cells. (*Metheny and Snively, p. 29.*)

**17 c**  Calcitonin is a hormone secreted by the thyroid gland. As the blood calcium level increases, calcitonin is released and acts directly on the bone to inhibit resorption. (*Langley, Telford, and Christensen, p. 729.*)

**18 a**  The normal serum calcium is 4.5 to 5.8 meq/L. (*Shafer et al., p. 117.*)

**19 a**  Numbness and tingling of the fingers, toes, lips, and fingers are early signs of calcium deficit. If calcium salts can be given intravenously at this time, they will prevent the more serious symptoms, such as tetany, laryngospasm, and convulsions from developing. (*Shafer et al., p. 117.*)

**20 b**  Calcium deficiency can be determined by the nurse by applying a blood pressure cuff on the patient's arm and inflating it. If carpopedal spasm (muscular contraction of the fingers and hands) occurs, the patient has a positive Trousseau's sign. (*Luckmann and Sorensen, p. 237. Shafer et al., p. 117.*)

**21 a**  A test used to determine calcium deficiency can be done by tapping the patient's facial nerve just below the temple. Tapping can be done with a percussion hammer. If the side of the face begins to contract, then the patient has a positive Chvostek sign. (*Luckmann and Sorensen, p. 237. Shafer et al., p. 117.*)

**22 d**  Calcium gluconate is used to correct hypocalcemia. Care should be exercised when it is being administered IV since it can cause severe tissue irritation and sloughing if it infiltrates into the surrounding tissue or if it is administered too quickly. It is given cautiously to patients receiving digitalis preparations because it potentiates the action of digitalis and produces serious cardiac arrhythmias. (*Bergersen, p. 422.*)

**23 a**  One cup of broccoli contains 132 mg of calcium, and 1 cup of spinach contains 167 mg. All the other foods listed are much lower sources of calcium. For example, cauliflower contains 25 mg, cooked peas contain 37 mg, and canned corn contains 10 mg. Although milk is the best source of calcium, green, leafy vegetables, such as spinach, broccoli, kale, turnip greens, and dandelion greens, are also good sources of calcium. (*Williams, pp. 625–629.*)

**24 b** Prolonged immobilization, as seen in patients with fractures and paraplegic patients, can lead to hypercalcemia. This occurs because the rate of bone destruction exceeds the rate of bone production. The prolonged immobilization causes calcium to be drained from the bones into the extracellular fluid, causing an elevation of serum calcium. (*Luckmann and Sorensen, p. 238. Shafer et al., p. 117.*)

**25 c** The Sulkowitch test is a diagnostic test used to determine the amount of calcium being excreted in the urine. To be most accurate, the patient should be on a low-calcium diet for 3 days prior to the test. Urine is collected for 24 hours and sent to the laboratory. (*Metheny and Snively, p. 32.*)

**26 b** As calcium is being drained from the bones and the serum calcium rises, increased amounts of calcium are being excreted by the kidneys in the form of calcium salts. These calcium salts can crystallize out and become renal calculi or stones. (*Luckmann and Sorensen, p. 301. Shafer et al., p. 117.*)

**27 c** Since patients with hypercalcemia tend to form kidney stones, the nurse should force fluids in an attempt to dilute the calcium salts as they move through the kidney. (*Shafer et al., p. 177. Moidel, Giblin, and Wagner, p. 693.*)

**28 d** The normal serum sodium level ranges between 138 and 145 meq/L. (*Shafer et al., p. 115.*)

**29 c** Sodium deficit can occur with diarrhea, vomiting, gastrointestinal suction, and diuretic therapy. Corticosteroid therapy can cause sodium retention with edema formation. (*Moidel, Giblin, and Wagner, p. 217.*)

**30 c** There is no direct method available for measuring the osmolarity of the intracellular fluid. Therefore, the only means currently available is to determine the serum sodium level. The intracellular fluid and the extracellular fluid normally have the same osmolarity. If the serum sodium level shows an increase, then we can conclude that intracellular-fluid osmolarity will be increased. (*Luckmann and Sorensen, p. 199.*)

**31 a** Hyperosmolarity occurs when there is a deficit of body water or an excess of extracellular fluid. The hyperosmolarity could be brought on by decreased water intake, increased water loss, or an increase of extracellular sodium from improper IV therapy. Hyperosmolarity is manifested by signs and symptoms of dehydration. If the dehydration is not corrected, then the blood flow to the kidneys is decreased, causing oliguria or anuria. (*Luckmann and Sorensen, pp. 214–215.*)

**32 c** When the body becomes dehydrated as a result of impaired fluid intake, the kidneys function in an effort to conserve water. The hypothalamus stimulates the pituitary gland to secrete greater amounts of ADH, which works directly on the kidney tubules to increase the reabsorpotion of water. As a result the urine is darker and more concentrated and the output is decreased. (*Reed and Sheppard, p. 67.*)

**33 c** Accurate intake and output is a vital aspect of caring for patients with fluid and electrolyte imbalance. According to Luckmann and Sorensen, a 200-mL glass of fluid with ice chips is equivalent to approximately 100 mL of fluid. (*Luckmann and Sorensen, p. 246.*)

**34 c** If hypertonic solutions of glucose are given too rapidly, this causes the blood sugar to suddenly rise, in turn causing an increased secretion of insulin. When the IV is discontinued, the hyperinsulinism can cause signs and symptoms of insulin shock. (*Metheny and Snively, p. 133.*)

**35 c** Patients with low plasma protein levels (hypoproteinemia) often develop edema, as seen in cirrhosis of the liver and nephrosis. Salt-poor serum albumin can bring some relief from the effects of low plasma proteins. (*Rodman and Smith, p. 655.*)

**36 d** Protein hydrolysates should be given slowly, since nausea and vomiting can develop if they are administered too rapidly. Slowing the rate of administration will relieve the untoward reactions. Some persons are sensitive or allergic to protein hydrolysate. In these situations, the infusion should be stopped and the physician notified immediately. (*Luckmann and Sorensen, pp. 252–253.*)

**37 a** The normal serum potassium is 5 meq/L. (*Shafer et al., p. 116.*)

**38 c** Diuretic therapy is one cause of potassium depletion. The diuretics most commonly associated with potassium loss are the thiazide diuretics, such as Diuril and Hydrodiuril (hydrochlorothiazide). These drugs act directly on the kidney tubules to increase excretion of electrolytes such as sodium, chloride, and potassium. (*Moidel, Giblin, and Wagner, p. 220.*)

**39 d** Normally, potassium is excreted daily via the kidneys. Any stressor that produces oliguria or anuria interferes with the excretion of potassium and produces an elevated serum potassium. Administration of potassium chloride in patients with oliguria or anuria can lead to severe cardiac arrhythmias. (*Jones, Dunbar, and Jirovec, p. 459. Metheny and Snively, p. 136.*)

**40 d** Lima beans contain 422 mg of potassium, and potatoes contain 407 mg. All the other combinations of foods are much lower sources of potassium. Foods high in potassium include potatoes, avocados, bananas, dried fruits, nuts, and legumes such as lima beans, peas, and beans. (*Williams, pp. 660–672.*)

**41 a** Aldosterone is an adrenocortical hormone that works directly on the kidney tubules to aid in the reabsorption of sodium and the excretion of potassium. Hypofunctioning of the adrenal cortex, as seen in Addison's disease, is characterized by retention of potassium and loss of sodium. (*Metheny and Snively, p. 28.*)

**42 d** Tall, peaked T waves occur on the electrocardiogram when the level of serum potassium is increased. Although other factors can cause tall, peaked T waves, measurement of blood and urine potassium levels will confirm the diagnosis of hyperkalemia. (*Passman and Drummond, p. 218.*)

**43 c** The normal pH of the blood is 7.4. The range is 7.35 to 7.45. Even the slightest variation of pH can be life-endangering.

**44 a** The kidneys play a vital role in regulating hydrogen-ion concentration. The kidney tubules exchange sodium ions for hydrogen ions. As a result, sodium ions are conserved by reabsorption and hydrogen ions are eliminated in the urine as carbonic acid, organic acids, and ammonium salts. (*Langley, Telford, and Christensen, p. 704.*)

**45 b** The arterial $P_{CO_2}$ normally ranges between 35 and 38 mmHg. (*Luckmann and Sorensen, p. 221.*)

**46 d** The arterial $P_{O_2}$ normally ranges between 95 and 100 mmHg. (*Luckmann and Sorensen, p. 221.*)

**47 a** Hydrogen-ion concentration is expressed in terms of pH. A method used to determine the acidity, neutrality, or alkalinity of a solution is to measure its pH. Water, which is a neutral solution, has a pH of 7 and contains 1/100,000,000 g of hydrogen per liter. A solution that has a pH of 4 contains 1/10,000 g of hydrogen per liter, has a higher hydrogen-ion concentration than water, and is more acid. A solution that has a pH of 10 contains 1/10,000,000,000 g of hydrogen per liter, has a lower hydrogen-ion concentration than water, and is more alkaline.

**48 a** The respiratory center of the medulla is stimulated if the pH of the blood is decreased, if the $P_{CO_2}$ is increased and if the $P_{O_2}$ is decreased. The effect of the stimulation is an increase in the depth and rate of respiration in an attempt to "blow off" excess carbon dioxide and hydrogen ions. (*Luckmann and Sorensen, pp. 221–223.*)

**49 c** The hallmark of respiratory acidosis is carbonic acid excess. The excessive retention of carbon dioxide results in the carbon dioxide ($CO_2$) combining with water ($H_2O$) to form carbonic acid ($H_2CO_3$). (*Luckmann and Sorensen, p. 229.*)

**50 c** The respiratory center in the medulla is very sensitive to changes in the pH and carbon dioxide levels in the blood. If the pH is decreased and the $CO_2$ level is increased, the respiratory center is stimulated to increase the rate and depth of respiration in an attempt to blow off excess carbon dioxide. (*Vander, Sherman, and Luciano, p. 312.*)

**51 c** If the hydrogen-ion concentration of the blood is decreased and the pH of the blood is increased above the normal range, a state of alkalosis is said to exist. Alkalosis, whether it is metabolic or respiratory, stimulates the central nervous system and is characterized by tetany, convulsions, and death if not corrected. (*Shafer et al., p. 117.*)

**52 a** Patients on gastric suction lose hydrogen, chloride, potassium, and sodium ions. If replacement therapy is not administered, the patient will develop bicarbonate excess or metabolic alkalosis. (*Metheny and Snively, p. 196.*)

**53 c** In caring for a patient with gastric suction, the nurse should weigh the patient daily to detect early signs of fluid imbalance. Loss of weight could be a sign of fluid deficit, and an increase of weight could be a sign of fluid excess. (*Metheny and Snively, p. 198.*)

**54 c** Nasogastric tubes should be irrigated with an isotonic solution, such as normal saline, to prevent the loss of valuable electrolytes as irrigating fluid is being withdrawn. (*Metheny and Snively, p. 198.*)

**55 b** The hourly rate can be determined by dividing 3000 mL by 24. Since the drop factor is 10 gtt/mL, the hourly rate can be divided by 6 to determine how many drops per minute the patient should receive. For example, the hourly rate is 125 mL. Divide 125 by 6 to determine how many drops per minute. The answer is 20.8 or 21 gtt per minute. (*Saxton, Ercolano, and Walter, p. 53.*)

**56 d** The hallmark of metabolic acidosis is a deficit of plasma bicarbonates which causes a decrease of the pH of the blood. The body then attempts to restore the normal pH of the blood. The respiratory center of the medulla is stimulated to increase the depth and rate of respirations. The increased hydrogen-ion concentration of the blood triggers the kidneys to excrete the excess in the form of a more acid urine. (*Luckmann and Sorensen, p. 226.*)

**57 a** Renal insufficiency is a stressor that can lead to metabolic acidosis. Other stressors include ketoacidosis, starvation, and intestinal suctioning. In renal failure, there is decreased hydrogen-ion excretion. As a result the hydrogen-ion concentration of the blood is increased, which leads to metabolic acidosis. (*Metheny and Snively, p. 39. Moidel, Giblin, and Wagner, p. 225.*)

**58 a** Metabolic acidosis is characterized by rapid, deep respiration (air hunger), weakness, disorientation, stupor, and coma. The symptoms are a result of the decreased pH of the blood, which stimulates the respiratory center in the medulla and also depresses the central nervous system. (*Luckmann and Sorensen, p. 227. Metheny and Snively, p. 39.*)

**59 c** To correct metabolic acidosis, sodium bicarbonate can be given intravenously. Since the person with metabolic acidosis has a bicarbonate deficit, administration of sodium bicarbonate will restore the bicarbonate/carbonic acid ratio to 1:20 (*Bergersen, p. 415.*)

**60 b** If the hourly rate and the drop factor of the infusion set are unknown, the following method can be used to calculate the number of drops per minute at which the infusion should be regulated:
   **1** If the drop factor is 10 gtt = 1 mL, divide the hourly rate by 6.
   **2** If the drop factor is 15 gtt = 1 mL, divide the hourly rate by 4.
   **3** If the drop factor is 60 gtt = 1 mL, divide the hourly rate by 60. For example, if the patient is receiving

75 mL per hour and the drop factor is 15 gtt = 1 mL, divide 75 by 4 and set the infusion to run at 18.75 or 19 gtt per minute. (*Saxton, Ercolano, and Walter, p. 53.*)

**61 a** "Skin turgor" refers to the firmness of the skin and is a means of determining the hydration of the skin. Normally when the skin is pinched it springs back to its original state immediately upon releasing the fingers. If the skin remains in the pinched position for a few seconds, the patient is said to have poor skin turgor and is dehydrated. (*Jones, Dunbar, and Jirovec, p. 439.*)

# UNIT 5
# Nursing care of the patient with a skin disorder

**OBJECTIVES**

To answer the questions in this unit, the reader should be able to

1. Identify the layers of the skin;
2. Review the functions of the skin and its appendages;
3. Describe primary and secondary skin lesions;
4. Describe the nursing management of a patient with a skin disorder.

## QUESTIONS RELATED TO OBJECTIVES

*Instructions*: Choose the *one best* answer to the following questions.

1. The outer, thinner layer of the skin, made up of epithelial cells, is the
   a  Surface ectoderm.
   b  Epidermis.
   c  Dermis.
   d  Hypodermis.

2. The layer of the skin composed of connective tissue is the
   a  "Ectoderm."
   b  "Epidermis."
   c  "Dermis."
   d  "Hypodermis."

3. The area of the epidermis responsible for the regeneration of skin is the stratum
   a  Corneum.
   b  Lucidum.
   c  Granulosum.
   d  Germinativum.

4. Which of the following statements *best* relates to the function of the skin?
   a  The sebaceous glands of the skin secrete sweat, which regulates body temperature.
   b  The skin plays a role in producing vitamin D on exposure to sunlight.
   c  The apocrine glands produce melanin, which is responsible for skin coloring.
   d  Bacterial flora that come in contact with the skin are absorbed via the eccrine glands into the bloodstream.

**5** In assessing Ms. L. in the skin clinic, the nurse observed that the skin lesion was flat, reddened, circumscribed, and covered the inner aspects of the arms and legs. The nurse described the rash as

　**a** "Macular."
　**b** "Papular."
　**c** "Vesicular."
　**d** "Pustular."

**6** While caring for Ms. L. the nurse noticed that she had multiple vesicles on her buttocks. A "vesicle" is a

　**a** Thickening of the skin into a dry plaque.
　**b** Solid, palpable, raised, "pea"-sized lesion.
　**c** Superficial, elevated lesion filled with fluid.
　**d** Flat, reddened, circumscribed area on the skin.

**7** Pruritus is a symptom associated with all of the following *except*

　**a** Dry skin.
　**b** Contact dermatitis.
　**c** Seborrhea.
　**d** Malignancies of the skin.

**8** Nursing measures for the patient with pruritus include

　**a** Bathing the patient with hot, soapy water.
　**b** Restraining the patient's hands at night.
　**c** Keeping the patient's fingernails trimmed short.
　**d** Applying talcum powder to the skin.

**9** When caring for a patient with pruritus, the nurse should recognize that pruritus is

　**a** Made more intense by cold and vasoconstriction.
　**b** Decreased when the body temperature goes up.
　**c** Relieved by bathing with hot, soapy water.
　**d** Increased by activities that cause perspiration.

**10** In pemphigus, the characteristic skin lesions are
   a   Scales.
   b   Pustules.
   c   Bullae.
   d   Wheals.

**11** In caring for a patient with pemphigus, the nurse should
   a   Place the patient on isolation because it is highly communicable.
   b   Discourage movement by the patient to minimize pain.
   c   Apply dry, sterile dressings to the lesions to minimize pain.
   d   Observe the patient for signs and symptoms of fluid and electrolyte imbalance.

**12** Psoriasis is a common skin disorder characterized by
   a   Pustules in the groin and perineal area.
   b   Excoriations on the legs.
   c   Groups of vesicles on the face and back.
   d   Dry, silvery scales on the elbows, scalp, and chest.

**13** Patients with psoriasis should be told that
   a   Clothing that covers the lesion should be avoided.
   b   An initial episode of the disease results in permanent immunity.
   c   Bathing is contraindicated.
   d   Emotional stress can precipitate a recurrence of the skin lesions.

**14** Severe forms of psoriasis may be successfully treated with
   a   Phenylbutazone.
   b   Ampicillin.
   c   Amphotericin B.
   d   Methotrexate.

15 The skin rash associated with exposure to poison ivy is an example of
   a  Atopic dermatitis.
   b  Contact dermatitis.
   c  Exfoliative dermatitis.
   d  Toxicoderma.

16 Jane had a pimple on her chin which she proceeded to squeeze and pick. At first her chin began to swell, but soon she noticed that the swelling was spreading. She was admitted to the hospital with cellulitis of the face and neck. The most common infecting microbiological stressor contributing to cellulitis is
   a  *Pseudomonas aeroginosa.*
   b  *Candida albicans.*
   c  Beta *Streptococcus.*
   d  Herpes simplex virus type I.

17 While caring for Jane, who has cellulitis of the face and neck, the nurse should
   a  Insist that she drink fluids.
   b  Observe for impaired breathing.
   c  Check for bleeding at the back of the neck.
   d  Place her on isolation technique.

18 Systemic lupus erythematosus has been classified as an "autoimmune" disorder. This means that the body
   a  Produces antibodies that are destructive and damaging to its own cells and tissues.
   b  Attempts to defend itself against microbiological stressors by producing antibodies.
   c  Responds to foreign proteins by producing immune bodies.
   d  Adapts to chemical stressors by producing immunoglobulins.

**19** Systemic lupus erythematosus is characterized by
   **a** A butterfly rash across the cheeks and the bridge of the nose.
   **b** Large bullae that are easily rubbed off by slight pressure.
   **c** Vesicular lesions running along the course of a peripheral sensory nerve.
   **d** Rose-colored macules and papules over the entire body.

**20** The medications that are used to control the symptoms of systemic lupus are
   **a** Antibiotics.
   **b** Glucocorticosteroids.
   **c** Antihistamines.
   **d** Immunosuppressives.

**21** In caring for the patient with systemic lupus erythematosus, the nurse should
   **a** Know that the course of the disease is confined to the skin and the joints.
   **b** Place the patient on isolation techniques because of its communicability.
   **c** Apply wet dressings to the lesions to decrease the pain associated with the denuded areas.
   **d** Tell the patient to avoid exposure to the sun.

**22** Herpes zoster is a viral infection characterized by
   **a** A unilateral pustule occurring at the junction of the lips.
   **b** Groups of vesicles running along the course of a peripheral sensory nerve.
   **c** Red, swollen, delineated plaques occurring on the face.
   **d** A rose-colored, well-demarcated oval lesion called a "herald patch."

**23** In caring for the patient with herpes zoster, the nurse should
  **a** Place the patient on isolation precautions.
  **b** Recognize that pain is usually severe.
  **c** Be aware that pruritus is not one of the usual symptoms.
  **d** Keep the lesions covered with dry, sterile dressings and loose clothing.

**24** While caring for Mr. P., a 76-year-old man, the nurse noted that his skin was very dry. Changes in the nursing-care plan included
  **a** Using a hexachlorophene soap for bathing.
  **b** Omitting a daily complete bath.
  **c** Adding bicarbonate of soda to the bath water.
  **d** Using witch hazel instead of alcohol to rub the back.

**25** Persons allergic to bee or wasp stings may go into anaphylactic shock. The medication that can be used to counteract the effects of anaphylactic shock is
  **a** Epinephrine.
  **b** Aminophylline.
  **c** Vasodilan.
  **d** Sodium bicarbonate.

**26** Which of the following statements relating to anaphylactic shock is true?
  **a** The first exposure to a foreign substance can cause anaphylactic shock.
  **b** Cardiopulmonary resuscitation is indicated if cardiac arrest occurs in anaphylactic shock.
  **c** Anaphylactic shock is slow in its onset and reaches its peak in 48 hours.
  **d** "Allergic asthma" is another name for anaphylactic shock.

**27** Toxic effects of epinephrine include
  **a** Hypertension, tachycardia, and tremors.
  **b** Hypotension, tremors, and circumoral flush.
  **c** Sloughing of subcutaneous tissue, dyspnea, and sweating.
  **d** Bradycardia, convulsions, and dyspnea.

**28** When teaching the patient who is hypersensitive to bee or insect bites, the nurse should tell the patient to *avoid* all the following *except*
  **a** Going barefoot.
  **b** Sitting in areas surrounded by flowers and bushes.
  **c** Wearing perfume.
  **d** Wearing dark clothing.

## ANSWERS, EXPLANATIONS, AND REFERENCES

**1 b**  The outer, thinner layer of the skin is called the "epidermis." During embryological development, the epidermis develops from the surface ectoderm. The epidermis prevents loss of body fluid and protects the body from the invasion of microorganisms and chemical irritants. (*Langley, Telford, and Christensen, p. 66.*)

**2 c**  The layer of the skin composed of connective tissue is called the "dermis" or "corium." It contains blood vessels, collagenous fibers, lymph vessels, sensory and motor neurons, and portions of glands of the skin. (*Langley, Telford, and Christensen, p. 68.*)

**3 d**  The epidermis has four distinct zones or strata. The stratum germinativum, or "growing layer," of the epidermis is subdivided into the basal and spinal layers. The cells in the basal layer are constantly reproducing. Damage or injury to this layer can cause scarring. (*Langley, Telford, and Christensen, p. 66.*)

**4 b**  The skin plays a role in the production of vitamin D. When the skin is exposed to the ultraviolet rays from the sun, vitamin D is produced. A deficiency of vitamin D impairs the absorpotion of calcium from the intestines. As a result, rickets can develop in children and osteomalacia in adults. (*Langley, Telford, and Christensen, p. 70.*)

**5 a** A "macule" is a primary skin lesion described as a flat, discolored, circumscribed area on the skin. The size of the lesion varies. (*Jones, Dunbar, and Jirovec, p. 296. Moidel, Giblin, and Wagner, p. 984.*)

**6 c** A "vesicle" is a small blister that is superficial and filled with serous or serosanguinous fluid. If it is larger than 0.5 cm in diameter, it is called a "bulla." (*Jones, Dunbar, and Jirovec, p. 297.*)

**7 d** Pruritus is not the usual symptom of skin malignancies. If a patient has a skin lesion that itches, malignancies can be ruled out. (*Luckmann and Sorensen, pp. 1254–1255.*)

**8 c** The scratching done by the patient to relieve pruritis traumatizes the skin and makes the patient more vulnerable to infection. Keeping the fingernails cut short helps to decrease the trauma inflicted by scratching. (*Luckmann and Sorensen, p. 1255.*)

**9 d** Pruritus is intensified by increased body temperature, heat, excessive drying of the skin, activities that cause increased perspiration, and stress. (*Shafer et al., p. 733.*)

**10 c** Pemphigus is a skin disorder of unknown etiology that is characterized by bullae on the skin and mucous membrane. Bullae are superficial elevated lesions that are larger than vesicles and filled with fluid. (*Shafer et al., p. 285.*)

**11 d** The fluid that collects in the bullae contains valuable electrolytes and protein. The escape of the fluid from the lesion can cause serious fluid and electrolyte imbalance. Therefore, the nurse should observe the patient very carefully for signs and symptoms of fluid and electrolyte imbalance. (*Moidel, Giblin, and Wagner, p. 1002.*)

**12 d** Psoriasis is a skin disease of unknown etiology characterized by dry, silver-scaled lesions on the elbows, chest, back, and scalp. (*Luckmann and Sorensen, p. 1270.*)

**13 d** Although psoriasis is a disease of unknown etiology, it is known that emotional stress, systemic illness, and drug allergy can influence the course of the disease and make it worse. (*Moidel, Giblin, and Wagner, p. 988.*)

**14 d** Severe forms of psoriasis are currently being treated successfully with methotrexate, a folic acid antagonist. Since the drug is so toxic, the physician prescribes the lowest dose that will relieve the skin lesion. (*Luckmann and Sorensen, p. 1272.*)

**15 b** Contact dermatitis is a skin rash that develops when certain irritants come in contact with the skin. Examples of chemical stressors or irritants causing local skin reactions are detergents, cosmetics, petroleum and coal tar products, and certain plants, such as poison ivy, sumac, and oak. (*Shafer et al., p. 784.*)

**16 c** Cellulitis is an inflammation of the skin and the subcutaneous tissue which can often spread from a primary focus of infection. The beta *Streptococcus* is the most common causitive microorganism. (*Moidel, Giblin, and Wagner, p. 86.*)

**17 b** If cellulitis spreads to the face and neck, the edematous tissue can exert pressure on the airway, leading to impaired respiration. The patient should be observed most carefully for difficulty in breathing, chewing, and swallowing. (*Moidel, Giblin, and Wagner, p. 86.*)

**18 a** There are many diseases of human beings that are now being classified as autoimmune disorders. It is believed that the body produces antibodies that are destructive or damaging to its own tissue. Examples of autoimmune disorders include systemic lupus erythematosus, rheumatoid arthritis, idiopathic thrombocytopenic purpura, Hashimoto's disease, etc. (*Luckmann and Sorensen, pp. 185–186. Vander, Sherman, and Luciano, p. 499.*)

**19 a** It is believed that systemic lupus erythematosus is an autoimmune disorder of connective tissue. A butterfly rash that occurs on the cheeks and crosses over the bridge of the nose is the characteristic skin lesion. (*Jones, Dunbar, and Jirovec, p. 399.*)

**20 b** The medications that are used to control the symptoms of systemic lupus erythematosus are the glucocorticosteroids. It is believed that they reduce the effects of inflammation and suppress antibody production. (*Luckmann and Sorensen, pp. 187, 1274.*)

**21 d** Exposure to the sun may contribute to an exacerbation of the disease. Therefore, patients with lupus should be told to avoid exposure to the sun and protect themselves from direct contact by using sun-screening agents and keeping the skin covered. (*Jones, Dunbar, and Jirovec, p. 400. Moidel, Giblin and Wagner, p. 1007.*)

**22 b** Herpes zoster, or "shingles," is a viral infection of the peripheral sensory nerves characterized by groups of vesicles running along the course of the nerve. It is usually unilateral. The virus causing herpes zoster is closely related to the virus causing chicken pox in children. (*Moidel, Giblin, and Wagner, p. 994.*)

**23 b** The pain associated with herpes zoster is usually persistent and severe. The nurse should recognize this and medicate the patient as prescribed by the physician. The pain is so severe that even clothing coming in contact with the lesions will intensify it. Another distressing symptom is pruritus. Systemic antipruritics and cool, wet dressings may be prescribed to relieve the itching. (*Moidel, Giblin, and Wagner, p. 994.*)

**24 b** Elderly persons have a tendency to develop dry skin because of the decreased activity of the sebaceous glands. In caring for persons with dry skin, the nurse should eliminate daily complete baths. Soap should not be used since it tends to increase dryness by removing protective oils from the skin. Bicarbonate of soda is also drying to the skin. (*Mitchell, p. 499. Shafer et al., p. 774.*)

**25 a** When a person develops anaphylactic shock as a result of an allergic reaction to a bee or an insect bite, drug therapy must be initiated immediately as an emergency measure. The drug most frequently used to halt the death-producing symptoms of anaphylactic·shock is epinephrine. (*Luckmann and Sorensen, p. 1262.*)

**26 b** One of the causes of cardiac arrest is anaphylactic shock. If the person stops breathing and has no pulse, cardiopulmonary resuscitation should be initiated immediately. (*Luckmann and Sorensen, p. 657.*)

**27 a** Epinephrine is an adrenergic drug that increases cardiac output and relieves the respiratory distress associated with anaphylactic shock. Toxic symptoms include hypertension, tachycardia, tremors, and anxiety. (*Luckmann and Sorensen, p. 178.*)

**28 d** Persons hypersensitive to bee or insect bites should carry an emergency insect kit and an identification card stating that they are sensitive to insect stings. These persons should also avoid wearing bright colors, since the bright colors attract insects. Furthermore, they should avoid going barefoot, wearing perfumes, and sitting in grassy areas surrounded by flowers and bushes. (*Luckmann and Sorensen, p. 180.*)

# UNIT 6

# Nursing care of the patient with a disorder of the blood

**OBJECTIVES**

To answer the questions in this unit, the reader should be able to
1. Identify the major components of the blood;
2. Describe the functions of the various blood components;
3. Explain how the body adapts to the various stressors causing a blood disorder;
4. Recognize the specific diagnostic tests relating to blood disorders;
5. Recognize the role of the nurse in administering the various medications used to treat blood disorders;
6. Describe the nursing management of the patient with a blood disorder.

## QUESTIONS RELATED TO OBJECTIVES

*Instructions*: Choose the *one best* answer to the following questions.

1. Examples of white blood cells formed in the red bone marrow are
   a. Leukocytes, agranulocytes, and granulocytes.
   b. Monocytes, lymphocytes, and eosinophils.
   c. Neutrophils, eosinophils, and basophils.
   d. Granulocytes, histiocytes, and monocytes.

2. The granulocyte that plays a role in acute infections is the
   a. Monocyte.
   b. Basophil.
   c. Eosinophil.
   d. Neutrophil.

3. The leukocyte that can be transformed into a macrophage in response to microbiological or foreign-body invasion is the
   a. Basophil.
   b. Lymphocyte.
   c. Monocyte.
   d. Eosinophil.

4. The blood cell that plays an essential role in the clotting mechanism is the
   a. Erythrocyte.
   b. Reticulocyte.
   c. Thrombocyte.
   d. Plasmacyte.

5. The normal platelet count range is how many per cubic millimeter of blood?
   a. 500 to 1500.
   b. 5000 to 10,000.
   c. 200,000 to 400,000.
   d. 4,500,000 to 5,000,000.

**6** An immature red blood cell is called a (an)
   **a** "Erythrocyte."
   **b** "Thrombocyte."
   **c** "Reticulocyte."
   **d** "Reticulum cell."

**7** The vitamin essential for the maturation of red blood cells is
   **a** Thiamine.
   **b** Niacin.
   **c** Pyridoxine.
   **d** Cyanocobalamin.

**8** The normal red-blood-cell count of each cubic millimeter of blood is
   **a** 500.
   **b** 5000.
   **c** 500,000.
   **d** 5,000,000.

**9** In addition to its function of serving as a buffer to maintain the acid-base balance of the blood, hemoglobin
   **a** Stimulates the bone marrow to manufacture red blood cells.
   **b** Aids in the maturation of reticulocytes.
   **c** Plays a role in differentiating reticulum cells.
   **d** Transports oxygen to all the cells.

**10** Persons living in high mountainous areas adapt to the high altitude by producing an increased number of
   **a** Erythrocytes.
   **b** Thrombocytes.
   **c** Leukocytes.
   **d** Plasmacytes.

**11** When preparing the patient for a bone marrow aspiration, the nurse should tell the patient that
  a  The procedure is painless.
  b  The specimen will be taken from the sternum.
  c  A small incision will be made over the hipbone.
  d  A consent is not necessary because the specimen is withdrawn with a needle and a syringe.

**12** Following a bone marrow aspiration on the sternum, the patient complained of soreness at the puncture site. The nurse checked the area and
  a  Notified the physician.
  b  Explained to the patient that this was normal and would subside in a few days.
  c  Applied hot compresses to the area.
  d  Told the patient that the doctor had had difficulty inserting the needle into the bone.

**13** A common symptom of the anemias is
  a  Achlorhydria.
  b  Fatigue.
  c  Bradycardia.
  d  Bleeding from the gums.

**14** Which of the following statements relating to sickle cell anemia is correct?
  a  A cure can be brought about by plasmapheresis.
  b  Sickle cell anemia is an acquired anemia transmitted by the anapheles mosquito.
  c  A sickle cell crisis can be precipitated by microbiological stressors causing an acute infection.
  d  The incidence is highest in persons of Mediterranean origin.

**15** Ms. A. is receiving ferrous sulfate for iron-deficiency anemia. The patient should be told that
   **a** Taking an antacid with each dose relieves nausea and vomiting.
   **b** Ferrous sulfate can cause the stool to be black.
   **c** If the oral route is not tolerated, ferrous sulfate can be given parenterally.
   **d** Orange juice impairs the absorption of oral iron preparations.

**16** The red blood cell adapts to a deficiency of iron by becoming
   **a** Microcytic and hypochromic.
   **b** Microcytic and hyperchromic.
   **c** Macrocytic and hypochromic.
   **d** Macrocytic and hyperchromic.

**17** Iron dextrose (Imferon) 30 mg IM has been ordered for the patient. When administering the medication the nurse should
   **a** Use a ¾-in, 22-gauge needle to administer the medication.
   **b** Administer the medication into the deltoid muscle.
   **c** Displace the subcutaneous tissue to one side before inserting the needle into the muscle.
   **d** Massage the injection site for 60 seconds to aid in absorption.

**18** Which of the following combinations of food is highest in iron?
   **a** Macaroni and cheese.
   **b** Hamburger and bun.
   **c** Cottage cheese and cantaloupe.
   **d** Tomato soup with rice.

**19** Mr. S. is a 45-year-old man who was admitted to the hospital with a diagnosis of pernicious anemia. The principal cause of the impaired absorption of vitamin $B_{12}$, as seen in pernicious anemia, is a lack of
  **a** Hydrochloric acid.
  **b** Intrinsic factor.
  **c** Hematopoietin.
  **d** Dietary intake of vitamin $B_{12}$.

**20** Symptoms of pernicious anemia include
  **a** Achlorhydria, sore tongue, and numbness of extremities.
  **b** Sore tongue, ataxia, and nosebleeds.
  **c** Fatigue, tingling of extremities, and smoky urine.
  **d** Ataxia, stress ulcer, and hematuria.

**21** The incidence of pernicious anemia is highest in
  **a** Southern Mediterraneans.
  **b** Northern Europeans.
  **c** Blacks.
  **d** Orientals.

**22** The Schilling test is a diagnostic test used to measure the intrinsic factor associated with pernicious anemia. The nurse should recognize that
  **a** All urine should be saved for 24 hours.
  **b** The patient should be NPO until blood samples are taken.
  **c** Gastric samples are taken via a nasogastric tube.
  **d** Red meats are omitted for 72 hours prior to the test.

**23** A gastric analysis was done on Mr. S. to determine gastric acidity. While assisting with the test, the nurse should
  **a** Position the patient flat in bed.
  **b** Attach the nasogastric tube to suction apparatus.
  **c** Encourage the patient to swallow frequently while the tube is being inserted.
  **d** Offer the patient food during the test to increase the flow of gastric juice.

**24** After a fasting gastric analysis specimen was collected, the nurse administered betazole hydrochloride (Histolog) subcutaneously to the patient. This medication

  **a** Is administered to neutralize the gastric secretions.
  **b** Causes an elevation of blood pressure, so the blood pressure should be monitored.
  **c** Is given with histamine phosphate to enhance its action.
  **d** Is preferred to histamine phosphate because it has less toxic effects.

**25** To alleviate the cold feet experienced by patients with pernicious anemia the nurse

  **a** Applied a heating pad to the feet.
  **b** Soaked the patient's feet in hot water.
  **c** Placed a hot water bag on her abdomen.
  **d** Encouraged the patient to wear warm socks.

**26** In planning a program of care for Mr. S.'s discharge, the nurse emphasized to him that

  **a** Eating foods high in vitamin $B_{12}$ will prevent an exacerbation.
  **b** Administration of hydrochloric acid with meals will aid in the absorption of vitamin $B_{12}$.
  **c** Periodic blood transfusions are indicated if the reticulocyte count decreases.
  **d** A maintenance dose of parenteral vitamin $B_{12}$ must be taken for life.

**27** About 1 week after discharge, Mr. S. returned to the hematology clinic for a follow-up visit. The nurse noted that his reticulocyte count was increased. This means that

  **a** Response to vitamin $B_{12}$ therapy is favorable and is causing a rise in red-cell production.
  **b** The bone marrow is being overstimulated because too much vitamin $B_{12}$ is being given.
  **c** There is a red-cell maturation failure that can be corrected by supplementing folic acid with vitamin $B_{12}$.
  **d** The dietary intake of foods high in vitamin $B_{12}$ should be reduced to stabilize the reticulocyte count.

**28** Reverse isolation is indicated for the patient with
   **a** Sickle cell anemia.
   **b** Pernicious anemia.
   **c** Aplastic anemia.
   **d** Iron-deficiency anemia.

**29** Patients who are on a phlebotomy regimen for polycythemia vera should be told
   **a** That plasma expanders will be given every 2 months.
   **b** To observe for bleeding tendencies.
   **c** To avoid foods high in iron.
   **d** That bed rest is essential for 72 hours after the phlebotomy.

**30** Alicia is a 35-year-old woman who has been admitted to the hospital with advanced chronic myelocytic leukemia (CML). While planning her nursing care the nurse should recognize that
   **a** Leukemia is a communicable disease, so Alicia should be placed on isolation.
   **b** Her complaints of fatigue and exhaustion are caused by the accompanying anemia.
   **c** The increased number of neutrophils enables Alicia to fight off acute infections.
   **d** Bleeding tendencies do not usually occur with chronic myelocytic leukemia.

**31** The nurse noticed that Alicia's thrombocyte count was decreased. Overt signs of a decreased thrombocyte count would be evidenced by
   **a** Ecchymoses, petechiae, and hematomas of the skin.
   **b** Leukoplakia and pallor of the mucous membrane of the mouth.
   **c** Dizziness, dyspnea, and fatigue on exertion.
   **d** Abdominal distention, ascites, and telangiectasis.

**32** In assessing the patient who has been admitted to the hospital with advanced chronic myelocytic leukemia, the nurse would expect to find
   a  Massive enlargement of the lymph glands.
   b  Marked splenomegaly.
   c  Alopecia.
   d  Joint pain.

**33** A laboratory finding associated with chronic myelocytic leukemia is the presence of
   a  Reed-Sternberg cells.
   b  Philadelphia chromosome.
   c  Leukemoid reaction.
   d  Cytolysin.

**34** Alicia was placed on chemotherapy to alleviate the symptoms of CML. One morning while combing her hair, you noticed large clumps of hair on the comb. Alicia said, "I'm losing all my beautiful hair." You should
   a  Agree with Alicia but assure her that it is not as much as she thinks it is.
   b  Tell her that it is a toxic symptom of the medication and the doctor will have to discontinue the therapy.
   c  Assure her that it will not be permanent and suggest that a wig can be worn until it grows back.
   d  Say to Alicia, "What makes you think you are losing your hair?"

**35** Patients with advanced leukemia tend to develop painful ulcerations of the oral mucosa. The nurse should
   a  Encourage the patient to use a soft toothbrush to cleanse the teeth.
   b  Instruct the patient to remove the plaque on the tongue with a toothbrush and a mild dentifrice.
   c  Use soft cotton applicators and a 1% solution of hydrogen peroxide to cleanse mouth and teeth.
   d  Omit mouth care because it just adds to the patient's discomfort.

**36** Leukapheresis was ordered to remove the increased number of white blood cells being formed in the patient with chronic lymphocytic leukemia. In caring for the patient, the nurse should recognize that
 **a** The rate of fluid replacement should exceed the rate at which the leukocytes are being removed.
 **b** The usual rate at which the pump circulates blood is 100 mL per hour.
 **c** At the end of the therapy, the blood in the tubing and centrifuge bowl should be discarded.
 **d** Staff members should wear rubber gloves to remove needles and to dismantle and wash centrifuge bowls.

**37** An early symptom of Hodgkin's disease is
 **a** Cough and dyspnea.
 **b** Painless enlargement of the cervical lymph nodes.
 **c** Enlargement of the liver and the spleen.
 **d** Nerve pain in the arms and hands.

**38** The characteristic cell found in Hodgkin's disease is the
 **a** Lymphoblast.
 **b** Plasmocyte.
 **c** Reed-Sternberg cell.
 **d** Atypical monocyte.

**39** The combination of drugs used to treat Hodgkin's disease are referred to as the "MOPP" combination. The names of the drugs used are
 **a** Mechlorethamine, Oncovin, prednisone, procarbazine.
 **b** Methotrexate, Oncovin, prednisone, Purinethol.
 **c** Mercaptopurine, Oncovin, prednisone, phosphotope.
 **d** Myleran, Oncovin, Purinethol, procarbazine.

**40** One of the drugs used to treat Hodgkin's disease is Oncovin (vincristine sulfate). Toxic symptoms of this medication include
   **a** Ringing in the ears and xanthopia.
   **b** Disturbance of gait and tingling and numbness of the fingers and toes.
   **c** Hypertrophied gums and deafness.
   **d** Irregular pulse and postural hypotension.

**41** While caring for the patient who is receiving procarbazine for Hodgkin's disease, the nurse recognizes that
   **a** It is inactivated by gastric juices.
   **b** It is an antibiotic with weak bacteriocidal activity.
   **c** Depression of bone marrow does not occur, so it is safer to use.
   **d** Foods such as bananas and cheese should be avoided.

**42** Toxic symptoms of prednisone include
   **a** Hematuria, skin rash, and peptic ulcer.
   **b** Alopecia, ulcerations of the mouth, and bleeding gums.
   **c** Cystitis, hypercalcemia, and gynecomastia.
   **d** Weight gain, rounding of the face, and acne.

**43** Other names for mechlorethamine are
   **a** Methotrexate and amethopterin.
   **b** Mercaptopurine and Purinethol.
   **c** Nitrogen mustard and Mustargen.
   **d** Cyclophosphamide and Cytoxan.

**44** Mrs. L. is a 54-year-old woman who has had multiple myeloma and suffers from severe bone pain that is controlled by medication. While caring for her you notice that her conversation is centered around herself, her body, and the pain. During the nursing conference, you interpret this to the team members as, "Mrs. L. is

    **a** So egocentric. I can't believe how much she talks about herself."

    **b** A poor conversationalist. I try to encourage her to talk about her husband and her family and she goes on and on about her illness."

    **c** Rude. No matter what I say to her, she manages to dominate the conversation."

    **d** Inner-directed because of the pain and the illness and is making an attempt to adapt to the illness."

**45** While caring for Mrs. L., who has multiple myeloma, the nurse should recognize that the patient

    **a** Is particularly vulnerable to pathological fractures.

    **b** Can develop hypertension from the increased production of red blood cells.

    **c** Responds well to steroid therapy and splenectomy.

    **d** Is prone to tetany and convulsions because of the hypocalcemia.

**46** Ms. O., who has advanced multiple myeloma, should

    **a** Be confined to bed because of the high risk of pathological fractures.

    **b** Have fluids restricted to reduce the work load of the kidneys.

    **c** Be observed for hypertension because of the increased blood volume.

    **d** Be protected from infection because of the decreased production of white blood cells.

**47** Persons with infectious mononucleosis produce antibodies that agglutinate the red blood cells of sheep. This test is called the
  **a** C-reactive protein agglutination test.
  **b** Latex agglutination test.
  **c** Complement fixation test.
  **d** Heterophil agglutination test.

**48** In acute infectious mononucleosis, there is an elevation of
  **a** Neutrophils.
  **b** Monocytes.
  **c** Lymphocytes.
  **d** Eosinophils.

**49** In idiopathic thrombocytopenic purpura, the following laboratory findings occur:
  **a** Prolonged partial thromboplastin time and increased coagulation time.
  **b** Decreased platelet count and prolonged bleeding time.
  **c** Prolonged bleeding time and prolonged prothrombin time.
  **d** Prolonged coagulation time and prolonged bleeding time.

**50** In caring for the patient with bleeding tendencies, the nurse should
  **a** Notify the physician if the patient becomes constipated.
  **b** Administer IM injections into the abdomen to prevent bleeding into the skin.
  **c** Tell the patient that the black stool is from the folic acid being used to combat the anemia.
  **d** Smoky urine occurs from the blood transfusions being given.

**51** The nurse plays an important role in the safe administration of blood and should recognize that
  **a** Blood that has been refrigerated should be placed in a pan of warm water before being administered.
  **b** In mild allergic reactions to blood, antihistamines can be added to the unit of blood.
  **c** Administration of mismatched blood can cause renal failure.
  **d** Pyrogenic reactions to contaminated blood occur 1 week after the initial administration.

## ANSWERS, EXPLANATIONS, AND REFERENCES

**1 c** The white blood cells produced in the red bone marrow are the granulocytes, which are subdivided into neutrophils, eosinophils, and basophils. (*Jones, Dunbar, and Jirovec, p. 279.*)

**2 d** The neutrophil is a granulocyte that plays an important role in acute infections. During the inflammatory process, the neutrophils engulf and inactivate the invading microorganism by a process called "phagocytosis." (*Beland and Passos, p. 324. Moidel, Giblin, and Wagner, p. 625.*)

**3 c** The monocyte is an agranulocyte that can be transformed into a macrophage during the inflammatory reaction. The macrophage engulfs the offending microorganism or other foreign material by a process called phagocytosis. (*Jones, Dunbar, and Jirovec, p. 280. Vander, Sherman, and Luciano, pp. 478–480.*)

**4 c** Another name for a blood platelet is a "thrombocyte." Thrombocytes are manufactured in the red bone marrow and play an important role in the clotting mechanism of the blood. (*Langley, Telford, and Christensen, p. 385.*)

**5 c** Platelets are necessary for blood coagulation. The normal platelet count ranges from 200,000 to 400,000 per cubic millimeter of blood. (*Langley, Telford, and Christensen, p. 385. Moidel, Giblin, and Wagner, p. 624.*)

**6 c** A reticulocyte is an immature form of a red blood cell. (*Beland and Passos, p. 541.*)

**7 d** Cyanocobalamin (vitamin $B_{12}$) is essential for the maturation of red blood cells and for normal functioning of the nervous system. It is also referred to as the "antianemic principle" and the "extrinsic" factor. (*Bergersen, p. 190.*)

**8 d** The normal red-blood-cell count is 5,000,000 per cubic millimeter of blood. (*Langley, Telford, and Christensen, p. 377.*)

**9 d** Hemoglobin, a protein constituent of red blood cells, is essential for transporting oxygen to the cells of the body. Any stressor leading to a reduction of hemoglobin can lead to tissue hypoxia. (*Langley, Telford, and Christensen, p. 377.*)

**10 a** Oxygen tension of the blood is greatly reduced in healthy individuals living in areas with a high altitude. As a result of the reduced oxygen tension of the blood, the kidneys release a substance called "erythropoietin," which stimulates the bone marrow to produce more red blood cells. This adaptation is referred to as a "physiological" or a "secondary" polycythemia. (*Beland and Passos, p. 552.*)

**11 b** Bone marrow aspiration is a diagnostic test used to examine the various types of blood cells being produced in the bone marrow. In adults, a special sternal needle and syringe is used to withdraw a sample of bone marrow tissue from the sternum or the iliac crest. The patient should be told that the puncture site will be anesthetized to reduce pain and discomfort. (*Massachusetts General Hospital, p. 75.*)

**12 b** Following a bone marrow aspiration, the patient may complain of soreness at the puncture site. The patient should be assured that this is normal and will subside in a few days. (*Luckmann and Sorensen, p. 752.*)

**13 b** Fatigue is a symptom common to disorders of the blood. The decrease of red blood cells and hemoglobin greatly reduces the oxygen being delivered to the tissues. Since physical activities increase the cells' requirements for oxygen, any physical exertion can cause fatigue. Patients should be taught to pace their activities and to rest frequently throughout the day to conserve energy. (*Beland and Passos, p. 549. Shafer et al., p. 410.*)

**14 c** Sickle cell anemia is an inherited blood disorder characterized by the presence of S hemoglobin. When the red blood is exposed to low oxygen tensions, it acquires the shape of a sickle. The incidence is highest in blacks. A sickle cell crisis, which is characterized by excruciating abdominal, muscle, and joint pain, can be precipitated by an acute infection. (*Beland and Passos, p. 547.*)

**15 b** Patients should be told that taking iron preparations by mouth can cause the stool to be black, since whatever iron is not absorbed will be eliminated in the stool. Administration of orange juice or vitamin C with the oral dose aids in the absorption. Although the medication is best absorbed on an empty stomach, if gastric irritation occurs, the patient should be advised to take the medication with meals. Ferrous sulfate cannot be given parenterally. (*Bergersen, p. 188.*)

**16 a** In iron-deficiency anemia, hemoglobin is reduced. As a result, the red blood cell is paler in color (hypochromic) and smaller in size (microcytic). Physiological stressors contributing to iron-deficiency include chronic blood loss, inadequate intake of iron, and impaired absorption of iron. (*Beland and Passos, p. 543.*)

**17 c** The nurse should exercise extreme caution when administering intramuscular iron preparation. A 2- or 3-in 19- or 20-gauge needle should be used to administer the preparation deeply into the upper outer quadrant of the buttocks. Prior to insertion of the needle, the subcutaneous tissue should be pulled aside to prevent leakage and discoloration of the skin along the injection tract. It is recommended that the nurse read the literature that accompanies the medication before administration. (*Luckmann and Sorensen, p. 761.*)

**18 b** Foods high in iron include meat, green, leafy vegetables, legumes, egg yolk, dried fruits, and shellfish. (*Williams, p. 151.*)

**19 b** Vitamin $B_{12}$ can be absorbed from the stomach only in the presence of intrinsic factors. Because of the gastric atrophy associated with pernicious anemia, it is believed that intrinsic factor cannot be produced and is therefore lacking. As a result, no matter how massive a dose is given by mouth, vitamin $B_{12}$ cannot be absorbed. (*Luckmann and Sorensen, p. 762.*)

**20 a** Pernicious anemia is a familial blood disorder characterized by gastrointestinal and neurological disorders. Atrophy of the gastric mucosa causes a decrease of hydrochloric acid, which is responsible for many of the gastrointestinal symptoms. Degeneration of the myelin sheath resulting from lack of vitamin $B_{12}$ contributes to the neurological symptoms. (*Jones, Dunbar, and Jirovec, p. 780. Luckmann and Sorensen, p. 762.*)

**21 b** The incidence of pernicious anemia is highest in persons of Northern European or Scandinavian extraction. It more commonly affects those persons who are blue-eyed and have white or gray hair. (*Jones, Dunbar, and Jirovec, p. 781.*)

**22 a** When the Schilling test is being done on a patient, a tracer dose of radioactive vitamin $B_{12}$ is given by mouth and a nonradioactive dose of vitamin $B_{12}$ is given intramuscularly. In pernicious anemia, the impaired absorption of vitamin $B_{12}$ causes a reduction of urinary excretion. (*Jones, Dunbar, and Jirovec, p. 782. Moidel, Gilblin, and Wagner, p. 629.*)

**23 c** While the nasogastric tube is being inserted, the patient should be encouraged to swallow or to take sips of water to facilitate the passage of the tube. The patient should be allowed to assume a sitting position while the tube is being inserted. Fluids and food are omitted for 6 to 8 hours prior to the test. To prevent leakage, the end of the tube is clamped after each specimen is collected. (*Shafer et al., p. 654.*)

**24 d** Betazole hydrochloride (Histolog), an analog of histamine, is administered to patients having a gastric analysis to increase the flow of gastric secretions. Since it has fewer side effects than histamine phosphate, it is the drug of choice. (*Shafer et al., p. 654.*)

**25 d** Patients with pernicious anemia often have a degeneration of the myelin sheath of the nerve fibers, which causes loss of sensation to heat and cold. Because of this, application of external heat can be extremely hazardous to these patients. Encouraging the patient to wear warm socks or applying extra blankets can alleviate complaints of cold feet. (*Beland and Passos, p. 551. Luckmann and Sorensen, p. 757.*)

**26 d** Patients with pernicious anemia should be told they will be committed to lifelong parenteral vitamin $B_{12}$ therapy. If the patient fails to take the medication as ordered, symptoms of pernicious anemia will recur. Since there is a lack of the intrinsic factor necessary for absorption of vitamin $B_{12}$, diet alone is inadequate for relieving symptoms. (*Luckmann and Sorensen, p. 764.*)

**27 a** Reticulocytes are an immature form of erythrocytes found in the peripheral blood. In pernicious anemia, the reticulocytes are decreased. However, once vitamin $B_{12}$ therapy is initiated, the reticulocyte count increases, signifying that red-cell production is being stimulated. (*Jones, Dunbar, and Jirovec, p. 782. Luckmann and Sorensen, p. 763.*)

**28 c** In aplastic anemia there is a severe decrease of the white blood cells and the platelets as well as the red blood cells. As a result, patients with aplastic anemia are particularly vulnerable to infections. Reverse isolation is indicated as a means of protecting the patient. (*Luckmann and Sorensen, p. 757.*)

**29 c** Patients with polycythemia vera who are on a phlebotomy regimen (venesection) will have approximately 500 mL of blood removed every 2 to 3 months once the hematocrit has been reduced. The phlebotomy aids in reducing blood volume and helps to relieve the symptoms of congestion associated with polycythemia vera.

Patients should be told to reduce the dietary intake of iron. Since thrombus formation is so common, bed rest should be avoided. (*Luckmann and Sorensen, p. 777.*)

**30 b** Chronic myelocytic leukemia is an abnormal proliferation of neutrophils and of their precursors, which are normally formed in the bone marrow. The abnormal production of immature neutrophils markedly reduces the production of red blood cells and platelets. This contributes to the anemia and bleeding tendencies characteristically seen in advanced CML. The severe anemia causes tissue hypoxia, which in turn results in shortness of breath, increased pulse rate, overwhelming fatigue, and exhaustion. (*Luckmann and Sorensen, p. 785. Moidel, Giblin, and Wagner, p. 639.*)

**31 a** Thrombocytes are manufactured in the bone marrow and play a role in controlling small-vessel bleeding. In advanced cases of chronic myelocytic leukemia, there is a decreased production of thrombocytes (platelets), which contributes to hemorrhagic lesions of the skin, such as petechiae, ecchymoses, and hematomas. The patient should also be observed for bleeding from any body orifice. (*Beland and Passos, p. 557.*)

**32 b** Chronic myelocytic leukemia is a blood disorder of unknown etiology. The marked enlargement of the spleen is characteristic of CML and is caused by invasive infiltration of immature neutrophils into the spleen. Hepatomegaly can also develop from the infiltration of immature neutrophils. (*Jones, Dunbar, and Jirovec, p. 244. Luckmann and Sorensen, p. 783.*)

**33 b** Many patients with chronic myelocytic leukemia have an abnormal chromosome called the "Philadelphia (Ph) chromosome." It is believed that this is an acquired genetic defect. (*Jones, Dunbar, and Jirovec, p. 243. Moidel, Giblin, and Wagner, p. 639.*)

**34 c** Alopecia is a common side effect of antineoplastic chemotherapeutic agents. The patient should be told that this is not permanent and the hair will grow back as soon as therapy is completed. Encouraging the patient to wear a wig will help her to maintain a positive self-image and maintain her dignity. (*Asperheim and Eisenhauer, p. 476. Moidel, Giblin, and Wagner, p. 640.*)

**35 c** Mouth care is important for the patient with painful ulcerations of the mouth. Frequent and gentle care is necessary. Cotton applicators are less traumatic than a toothbrush. Cleansing the mouth and teeth with a dilute solution of hydrogen peroxide or glycerin and lemon is more soothing to the ulcerated lesions than toothpaste or harsh mouthwashes. (*Luckmann and Sorensen, p. 784. Moidel, Giblin, and Wagner, p. 640.*)

**36 d** Leukapheresis is a process currently being used to separate leukocytes from blood. Blood is withdrawn from the patient, centrifuged, and separated into each blood component. Separate pumps remove the unwanted leukocytes. The remaining blood is then pumped back to the patient. In caring for these patients, staff members run a high risk of contracting hepatitis; therefore they should be advised to wear rubber gloves when handling any equipment or material that comes in contact with the patient's blood. Special care of contaminated syringes and needles is recommended. (*Russman, Slavin, and Taft*, American Journal of Nursing, *July 1977, pp. 1138–1139.*)

**37 b** One of the first early symptoms of Hodgkin's disease is painless lymphadenopathy. The lymph glands most frequently affected at this time are the cervical glands. (*Jones, Dunbar, and Jirovec, p. 261. Shafer et al., p. 416.*)

**38 c** It is the presence of Reed-Sternberg cell, a giant atypical cell differentiating Hodgkin's disease from other tumors of the lymph nodes. (*Jones, Dunbar, and Jirovec, p. 260.*)

**39 a** Successful treatment of Hodgkin's disease has occurred with a combination of chemotherapeutic agents. This combination of drugs is referred to as MOPP and includes mechlorethamine (Mustargen), Oncovin (vincristine), prednisone, and procarbazine. (*Jones, Dunbar, and Jirovec, p. 264. Rodman and Smith, p. 646.*)

**40 b** Oncovin is an antineoplastic alkaloid extracted from the periwinkle plant and is being used with other neoplastic agents to treat Hodgkin's disease. Oncovin has many adverse reactions and toxic symptoms. Neurotoxicity is the most troublesome and is manifested by numbness and tingling of the fingers and toes and disturbance of gait. (*Rodman and Smith, pp. 639–640.*)

**41 d** Procarbazine is an antineoplastic agent used in the treatment of Hodgkin's disease. It is believed that procarbazine interferes with protein, RNA and DNA synthesis. Foods and drugs with a high tyramine content (such as ripe cheese and bananas) should be avoided.

**42 d** Prednisone is an adrenocorticosterioid drug used in the palliative treatment of chronic lymphocytic leukemia, Hodgkin's disease, and lymphosarcoma. Toxic symptoms and side effects include fluid retention; weight gain; psychic disturbance; and Cushing's signs, such as rounding of the face, buffalo hump, acne, etc. Peptic ulcer and gastrointestinal hemorrhage are also encountered in patients on prednisone. (*Rodman and Smith, p. 233.*)

**43 c** Mechlorethamine is the generic name for Mustargen and nitrogen mustard. It is a potent alkylating agent that is used in combination with Oncovin, prednisone, and procarbazine to treat Hodgkin's disease.

**44 d** According to Luckmann and Sorensen, self-interest during illness is a common finding. If the patient is experiencing psychological or physical pain, he or she can become inner-directed and it may become difficult to think of others. As Mrs. L. speaks about herself, she is attempting to adapt to the illness so that she can tolerate the situation. If patients wish to talk about their illness, they should be encouraged to do so. (*Luckmann and Sorensen, p. 60.*)

**45 a** Multiple myeloma is a neoplastic disorder of the bone that causes destruction of the bone and impaired production of the blood cells normally produced in the bone marrow. Destruction of the bone causes a loss of calcium in the bone, hypercalcemia, and hypercalciuria. This makes patients particularly vulnerable to pathological fractures, kidney stones, and renal damage. (*Luckmann and Sorensen, p. 786.*)

**46 d** Nursing care of the patient with multiple myeloma includes observing the patient for bleeding tendencies and protecting the patient from infection. Encouraging the patient to ambulate the forcing fluids are important nursing responsibilities. (*Luckmann and Sorensen, p. 786.*)

**47 d** The heterophil agglutination test is elevated in infectious mononucleosis. Although the test can be positive in other conditions, the diagnosis of infectious mononucleosis is confirmed if the white-blood-cell count is elevated, if the mononuclear leukocytes are increased, and if the patient presents clinical signs and symptoms.

**48 c** In infectious mononucleosis there is an enlargement of the spleen, tonsils, and lymph glands. In addition, there is an elevation of the lymphocytes, many of which are atypical. (*Jones, Dunbar, and Jirovec, p. 325. Moidel, Giblin, and Wagner, p. 644.*)

**49 b** Idiopathic thrombocytopenic purpura is a disease characterized by destruction of blood platelets. As a result the patients are very prone to bleeding from body orifices, under the skin, and from mucous membranes. The diagnosis is confirmed by decreased platelet count, prolonged bleeding time, and increased capillary fragility test. Coagulation factors are normal. (*Luckmann and Sorensen, pp. 795–796.*)

**50 a** Patients with bleeding tendencies should avoid constipation. Straining at the stool can precipitate rectal bleeding and cause an increased intracranial pressure. Cerebral hemorrhage can be caused by the increased intracranial pressure. If the patient becomes constipated, the physician should be notified. (*Luckmann and Sorensen, pp. 794–796.*)

**51 c** Patients who have received mismatched blood develop hemolysis of red blood cells, which releases free hemoglobin into the plasma. The greatest threat occurs if the free hemoglobin plugs the kidney tubules, resulting in renal failure and, ultimately, death. The patient should be observed very carefully for oliguria and anuria. (*Luckmann and Sorensen, p. 749. Shafer et al., p. 95.*)

# UNIT 7

# Nursing care of the patient with a disorder of cerebral function

**OBJECTIVES**

To answer the questions in this unit, the reader should be able to

1 Identify the major components of the central nervous system;
2 List the functions of the various parts of the cerebral cortex;
3 Identify those adaptations that result from disorders of cerebral function;
4 Describe the various levels of consciousness;
5 Describe the various types of seizure disorders;
6 Recognize the nurse's role in preparing the patient for the major diagnostic tests;
7 Describe the nursing managment of the patient with a disorder of cerebral function.

## QUESTIONS RELATED TO OBJECTIVES

*Instructions*: Choose the *one best* answer to the following questions.

1. The components of the central nervous system are the
   a. Spinal nerves and the cranial nerves.
   b. Cerebrum and the cerebellum.
   c. Brain and the spinal cord.
   d. Autonomic nervous system and the voluntary nervous system.

2. The primary divisions of the brain are the
   a. Cerebrum, pons, and cerebellum.
   b. Medulla, pons, and midbrain.
   c. Cerebrum, cerebellum, and medulla.
   d. Brainstem, cerebellum, and cerebrum.

3. That portion of the central nervous system which initiates voluntary movements of the body is found in the
   a. Frontal lobe of the cerebral cortex.
   b. Posterior portion of the cerebellum.
   c. Gray matter of the basal ganglia.
   d. White matter of the spinal cord.

4. The band of white matter that lies between the thalamus and the basal ganglia is called the
   a. "Caudate nucleus."
   b. "Reticular formation."
   c. "Internal capsule."
   d. "Tenticular nucleus."

5. The center for the regulation of heat production and heat loss is in the
   a. Reticular formation of the medulla.
   b. Skin.
   c. Hypothalamus.
   d. Cerebellum.

6 In most individuals, the speech center of the brain is located in the
  a Left hemisphere of the cerebrum.
  b Right hemisphere of the cerebrum.
  c Left hemisphere of the cerebellum.
  d Right hemisphere of the cerebellum.

7 That portion of the cerebral cortex associated with vision is located in the
  a Frontal lobe.
  b Parietal lobe.
  c Occipital lobe.
  d Temporal lobe.

8 The center for hearing is in the
  a Parietal lobe.
  b Temporal lobe.
  c Occipital lobe.
  d Frontal lobe.

9 The network of capillaries in the ventricles of the brain which produces cerebrospinal fluid is the
  a Carotid sinus.
  b Circle of Willis.
  c Choroid plexus.
  d Arachnoid villi.

10 The normal spinal fluid pressure ranges between
  a 0 and 10 mm of water.
  b 15 and 50 mm of water.
  c 80 and 180 mm of water.
  d 200 and 300 mm of water.

**11** A core of tissue that runs through the brain stem and controls wakefulness is the
   **a** Reticular formation.
   **b** Internal capsule.
   **c** Basal ganglia.
   **d** Limbic system.

**12** Severe damage to the reticular formation of the brain stem can lead to
   **a** Convulsion.
   **b** Coma.
   **c** Aphasia.
   **d** Intention tremors.

**13** The nurse described the stuporous patient as
   **a** Being extremely drowsy and responding inappropriately when aroused.
   **b** Having clouding of consciousness, confusion, and being aroused by light shaking.
   **c** Being unresponsive; being aroused only by vigorous, continuous stimulation and by painful stimulation.
   **d** Experiencing loss of consciousness, lack of response to painful stimuli, and loss of gag reflex and corneal reflexes.

**14** Which of the following nursing actions has the priority while caring for the comatose patient?
   **a** Monitoring vital signs.
   **b** Maintaining a patent airway.
   **c** Monitoring urinary output.
   **d** Maintaining adequate fluid and electrolyte intake.

15 One means of maintaining a patent airway for the comatose patient is to suction the oral and nasopharyngeal secretions. A Y tube has been attached to the suction catheter. The nurse
   a  Advanced the catheter via the nose as far as it would go.
   b  Created suction while inserting the catheter by clamping the free end of Y tube.
   c  Applied suction for no more than 30 seconds.
   d  Withdrew the catheter by using a rotary motion.

16 To test the corneal reflex the nurse
   a  Used a flashlight to determine the pupil's reaction to light.
   b  Touched the cornea with a small wisp of cotton.
   c  Used an ophthalmoscope to look into the pupils of the eye.
   d  Asked the patient to follow the nurse's finger as the nurse moved it into the patient's field of vision.

17 To assess the plantar reflex of the patient, the nurse used a sharp object to stroke the lateral aspect of the foot from the heel to the base of the toes. The normal response is
   a  Flexion of the toes.
   b  Dorsiflexion of the great toe with fanning of the other toes.
   c  External rotation of the foot.
   d  Plantar flexion of the foot.

18 To test for the gag reflex, the nurse
   a  Stimulated the back of the pharynx with a tongue blade.
   b  Placed small quantities of ice chips on the patient's tongue.
   c  Placed the fingers over the larynx and asked the patient to swallow.
   d  Inserted small quantities of water into the patient's mouth with an asepto syringe.

**19** While assessing the plantar reflex, the nurse noticed that there was dorsiflexion of the great toe and fanning of the other toes. The nurse noted on the chart that the patient had a positive

   **a** Hoffman's sign.
   **b** Brudzinski's sign.
   **c** Babinski response.
   **d** Ankle clonus.

**20** While caring for Mrs. Schmidt, who was comatose, the nurse spoke to the patient and explained each part of the care being given. The nurse

   **a** Recognized that hearing is the last sense to be lost in the unconscious patient.
   **b** Was attempting to cope with the anxiety of caring for a comatose patient.
   **c** Was increasing the noise level in order to assess the patient's response.
   **d** Wanted the family to understand what was being done for the patient.

**21** Mrs. Schmidt is a patient you are caring for who is comatose. The doctor has ordered gavage feedings. You

   **a** Aspirate the stomach contents to determine that the tube is in place, and then discard the aspirated contents.
   **b** Administer the feeding by using a slow, gentle pressure on the plunger.
   **c** Follow the feeding with approximately 30 mL of water to flush out the tubing.
   **d** Lower the head of the bed during and after the feeding.

**22** Mr. Jones is a patient you are caring for who has a lesion of the left hemisphere of the cerebrum. You notice that he is able to recognize various objects but is unable to form the words to describe them. Mr. Jones probably has

   **a** Motor aphasia.
   **b** Sensory aphasia.
   **c** Global aphasia.
   **d** Visual agnosia.

23 Motor aphasia is due to damage or injury to the
   a   Angular gyrus region.
   b   Broca's area.
   c   Wernicke's area.
   d   Anterior occipital lobe.

24 While being prepared for a computerized transaxial brain scan, Mr. Jones asked the nurse if there would be any aftereffects of the scan. The nurse told Mr. Jones that
   a   Patients sometimes have a headache, but keeping the bed flat would relieve this.
   b   He will not be allowed to eat or drink for 1 hour after the scan.
   c   He will experience mild tingling of the arms and legs, which will subside with 24 hours.
   d   There should be no aftereffects of the scan.

25 In preparing the patient for a cerebral arteriogram, the nurse told the patient that
   a   No special preparation is required prior to the procedure.
   b   A radioactive isotope is taken by mouth ½ hour before the procedure.
   c   A warm, flushed feeling will be experienced after the dye is injected.
   d   There is no special care following the procedure.

26 The nursing-care plan for Mr. Jones stated, "Observe for signs of increased intracranial pressure." Which of the following assessments made by the nurse suggests increasing intracranial pressure?
   a   Constricted pupils.
   b   Rapid pulse and respirations.
   c   Decreased body temperature.
   d   Widening of pulse pressure.

27. Mr. Jones became restless and started thrashing about in bed. The nurse
   a. Loosely restrained the patient's hands and feet to prevent self-injury.
   b. Placed the patient in a Trendelenberg position to relieve pressure on the brain stem.
   c. Recognized that this could be an indication of increasing intracranial pressure and notified the physician.
   d. Did nothing, since restlessness is part of the patient's behavior.

28. While caring for a patient on a hypothermia blanket, the nurse
   a. Covered the hypothermia blanket with a bath blanket so that the patient's skin would not be in direct contact.
   b. Recognized that shivering is an expected effect of hypothermia.
   c. Recognized that drug absorption from the intramuscular route is enhanced while the patient is on the hypothermia blanket.
   d. Turned the machine off when the patient's temperature was within 2°F of the desired level.

29. The doctor ordered 500 mL of a 10% solution of Mannitol to be administered over 24 hours. The nurse recognized that this was being administered to
   a. Correct severe dehydration.
   b. Act as a central nervous system stimulant.
   c. Reduce intracranial pressure.
   d. Relieve pulmonary edema.

**30** Mrs. Olivia is a 59-year-old woman who was admitted to the hospital with a diagnosis of cerebral hemorrhage. In preparing her for a lumbar puncture, the nurse placed Mrs. Olivia on her side and told her to
  **a** Draw her knees up onto her chest and slightly bend her head onto the chest.
  **b** Keep her legs extended and her head sharply bent onto her chest.
  **c** Bend the upper leg, extend the lower leg, and bend the head backward.
  **d** Keep both legs slightly bent and keep the head still by looking straight ahead.

**31** The patient was having a lumbar puncture done. As the nurse collected the three specimens, it was noted that they contained bright red blood. The nurse realized that this
  **a** Is the normal color of cerebrospinal fluid.
  **b** Could mean a ruptured cerebral aneurysm.
  **c** Is a sign of bacterial infection of the central nervous system.
  **d** Was caused by trauma from the puncture needle.

**32** Following the lumbar puncture the patient may complain of headache. To prevent the headache, the patient should be
  **a** Placed in a Trendelenberg position.
  **b** Told to lie flat in bed.
  **c** Encouraged to ambulate.
  **d** Maintained in a high-Fowler's position.

**33** The contractures that develop in the lower extremity of the patient with a stroke are
  **a** Internal rotation of the hip, hyperextension of the hip and knee, and plantar extension of the foot.
  **b** External rotation of the hip, flexion of the knee, and plantar flexion of the foot.
  **c** Adduction of the hip, hyperextension of the knee, and plantar flexion of the foot.
  **d** Abduction of the hip, flexion of the knee, and dorsiflexion of the ankle.

**34** Contractures of the upper extremity which can develop in the hemiplegic patient are
   **a** Abduction of the shoulder, flexion of the elbow, and ulnar flexion and abduction of the fingers.
   **b** Adduction of the shoulder, and flexion of the elbow, wrist, fingers, and thumb.
   **c** Outward rotation of the shoulder joint and hyperextension of the elbow, wrist, fingers, and thumb.
   **d** Internal rotation of the arm, extension of elbow, and flexion of the wrist and fingers.

**35** One of the goals of nursing care for the patient with a stroke is prevention of contractures. This can be done by
   **a** Placing a pillow between the upper arm and body, using a hand roll, a trochanter roll, and a footboard.
   **b** Supporting the arm on a small pillow placed on the chest, placing pillows between the legs, and using a footboard for the feet.
   **c** Supporting the arm on a pillow with the elbow flexed, using a hand roll, and placing a pillow between the legs.
   **d** Placing the arm on a pillow with the elbow extended, placing a pillow under the neck, using a trochanter roll, and keeping fingers and thumb extended.

**36** Frequent passive range-of-motion exercises can be done by the nurse to prevent contractures in the patient with a stroke. The nurse
   **a** Performed range-of-motion exercises to the affected side and to the unaffected side.
   **b** Recognized that range-of-motion exercises are contraindicated until the patient regains consciousness.
   **c** Supported the body part at the muscle and moved the joint through a complete range of motion.
   **d** Exercised the joint just beyond the point that the patient experienced pain.

**37** Rehabilitation is a major part of care for the patient with a stroke. Which of the following statements is true?
   **a** Rehabilitation is a separate program carried out by the physical therapist.
   **b** The family plays an important role in the rehabilitation program.
   **c** Rehabilitation begins after other therapies are completed.
   **d** To be most successful, the person being rehabilitated should be a passive recipient of care.

**38** Patients with hemiplegia have nutritional problems resulting from dysphagia. When feeding these patients, the nurse should
   **a** Offer them milk since it slides down so easily.
   **b** Place food in the affected side so that the patient can swallow more easily.
   **c** Offer foods with minimal texture and viscosity.
   **d** Give mouth care after feeding since food tends to accumulate in the affected side.

**39** The most common cause of aphasia is cerebrovascular disorders that involve the
   **a** Anterior communicating artery.
   **b** Common carotid artery.
   **c** Posterior cerebral artery.
   **d** Middle cerebral artery.

**40** Speech therapy had been ordered for Mrs. Olivia. The nurse reported that she shouted obscenities to all persons who administered care to her. The nurse recognized that this
   **a** Was probably her speech pattern before the stroke and there is little that can be done.
   **b** Is a sign of regression and should be reported to the speech therapist.
   **c** Is a form of automatic speech and therefore an early expression of speech.
   **d** Is a sign of hostile behavior and a psychiatric consultation should be recommended.

**41** One day while Mr. Olivia was visiting his wife, she began to cry uncontrollably as soon as he entered the room. Mr. Olivia came out to the nurse's station and said to the nurse: "I'm just not coming to visit anymore. Every time I come, my wife cries!" The nurse told Mr. Olivia that
   **a** Mrs. Olivia has been fine all day and there is no reason for the crying.
   **b** Mrs. Olivia has no control over this crying and it does not mean that she is unhappy.
   **c** Mr. Olivia should ask the attending physician for a psychiatric consult.
   **d** Staying away for a few days will help the situation.

**42** While the nurse was bathing Miriam, who was admitted with a tentative diagnosis of idiopathic epilepsy, she experienced a grand mal seizure. The nurse
   **a** Forced the jaws open and inserted a padded tongue blade.
   **b** Restrained Miriam's arms and legs to protect her from injury.
   **c** Turned her head to the side to facilitate drainage.
   **d** Left the patient for 1 minute to call for help.

**43** Which of the following statements relating to grand mal seizures is true? Grand mal seizures
   **a** Start with a clonic rhythmic twitching on one side of the body and spread in an orderly fashion down the opposite side.
   **b** Are characterized by an "epileptic cry," which is caused by air being forced across the closed glottis.
   **c** Produce erratic asymmetrical contractions of voluntary and involuntary muscles.
   **d** Are generalized but do not always cause unconsciousness.

**44** During the clonic stage of a grand mal seizure
   **a** Symmetrical rigidity of skeletal muscles occur.
   **b** The patient does not breathe and becomes cyanotic.
   **c** Foaming at the mouth and incontinence occur.
   **d** The jaw clamps shut and salivation decreases.

**45** The cause of most recurrent seizures is
   **a** Central nervous system infections.
   **b** Brain tumors.
   **c** Metabolic disturbances.
   **d** Unknown.

**46** When preparing Miriam for an electroenchephalogram (EEG), the nurse told the patient
   **a** To withhold fluids and food for 6 to 8 hours prior to the test.
   **b** That the hair at the temporal area will have to be shaved.
   **c** That little needles will be stuck into the scalp.
   **d** That the procedure is noninvasive and no special preparation is needed.

**47** The generic name for Dilantin is
   **a** Primidone.
   **b** Trimethadione.
   **c** Ethosuximide.
   **d** Phenytoin.

**48** Gingival hyperplasia is a side effect seen with continued use of
   **a** Phenobarbital.
   **b** Phenytoin.
   **c** Primidone.
   **d** Trimethadione.

**49** Medications that can increase the toxicity of antiepileptic drugs include
 a Tranquilizers and barbiturates.
 b Antiemetics and antipyretics.
 c Antibiotics and narcotics.
 d Antitubercular drugs and anticoagulants.

**50** Which of the following statements relating to antiepileptic drugs is true?
 a The chief disadvantage of Dilantin is its sedative effect.
 b Primidone and phenobarital are given concomitantly to control grand mal seizures.
 c Trimethadione can be used to control grand mal seizures.
 d The usual oral maintenance dose of phenytoin is 300 mg per day.

**51** In teaching the patient who is taking phenytoin for grand mal seizures, the nurse should tell the patient that
 a Once the seizures have been controlled the medications can be discontinued.
 b Sudden withdrawal of the medication can lead to status epilepticus.
 c Aspirin can inhibit the action of phenytoin.
 d Phenytoin potentiates the action of the corticosterioids and digitalis.

**52** In preparing Miriam for discharge, the nurse pointed out that the following stressors may precipitate a seizure:
 a Sudden change of environmental temperature and fluid retention.
 b Alcohol consumption and low-fat diet.
 c Premenstrual edema and emotional stress.
 d Straining at the stool and tight clothing.

**53** In planning long-term care for Miriam, the nurse will be expected to clarify some misconceptions about epilepsy. Which of the following statements is true?

   **a** Marriage of epileptics is prohibited in some parts of the United States.

   **b** The learning ability of an epileptic is impaired.

   **c** Job performance of epileptics is less effective than that of nonepileptics.

   **d** Brain damage can result if persons with status epilepticus suffer hypoxia.

## ANSWERS, EXPLANATIONS, AND REFERENCES

**1 c** The nervous system can anatomically be divided into the central nervous system and the peripheral nervous system. The components of the central nervous system are the brain and the spinal cord. The peripheral nervous system is composed of cranial nerves and the spinal nerves. (*Langley, Telford, and Christensen, p. 209. Price and Wilson, p. 577. Vander, Sherman, and Luciano, p. 166.*)

**2 d** The primary divisions of the brain are the cerebrum, the cerebellum, and the brain stem. The brain stem, or "stalk," of the brain is composed of the medulla, the pons, and the midbrain. (*Langley, Telford, and Christensen, p. 227. Vander, Sherman, and Luciano, p. 166.*)

**3 a** A large number of motor fibers originate in the frontal lobe of the cerebral cortex. These motor fibers innervate voluntary movements and affect movement of the toes, feet, legs, trunk, arms, fingers, face, etc. Damage to the motor cortex causes impaired motor function. (*Vander, Sherman, and Luciano, p. 546.*)

**4 c** The internal capsule is a band of white matter that lies between the thalamus and the basal ganglia. It is made up of motor and sensory fibers that run to and from the cerebral cortex. Damage to the internal capsule impairs the transmission of motor and sensory impulses. (*Beland and Passos, p. 255.*)

**5 c** The hypothalamus is the center for the regulation of heat production and heat loss. Input comes from thermoreceptors in the skin and from the blood that perfuses the hypothalamus. (*Langley, Telford, and Christensen, p. 301.*)

**6 a** In most individuals the speech center of the brain is located in the left hemisphere. (*Langley, Telford, and Christensen, p. 362.*)

**7 c** The occipital lobe of the cerebrum controls vision. (*Jones, Dunbar, and Jirovec, p. 1077. Langley, Telford, and Christensen, p. 230.*)

**8 b** The temporal lobe of the cerebrum is the center for hearing. (*Jones, Dunbar, and Jirovec, p. 1077. Langley, Telford, and Christensen, p. 230.*)

**9 c** The ventricles of the brain play an important role in the production and circulation of cerebrospinal fluid. Projecting into the ventricles is a network of capillaries, called the "choroid plexus," which are responsible for the formation of cerebrospinal fluid. (*Jones, Dunbar, and Jirovec, p. 1077. Langley, Telford, and Christensen, p. 237.*)

**10 c** The normal pressure of spinal fluid ranges from 80 to 180 mm of water. Any increase of pressure can be caused by a tumor, an obstruction, or hydrocephalus. (*Shafer et al., p. 865.*)

**11 a** The reticular formation is a core of tissue that runs through the entire brain stem. In addition to controlling wakefulness, the reticular formation contains centers that regulate circulation, respiration, and gastrointestinal activities. (*Jones, Dunbar, and Jirovec, p. 1078. Langley, Telford, and Christensen, pp. 355–356. Vander, Sherman, and Luciano, pp. 167–168.*)

**12 b** Ascending neurons of the reticular formation control wakefulness. Tumors or hemorrhage that cause damage to the reticular formation can lead to coma. (*Jones, Dunbar, and Jirovec, p. 1078. Langley, Telford, and Christensen, p. 356. Vander, Sherman, and Luciano, p. 168.*)

**13 c** "Stupor" is a term used to describe a level of consciousness. The patient can be aroused only by vigorous, continuous stimulation and responds to painful stimuli by grimacing, groaning, or uttering unintelligible sounds. Once the stimulation ceases, the patient returns to a state of decreased consciousness. (*Beland and Passos, p. 263. Jones, Dunbar, and Jirovec, p. 1207.*)

**14 b** In caring for a comatose patient, maintaining a patent airway has the highest priority. Maintaining a patent airway can be accomplished by turning the patient's head to the side, inserting an airway, suctioning, mouth care, etc. (*Beland and Passos, p. 261. Moidel, Giblin, and Wagner, p. 275.*)

**15 d** Nasopharyngeal secretions tend to increase in the unconscious patient. Oral and nasopharyngeal suctioning is a means employed to clear the airway. To assure maximum removal of secretions, the catheter should be withdrawn with a rotary motion and the free end of the Y tube should be occluded. (*Bushnell, p. 50. Massachusetts General Hospital, p. 268. Shafer et al., p. 187.*)

**16 b** One means of assessing the level of consciousness is to test the corneal reflex. If the reflex is normal, the patient blinks when a wisp of cotton touches the cornea. (*Jones, Dunbar, and Jirovec, p. 1097. Luckmann and Sorensen, p. 403. Price and Wilson, p. 587.*)

**17 a** The normal response is flexion of the toes. (*Price and Wilson, p. 591.*)

**18 a** The gag reflex can be determined by stimulating the pharynx with a tongue blade. If the patient "gags" or chokes, the reflex is intact. (*Jones, Dunbar, and Jirovec, p. 1097. Luckmann and Sorensen, p. 403.*)

**19 c** The Babinski response is an abnormal neurological finding that is produced by abnormalities of the corticospinal motor system. (*Guyton, p. 681. Luckmann and Sorensen, p. 403. Price and Wilson, p. 591.*)

**20 a** One of the last senses to leave the unconscious patient is hearing. Therefore it is important for the nurse to speak to the patient and explain each part of the nursing care being given. Situations have been reported in which a comatose patient regained unconsciousness and repeated conversations that were heard during the period of unconsciousness. (*Luckmann and Sorensen, p. 430. Shafer et al., p. 186.*)

**21 c** In a gavage feeding, the head of the bed should be elevated during and after the feeding to prevent aspiration. One means of determining if the gastric tube is in place is to aspirate the stomach contents. However, the aspirated contents must be returned to the stomach. Gavage feedings must be administered by gravity drainage. After the feeding, the tubing is flushed with approximately 30 mL of water to maintain the patency of the tube. (*Jones, Dunbar, and Jirovec, p. 569. Massachusetts General Hospital, p. 149. Shafer et al., p. 127.*)

**22 a** Hemorrhage, tumors, or disease can cause damage to various portions of the brain that control language and speech. If the patient recognizes the object but is unable to form the words to describe it then the patient is suffering from motor aphasia. (*Beland and Passos, p. 253.*)

**23 b** Broca's area is the frontal portion of the cerebral cortex. It controls the muscles that are used for speech. Damage to this area of the motor cortex causes motor aphasia. (*Guyton, p. 728. Langley, Telford, and Christensen, p. 363. Moidel, Giblin, and Wagner, p. 884.*)

**24 d** The patient should be told that there will be no after-effects from the scan. Although the procedure is painless, the patient should be told to keep her head still throughout the entire procedure. Uncooperative patients or infants may have to be sedated. (*Jones, Dunbar, and Jirovec, p. 1108. Stone,* American Journal of Nursing *, p. 1601.*)

**25 c** Cerebral anteriogram is a comparatively dangerous procedure that is used to diagnose abnormalities of cerebral circulation. The preparation prior to the procedure is similar to that for a patient going to surgery. After the dye is injected, the patient may experience a warm, flushed feeling. Aftercare includes monitoring vital signs and doing a careful neurological check. (*Jones, Dunbar, and Jirovec, p. 1110.*)

**26 d** Widening of the pulse pressure (the difference between the systolic and diastolic pressures) is a sign of increasing intracranial pressure. If it occurs, the physician should be notified. (*Luckmann and Sorensen, p. 421.*)

**27 c** Restlessness is an early sign of increased intracranial pressure. As the pressure increases, the patient's level of consciousness declines. Since early recognition of increased intracranial pressure is necessary for successful treatment, the physician should be notified. (*Luckmann and Sorensen, p. 430. Moidel, Giblin, and Wagner, p. 871.*)

**28 d** After the hypothermia blanket has been discontinued, there is a tendency for the body temperature to drift downward about 1° to 2°F. The nurse should recognize that the hypothermia blanket is usually turned off when the patient's temperature is within 2°F of the desired level. (*Luckmann and Sorensen, p. 439. Massachusetts General Hospital, p. 139.*)

**29 c** Mannitol is an osmotic diuretic used to reduce increasing intracranial pressure. Diuresis is produced by interfering with tubular reabsorption of water. It is contraindicated in persons with severe kidney, liver, and cardiac disorders. (*Bergersen, p. 453. Rodman and Smith, p. 337.*)

**30 a** When positioning a patient for a lumbar puncture, it is important for the patient to lie on her side, flex both legs as high up onto the chest as possible, and bend the head onto the chest. This position allows the physician to insert the needle into the lumbar spine with minimal trauma. (*Jones, Dunbar, and Jirovec, p. 1111. Massachusetts General Hospital, p. 74. Shafer et al., p. 866.*)

**31 b** Cerebrospinal fluid is normally colorless and clear. In some instances the first specimen collected may be blood-tinged because of trauma caused by the needle's being inserted. However, the subsequent specimens should be clear. If all three specimens contain blood, this could mean that there is bleeding into the cerebrospinal space, for example, cerebral hemorrhage, ruptured aneurysm, etc. (*Shafer et al., p. 866.*)

**32 b** After a lumbar puncture, some patients complain of headache. Keeping the patient flat in bed after the procedure will help to prevent headache. The patient can move from side to side. (*Jones, Dunbar, and Jirovec, p. 1111.*)

**33 b** In cerebrovascular lesions, the strong adductor muscles and flexor muscles draw the limbs into positions of flexion and adduction. The contractures seen in the lower extremity are external rotation of the hip, flexion of the knee, and plantar flexion of the foot. (*Jones, Dunbar, and Jirovec, p. 1105. Moidel, Giblin, and Wagner, pp. 881–883. Shafer et al., p. 895.*)

**34 b** The hemiplegic patient can develop disabling contractures of the upper and lower extremities. The contractures that can develop in the upper extremities include adduction of the shoulder and flexion of the elbow, wrist, fingers, and thumb. (*Moidel, Giblin, and Wagner, p. 881. Shafer, Sawyer, et al., p. 895.*)

**35 a** To prevent disabling contractures from forming, the nurse should place a pillow between the upper arm and the body to prevent adduction of the shoulder and should position a hand roll to prevent plantar flexion of the fingers. Using a trochanter roll or a sandbag will prevent external rotation of the hip. Placing the foot at a 90° angle on the footboard prevents foot drop. (*Jones, Dunbar, and Jirovec, p. 1185. Moidel, Giblin, and Wagner, p. 881. Shafer et al., p. 895.*)

**36 a** In doing passive range-of-motion exercises with the patient with a cardiovascular accident (CVA), the nurse performs the exercises on both the affected and the unaffected sides. If the patient experiences pain, then the nurse has exceeded the range of motion for that particular joint. The body part is supported at the joint rather than at the muscle. Passive range of motion can be performed while the patient is comatose. (*Moidel, Giblin, and Wagner, pp. 342–350.*)

**37 b** Rehabilitation is an integral part of health care that focuses on helping a person regain independence. Actually, rehabilitation should begin as soon as the patient is admitted to the hospital. All members of the health team play a vital role in the successful rehabilitation of the patient. Both the family and the patient should actively participate in the rehabilitation program. (*Henderson and Nite, p. 600.*)

**38 d** Once the swallowing reflex returns, the patient will be allowed to take food by mouth. Milk and milk products tend to produce a thick saliva, so should not be given. Foods with some texture stimulate the swallowing reflex and are better tolerated. When feeding the patient, the food is best placed in the unaffected side to assure swallowing. Since food tends to accumulate in the unaffected side, mouth care should be given after meals. (*Jones, Dunbar, and Jirovec, p. 1186. Moidel, Giblin, and Wagner, p. 881.*)

**39 d** The middle cerebral artery supplies blood to the speech and language center of the brain. Cerebrovascular disorders that involve the middle cerebral artery are the most common cause of aphasia. (The middle cerebral artery also supplies blood to the internal capsule, the basal ganglia, and the thalamus.) (*Moidel, Giblin, and Wagner, p. 884. Price and Wilson, p. 585.*)

**40 c** When the patient begins speech therapy, it is not unusual for the person to become angry and frustrated. This is a method of coping with the incapacity to speak. Shouting of obscenities is a form of automatic speech and therefore an early expression of speech. The patient needs support and understanding. (*Jones, Dunbar, and Jirovec, p. 1187.*)

**41 b** Emotional lability is a condition that occurs following a CVA. The crying or laughing is inappropriate to the situation and occurs without any reason. The family should be assured that the patient has no control over this and it does not mean the patient is unhappy. Both patient and family need support and encouragement. (*Haber, Leach, et al., p. 484. Jones, Dunbar, and Jirovec, p. 1184. Luckmann and Sorensen, p. 472.*)

**42 c** During a grand mal seizure, it is important to maintain a patent airway. Once the patient's jaw has been clamped shut, attempts should not be made to insert a tongue blade. Turning the head to the side is done to facilitate drainage and prevent the tongue from occluding the airway. (*Jones, Dunbar, and Jirovec, p. 1164.*)

**43 b** Grand mal seizures are generalized seizures that always produce unconsciousness. The characteristic epileptic cry is caused by contraction of the abdominal and thoracic muscles, which forces air out of the lungs and through the contracted vocal cords or glottis. (*Jones, Dunbar, and Jirovec, p. 1608. Luckmann and Sorensen, p. 508.*)

**44 c** The clonic stage is the second stage of the grand mal seizure. The tonic rigidity of the first stage is replaced by violent jerking movements of the entire body. The patient usually foams at the mouth and often becomes incontinent of urine as the bladder sphincter relaxes. (*Luckmann and Sorensen, p. 508.*)

**45 d** Approximately 75 percent of all adults with seizures have idiopathic epilepsy. The cause of idiopathic epilepsy is unknown. (*Luckmann and Sorensen, p. 507.*)

**46 d** An EEG is a noninvasive procedure, is painless, and requires no special preparation. However, the patient should be told not to move the head during the procedure. There is no special aftercare. (*Jones, Dunbar, and Jirovec, p. 1108.*)

**47 c** Phenytoin is the latest generic name for Dilantin. It was formerly called phenylhydantoin. (*Bergersen, p. 263. Bruya and Bolin*, American Journal of Nursing, *p. 393.*)

**48 b** Continued use of phenytoin causes gingival hyperplasia. Meticulous mouth care and proper brushing of the teeth are imperative to prevent painful gingivitis. In severe cases, the hypertrophied gums can be removed surgically. (*Jones, Dunbar, and Jirovec, p. 1168. Rodman and Smith, p. 150.*)

**49 d** Certain groups of drugs tend to increase the toxicity of antiepileptic and antitubercular drugs. Examples of these drugs include warfarin, Dicumarol, isoniazid, and para-aminosalicylic acid. (*Rodman and Smith, p. 148–149.*)

**50 d** Although the dosage of phenytoin must be adjusted to the individual patient, the most common oral maintenance dose is 100 mg tid or 300 mg daily. The usual daily range is 100 to 600 mg daily. (*Bergersen, p. 263. Rodman and Smith, p. 155.*)

**51 b** In teaching the patient who is taking phenytoin or other antiepileptics, the patient should be told never to suddenly discontinue the medications, since doing this can lead to status epilepticus. Patients should be cautioned to exercise extreme care when taking any other medications, since these can cause unexpected responses. (*Bergersen, p. 263. Rodman and Smith, p. 154.*)

**52 c** Stressors that may precipitate a seizure include alcohol consumption, fluid retention, premenstrual edema, and emotional stress. (*Bruya and Bilin*, American Journal of Nursing, *p. 394.*)

**53 d** The role of the nurse in planning long-term nursing care for the patient with epilepsy involves clarifying the many misconceptions that exist. Marriage is no longer prohibited in the United States; the learning ability of epileptics is not impaired, nor is it a mental disease. Persons with status epilepticus can suffer brain damage from hypoxia. (*Bruya and Bolin*, American Journal of Nursing., *pp. 396–397.*)

# UNIT 8

# Nursing care of the patient with a disorder of body movement

**OBJECTIVES**

To answer the questions in this unit, the reader should be able to

1. List the components of the central nervous system and the peripheral nervous system;
2. Identify the structures involved in body movement;
3. List the functions of the major motor and sensory pathways;
4. Describe how the body adapts to disorders of body movement;
5. Identify the signs and symptoms of major disorders of body movement;
6. Describe the nursing management of the patient with a disorder of body movement.

## QUESTIONS RELATED TO OBJECTIVES

*Instructions*: Choose the *one best* answer to the following questions.

1. The main components of the peripheral nervous system include the
   a. Parasympathetic and the sympathetic nervous system.
   b. Spinal nerves and the cranial nerves.
   c. Hypothalamus and the autonomic nervous system.
   d. Brain and the spinal cord.

2. Which of the following statements relating to the autonomic nervous system is true? Autonomic neurons
   a. Arise in the cerebrum and the brain stem.
   b. Do not have dual innervation on effector organs.
   c. Are regulated primarily by voluntary control.
   d. Are termed "preganglionic" and "postganglionic" neurons.

3. Which of the following statements relating to the autonomic nervous system is true?
   a. Postganglionic fibers of the parasympathetic nervous system liberate acetylcholine when activated.
   b. Cholinesterase inactivates norepinephrine released by postganglionic fibers.
   c. Sympathetic and parasympathetic fibers are adrenergic.
   d. Postganglionic fibers that release norepinephrine are termed "cholinergic".

4. The main function of the cerebellum is to
   a. Serve as a relay station for sensory pathways.
   b. Integrate the functions of the autonomic nervous system and the endocrine system.
   c. Regulate thirst and appetite.
   d. Control equilibrium and muscular coordination.

**5** Damage to the cerebellum causes
  **a** Loss of touch and pressure sensations.
  **b** Paralysis of voluntary movement.
  **c** Loss of intellectual function.
  **d** Intention tremors and ataxia.

**6** The function of the thalamus is to
  **a** Integrate autonomic nervous system functions with endocrine functions.
  **b** Serve as a relay station for major sensory pathways.
  **c** Regulate body temperature.
  **d** Control equilibrium and muscle coordination.

**7** A major sensory tract is the
  **a** Extrapyramidal.
  **b** Spinothalamic.
  **c** Corticospinal.
  **d** Corticobulbar.

**8** Damage to the lateral spinothalamic tract causes loss of
  **a** Pain and temperature sensations.
  **b** Muscle coordination for maintaining posture and for limb movement.
  **c** Touch and pressure sensations.
  **d** Voluntary movements.

**9** It is generally believed that the major function of the basal ganglia is to
  **a** Coordinate muscular movements, especially the automatic associated movements of the body.
  **b** Serve as a relay station for major sensory pathways.
  **c** Control voluntary movement.
  **d** Transmit motor and sensory impulses.

**10** Damage or injury to the pyramidal tract produces
   **a** Paralysis of voluntary movement.
   **b** Intention tremors.
   **c** Loss of posture sense.
   **d** Loss of pain and temperature sense.

**11** Most motor pathways decussate in the
   **a** Cerebral cortex.
   **b** Spinal cord.
   **c** Medulla oblongata.
   **d** Thalamus.

**12** Examples of upper motor neurons are the
   **a** Corticospinal and corticobulbar neurons.
   **b** Motor neurons of the spinal and cranial nerves.
   **c** Rubrospinal and vestibulospinal neurons.
   **d** Spinothalamic and spinocerebellar neurons.

**13** Damage to upper motor neurons causes
   **a** Tetanic spasms.
   **b** Flaccid paralysis.
   **c** Spastic paralysis.
   **d** Myoclonic spasms.

**14** Examples of lower motor neurons are
   **a** Corticospinal and corticobulbar neurons.
   **b** Motor neurons of the spinal and cranial nerves.
   **c** Rubrospinal and vestibulospinal neurons.
   **d** Spinothalamic and spinocerebellar neurons.

**15** Lower motor neurons
   **a** Activate the muscle they innervate.
   **b** Initiate voluntary movement.
   **c** Facilitate the transmission of impulses at the synapse.
   **d** Control reflex movement.

**16** Damage to the lower motor neurons causes
  **a** Flaccid paralysis.
  **b** Spastic paralysis.
  **c** Hemiplegia.
  **d** Monoplegia.

**17** The substance liberated at the neuromuscular junction which stimulates the muscle is called
  **a** "Epinephrine."
  **b** "Cholinesterase."
  **c** "Acetylcholine."
  **d** "Creatine."

**18** The action of acetylcholine is inactivated by
  **a** Epinephrine.
  **b** Creatine.
  **c** Histamine.
  **d** Cholinesterase.

**19** The muscles of the body that respond to conscious control are
  **a** Cardiac.
  **b** Smooth.
  **c** Striated.
  **d** Visceral.

**20** The knee is an example of a freely movable joint that is essentially what type of joint?
  **a** Ball and socket.
  **b** Saddle.
  **c** Hinge.
  **d** Condyloid.

**21** The type of joint most frequently involved in rheumatoid arthritis is the
  **a** Synarthroidal.
  **b** Amphiarthroidal.
  **c** Synovial.
  **d** Ginglymus.

**22** The onset of rheumatoid arthritis can be precipitated by
  **a** Trauma to the joints.
  **b** Emotional stress.
  **c** The aging process.
  **d** Obesity.

**23** In addition to the many physical findings associated with rheumatoid arthritis, the following diagnostic tests are elevated during the acute and the chronic stage
  **a** RBC and lactodehydrogenase.
  **b** Erythrocyte sedimentation rate and C-reactive protein.
  **c** SGOT and white-blood-cell count.
  **d** Latex fixation and hematocrit.

**24** The "rheumatoid factor" refers to the
  **a** Autoantibody found in the serum of patients with rheumatoid arthritis.
  **b** Joint deformities typically seen in rheumatoid arthritis.
  **c** Triad of symptoms characterizing rheumatoid arthritis.
  **d** Systemic effects that develop in severe rheumatoid arthritis.

**25** The nurse noted that the patient has bony ankylosis. This means that the joint
  **a** Is freely movable, but there is severe pain on movement.
  **b** Can be moved only with effort and excruciating pain.
  **c** Is partially fixed and there is deformity.
  **d** Is fixed and there is complete loss of motion.

**26** The drug of choice for treating rheumatoid arthritis is
   **a** Acetylsalicyclic acid.
   **b** Aurothioglucose.
   **c** Corticosteroids.
   **d** Phenylbutazone.

**27** Which of the following statements relating to the use of corticosteroids in the treatment of rheumatoid arthritis is true? Corticosteroids
   **a** Are the drugs of choice in the treatment of rheumatoid arthritis.
   **b** Bring about a cure of rheumatoid arthritis.
   **c** Relieve the symptoms of rheumatoid arthritis but do not arrest the pathological process.
   **d** Are usually indicated during the initial or the acute phase of the disease.

**28** Ms. Browne, a patient who is receiving gold salts for rheumatoid arthritis, tells you that she has a skin rash and sores in her mouth. The nurse should
   **a** Recognize that there are toxic symptons of gold therapy and the physician should be notified.
   **b** Tell the patient to omit using soap for bathing and to rinse her mouth with a weak solution of hydrogen peroxide.
   **c** Explain to the patients that these are side effects and will subside as soon as she builds up a tolerance.
   **d** Recognize that these symptoms are unrelated to gold therapy and attempt to elicit more data.

**29** The antidote used to treat overdosage from gold salts is
   **a** Naloxone hydrochloride.
   **b** Dimercaprol.
   **c** Pyridoxine.
   **d** Neostigmine methylsulfate.

**30** While Ms. Browne is being maintained on bed rest, the nurse positioned the patient
- **a** On her side with pillows supporting the uppermost leg and the uppermost arm.
- **b** Flat on her back with the affected joints in the position of extension.
- **c** In semi-Fowler's position with a pillow under the head and under the knees.
- **d** With the head of the bed slightly elevated, the elbows flexed on pillows, and the legs hyperextended.

**31** While caring for Ms. Browne the nurse
- **a** Performed range-of-motion exercises during the acute phase.
- **b** Placed pillows under her knees to relieve pain.
- **c** Notified the physician when the patient complained of pain while exercising.
- **d** Recognized that taking aspirin $\frac{1}{2}$ hour before performing exercises relieves pain.

**32** While preparing Ms. Browne for discharge, the nurse pointed out that
- **a** A diet high in vitamin C relieves inflammation.
- **b** Eliminating red meats from the diet improves circulation to the diseased joints.
- **c** Milk and milk products foster calcification of the joints.
- **d** No special diet is recommended.

**33** While administering phenylbutazone the nurse should recognize that this drug
- **a** Can cause bone marrow depression.
- **b** Inhibits the action of penicillin and the sulfonamides.
- **c** Enhances the action of the barbiturates.
- **d** Can be used safely for prolonged therapy.

**34** Stressors that contribute to the development of osteoarthritis include
  **a** Repeated sore throats, infected teeth, and emotional stress.
  **b** Aging, trauma, and obesity.
  **c** Emotional stress, psoriasis, and autoantibodies.
  **d** High-purine diet, trauma, and obesity.

**35** In gouty arthritis, a deposition of sodium urate crystals in the subcutaneous tissue or near the joints causes the production of
  **a** Subcutaneous nodules.
  **b** Heberden's nodes.
  **c** Tophi.
  **d** Uremic frost.

**36** A medication that is used to treat gouty arthritis is
  **a** Para-aminosalicylic acid.
  **b** Allopurinol.
  **c** Robaxin.
  **d** Aurothioglucose.

**37** While administering allopurinol, the nurse recognizes that
  **a** The medication should be given with antacids.
  **b** Aspirin inactivates the effects of allopurinol.
  **c** The patient should be encouraged to drink extra fluids.
  **d** Minimal side effects are associated with the drug.

**38** The doctor ordered a low-purine diet for the patient. Which of the following groups of food is lowest in purines?
  **a** Milk, grilled-cheese sandwich, apple pie.
  **b** Roast beef with mushroom gravy, peas, mashed potatoes.
  **c** Beef consomme, roast turkey, asparagus.
  **d** Liver with bacon, baked potato, carrots.

**39** The most common early symptom of myasthenia gravis is
   **a** Increased fatigue.
   **b** Ptosis and diplopia.
   **c** Regurgitation of food and fluid through nares.
   **d** Transient paralysis of extremities.

**40** The diagnosis of myasthenia gravis can be confirmed by the Tensilon test. In this test, endrophonium chloride (Tensilon) is given intravenously. If the patient has myasthenia gravis, there is an increase of
   **a** Muscle strength.
   **b** Blood pressure.
   **c** Urinary output.
   **d** Oral secretions.

**41** The symptoms of myasthemia gravis can be relieved by the administration of anticholinesterase medications. An example of an anticholinesterase medication is
   **a** Atropine.
   **b** Epinephrine.
   **c** Neostigmine.
   **d** Levodopa.

**42** Which of the following anticholinesterase drugs has a longer action than neostigmine and less severe side effects?
   **a** Eserine.
   **b** Urecholine.
   **c** Tensilon.
   **d** Mestinon.

**43** "Cholinergic crisis" can occur from an overdose of anticholinesterase medications. The antidote is
   **a** Curare.
   **b** Atropine.
   **c** Epinephrine.
   **d** Endrophonium.

**44** The major symptom of "myasthenia crisis" is
   a  Respiratory distress.
   b  Abdominal cramps.
   c  Inability to open eyelid.
   d  Nasal speech.

**45** In planning a schedule of activities for the patient with myasthenia gravis, one should tell the patient to plan important activities so that they fall within
   a  The morning hours.
   b  The peak activity of the medication.
   c  2 hours after meals.
   d  The evening hours.

**46** An example of a disorder caused by degeneration of the basal ganglia is
   a  Guillain-Barre syndrome.
   b  Multiple sclerosis.
   c  Myasthenia gravis.
   d  Parkinson's disease.

**47** Which of the following statements relating to Parkinson's disease is true?
   a  It is an autoimmune response that causes damage to the corticospinal pathways.
   b  It is a muscle defect caused by decreased amounts of acetylcholine at the motor end plate.
   c  There is decreased dopamine secretion in the corpus striatum of the basal ganglia.
   d  There is demyelination of the pyramidal tracts and the posterior columns.

**48** Symptoms of Parkinson's disease include
   a  "Pill-rolling" tremors and cogwheel muscle rigidity.
   b  Muscle fasciculations and flaccid paralysis.
   c  Hemiballismus and tetanic muscle spasms.
   d  Intention tremors and ataxia.

**49** While the nurse was assessing the patient with Parkinson's disease, the gait was described as
   a  Shuffling.
   b  Ataxic.
   c  Scissors.
   d  Slapping.

**50** Mr. Stein is a 72-year-old man who is taking levodopa for Parkinson's disease. During the nursing conference, it was pointed out that while caring for Mr. Stein it was not uncommon for him to have an erection. The nurses
   a  Decided that it was necessary to speak to him about his perverted behavior.
   b  Refused to care for him.
   c  Requested that he be transferred to another unit.
   d  Recognized that it could be a side effect of the levodopa.

**51** While preparing Mr. Stein, who is receiving levodopa, for discharge, the nurse stressed that
   a  Levodopa should be given on an empty stomach to facilitate absorption.
   b  Rapid position changes can cause blood pressure to drop.
   c  Bananas and ripe cheeses can decrease the adrenergic effects of levodopa.
   d  Medications used to decrease blood pressure increase the action of levodopa.

**52** When Mr. Stein returned to the outpatient clinic, he told the nurse that his urine was red. The nurse told Mr. Stein
   a  That this was a harmless effect of the drug.
   b  To discontinue the drug for a few days.
   c  To take the medication with sodium bicarbonate.
   d  That this was a sign of prostate problems and to tell the doctor.

**53** Which of the following vitamins interferes with the action of levodopa?
  **a** Cyanocobalamin.
  **b** Pyridoxine.
  **c** Niacin.
  **d** Thiamine.

**54** Which of the following statements relating to multiple sclerosis is true?
  **a** The demyelination affects the motor pathways only.
  **b** Involvement of the motor pathways causes flaccid paralysis.
  **c** Emotional instability is a common symptom.
  **d** Total physical disability occurs early in the course of the disease.

**55** "Charcot's triad" refers to a group of symptoms seen in patients with multiple sclerosis. The triad of symptoms includes
  **a** Involuntary movement of muscles, unconsciousness, and incontinence.
  **b** Ptosis, blurred vision, and headache.
  **c** Dizziness, tinnitus, and vomiting.
  **d** Intention tremors, scanning speech, and nystagmus.

**56** The patient with intention tremors has
  **a** Increased tremors while asleep.
  **b** Maximum tremors while the arms are at rest.
  **c** Increased tremors when attempts are made to grasp an object.
  **d** No tremors during voluntary movement.

**57** The patient with multiple sclerosis has hyperactive deep-tendon reflexes. Examples of deep-tendon reflexes are the
  **a** Patellar reflex and the biceps reflex.
  **b** Plantar reflex and the triceps reflex.
  **c** Cremasteric reflex and the ankle reflex.
  **d** Abdominal reflex and the brachioradialis.

**58** Mrs. Collins is a 35-year-old woman who has multiple sclerosis. To test for proprioception sense, the nurse asked the patient to stand with her feet together and then close her eyes. As Mrs. Collins did this, she began to fall. The nurse recorded this as a positive

   a   Brudzinski sign.
   b   Romberg sign.
   c   Rinne test.
   d   Kernig's sign.

**59** While reading Mrs. Collins' chart the nurse noted that there was bulbar involvement. Nursing action for this problem would be to

   a   Monitor the blood pressure and pulse.
   b   Observe for chewing and swallowing difficulties.
   c   Monitor the urinary output.
   d   Observe for elevated temperature.

**60** While attempting to teach Mrs. Collins catheter care in preparation for discharge, she states that she is too weak to go home and no way can she learn to care for that "hose." In evaluating the situation the nurse recognizes that

   a   Mrs. Collins can learn only when she is emotionally and physically ready
   b   Learning requires participation, so Mrs. Collins is asked to give a return demonstration.
   c   Mrs. Collins will learn in spite of her reluctance if repeated demonstrations are given.
   d   Mrs. Collins can be stimulated to learn by leaving written material at the bedside.

## ANSWERS, EXPLANATIONS, AND REFERENCES

**1 b**   The main components of the peripheral nervous system include the 31 pairs of spinal nerves and the 12 cranial nerves. The peripheral nervous system is located outside the central nervous system and carries motor and sensory impulses to and away from the brain. (*Langley, Telford, and Christensen, p 239.*)

**2 d** The neurons of the autonomic nervous system are termed preganglionic and postganglionic neurons. The preganglionic neurons originate in the nerve cell bodies located in the spinal cord or the brain stem, and terminate in ganglia located outside the central nervous system. The postganglionic neurons originate in the ganglia and terminate in muscles or glands. (*Langley, Telford, and Christensen, p. 291. Vander, Luciano, and Sherman, p. 164.*)

**3 a** All preganglionic fibers release acetylcholine and are classified as cholinergic. The postganglionic fibers of the parasympathetic nervous system release acetylcholine, causing the muscle or gland to react. Acetylcholine is inactivated by cholinesterase. Autonomic fibers that release acetylcholine are classified as cholinergic; those that release norepinephrine are classified as adrenergic. (*Langley, Telford, and Christensen, p. 297.*)

**4 d** The cerebellum controls equilibrium and muscular coordination. It plays a major role in controlling those muscles used to maintain posture and to perform rapid movements smoothly and precisely. (*Langley, Telford, and Christensen, pp. 359–360. Vander, Sherman, and Luciano, p. 548.*)

**5 d** Damage or injury to the cerebellum causes intention tremors and ataxia. The person can no longer perform movements smoothly. The person has difficulty maintaining balance, and the gait resembles that of a drunken person. Intellectual or sensory capacity is not impaired. (*Langley, Telford, and Christensen, p. 360. Vander, Sherman, and Luciano, pp. 547–548.*)

**6 b** All major sensory impulses are relayed from the spinal cord to the thalamus and then to the sensory cortex. Not only does the thalamus serve as a relay station for the major sensory pathways, but it also plays a major role in the emotional response to perception and in the interpretation of sensory stimulation. (*Jones, Dunbar, and Jirovec, p. 1077. Langley, Telford, and Christensen, pp. 232, 272.*)

**7 b** A major ascending sensory tract is the spinothalamic tract. The neurons originate in the spinal cord and terminate in the thalamus. The lateral spinothalamic tract transmits pain and temperature sensation from the opposite side of the body, and the anterior spinothalamic tract transmits touch and pressure sensations from the opposite side of the body. (*Langley, Telford, and Christensen, p. 268.*)

**8 a** The lateral spinothalamic tract carries pain and temperature sensation from the lateral white columns of the spinal cord to the thalamus. Damage or injury to the lateral spinothalamic tract causes loss of pain and temperature sensations on the opposite side of the body. (*Jones, Dunbar, and Jirovec, p. 1077. Price and Wilson, p. 593.*)

**9 a** It is believed that the basal ganglia are important constituents of the extrapyramidal tract. The basal ganglia play a major role in coordination and in the control of automatic associated movements. As a result, muscular movements are orderly, precise, and purposeful. (*Beland and Passos, p. 247. Langley, Telford, and Christensen, p. 361.*)

**10 a** The pyramidal tract is a motor pathway that originates in the cerebral cortex and terminates in the spinal cord. The primary function is to control voluntary movement. Damage or injury to the pyramidal tract produces paralysis of voluntary movement. Patients suffering from a cerebrovascular accident best exemplify damage to the pyramidal tract. (*Beland and Passos, pp. 254–255. Price and Wilson, p. 579.*)

**11 c** Most motor pathways that originate in the cerebral cortex decussate (cross over) in the medulla. Motor pathways that originate in the right cerebral cortex control muscles on the left side of the body and vice versa. (*Langley, Telford, and Christensen, p. 285. Luckmann and Sorensen, p. 394.*)

**12 a** Most motor neurons involve two neurons, the upper motor neurons and the lower motor neurons. If the cell body of the motor neurons lies in the cerebral cortex, it is classified as an upper motor neuron. Examples of upper motor neurons are the corticospinal and the corticobulbar neurons. (*Langley, Telford, and Christensen, p. 285.*)

**13 c** Damage or injury to upper motor neurons causes spastic paralysis. In this type of paralysis, voluntary control is lost, the reflex arc remains functional, and the muscle responds to stretch. Cerebrovascular accidents are the most common cause of damage to upper motor neurons. (*Langley, Telford, and Christensen, p. 288. Shafer et al., p. 864.*)

**14 b** The neurons that innervate the muscle are called "lower motor neurons." The motor neurons of the cranial and spinal nerves are examples of lower motor neurons. (*Langley, Telford, and Christensen, p. 285.*)

**15 a** According to Langley et al., the lower motor neuron's function is to activate the muscles it innervates. (*Langley, Telford, and Christensen, p. 285.*)

**16 a** If there is damage to the lower motor neurons, paralysis develops which does not respond to stretch. This type of paralysis is termed "flaccid" paralysis. (*Langley, Telford, and Christensen, p. 287.*)

**17 c** A substance liberated by the axon at the neuromuscular junction is called "acetylcholine." This substance stimulates the muscle to contract. (*Langley, Telford, and Christensen, p. 195.*)

**18 d** Cholinesterase inactivates acetylcholine. As the acetylcholine is inactivated, the muscle relaxes (*Langley, Telford, and Christensen, p. 195.*)

**19 c** Striated muscle or skeletal muscle is responsible for the movement of parts of the skeleton. Most striated muscle is attached to the bones and responds to conscious control. (*Langley, Telford, and Christensen, p. 120. Vander, Sherman, and Luciano, p. 189.*)

**20 c** The knee is freely movable joint that is essentially a hinge joint. It also has some pivotal and gliding movement. (*Langley, Telford, and Christensen, p. 114.*)

**21 c** Rheumatoid arthritis primarily affects synovial joints. The joints most frequently affected are the small joints of the hands and feet, wrists, knees, and elbows. (*Luckmann and Sorensen, p. 1222.*)

**22 b** Rheumatoid arthritis is an inflammatory disease of the joints characterized by remissions and exacerbations. Emotional stress can trigger an exacerbation and precipitate the onset of rheumatoid arthritis. (*Luckmann and Sorensen, pp. 1220–1221.*)

**23 b** During the acute and chronic stage of rheumatoid arthritis, the erythrocyte sedimentation rate (ESR) and the C-reactive proteins are elevated. Other significant findings are a decreased red-blood-cell count, elevated white blood count, and positive latex fixation test. (*Luckmann and Sorensen, p. 1222.*)

**24 a** The "rheumatoid factor" refers to an autoantibody that is found in many patients with rheumatoid arthritis. Since these autoantibodies have been identified in patients with autoimmune diseases, it is believed by some authorities that rheumatoid arthritis is an autoimmune disorder. (*Price and Wilson, pp. 139, 749.*)

**25 d** If the inflammatory process of rheumatoid arthritis is allowed to progress, the joints become calcified and fixed. This bony ankylosis results in complete loss of motion in the joint. (*Luckmann and Sorensen, p. 1120. Price and Wilson, p. 748. Shafer et al., p. 941.*)

**26 a** Although there are many different kinds of drugs being used to treat rheumatoid arthritis, acetylsalicylic acid (aspirin) continues to be the drug of choice. Not only is aspirin an analgesic, but it also has anti-inflammatory effects. (*Price and Wilson, p. 751. Shafer et al., p. 940.*)

**27 c** The corticosteroids are used after all other modes of therapy have been tried. Although the corticosteroids are beneficial in relieving the overt symptoms of rheumatoid arthritis, they do nothing to arrest the joint destruction and the development of deformities. They are rarely used in the initial or the acute phases of the disease. (*Shafer et al., p. 936.*)

**28  a**  Gold therapy is indicated for those patients with rheumatoid arthritis if the more conservative modes of therapy have been unsuccessful. The drug has many toxic effects and should be used with great caution. The most common toxic effects are skin reactions and lesions of the mucous membrane. Since the drug is discontinued at the first sign of toxicity, the physician should be notified. Other toxic effects include aplastic anemia, photosensitization, purpura, etc. (*Luckmann and Sorensen, p. 1228. Price and Wilson, p. 752.*)

**29  b**  Dimercaprol (British anti-Lewisite) is the antidote used for arsenic, gold, or mercury poisoning. Since the antidote for these metals is a potentially dangerous drug, patients receiving it should be carefully observed for renal failure. (*Bergersen, p. 705.*)

**30  b**  In caring for the patient with rheumatoid arthritis, the side-lying position and the semi-Fowler's position should not be encouraged. The patient can be positioned flat in bed with the affected joints placed in a position of extension. Lying prone is another position that should be encouraged. The head rests and the knee rests should never be elevated since these positions foster the development of flexion contractures. (*Luckmann and Sorensen, p. 1224.*)

**31  d**  Since the patient with rheumatoid arthritis usually experiences pain while performing exercises, the patient should be encouraged to take aspirin about ½ hour before beginning exercises. (*Luckmann and Sorensen, p. 1225. Shafer et al., p. 938.*)

**32  d**  There are many dietary food fads associated with "curing" rheumatoid arthritis. Patients should be cautioned about adhering to these dietary fads and should be told that no special diet is recommended as long as the dietary intake is well balanced and nutritious. (*Shafer et al., p. 938.*)

**33 a** Phenylbutazone (Butazolidin) is an anti-inflammatory medication used to treat many forms of arthritis. Since the drug has such a high incidence of side effects, it is not recommended for prolonged use. Side effects include bone marrow depression, visual disturbances, hepatitis, gastric irritation, etc. The drug enhances the action of penicillin, the sulfonamides, and warfarin. It inhibits the action of steroids, sex hormones, barbiturates, etc. (*Bergersen, pp. 237–238.*)

**34 b** Osteoarthritis is a common disorder of the elderly. There is degeneration of the weight-bearing joints and the distal joints of the fingers. Aging, obesity, and trauma contribute to the development of osteoarthritis. (*Luckmann and Sorensen, p. 1228.*)

**35 c** Gout is a disorder of purine metabolism that causes an elevation of the uric acid in the blood. The elevated uric acid contributes to the formation of tophi in the subcutaneous tissue or near the joints. These urate crystals settle in the joints and cause an inflammatory response that produces severe pain. (*Luckmann and Sorensen, p. 1234. Shafer et al., p. 943.*)

**36 b** Allopurinol is the drug of choice for treating gouty arthritis. It inhibits the production of uric acid by interfering with the metabolism of purines. This in turn decreases the deposit of urate crystals in the kidneys and joints. (*Asperheim and Eisenhauer, p. 454.*)

**37 c** Allopurinol is excreted by way of the kidneys. The patient receiving allopurinol should be encouraged to drink extra fluids to prevent the formation of urinary calculi. Salicylates and uricosuric agents can be given concurrently with allopurinol without causing any adverse effects. The drug has many side effects, and patients should be observed carefully for toxicity. (*Bergersen, p. 240. Luckmann and Sorensen, p. 1235.*)

**38 a** Foods that have negligible amounts of purines and may be used as desired include cheeses of all kinds, milk, eggs, butter, pies, sugar and other sweets, most vegetables, cereal, breads, and fruits of all kinds. Foods high in purine include consommés and other meat extracts, liver and other organ meats, gravies, anchovies, and sardines. Moderate amounts of purines are found in meats, fish, fowl, legumes, spinach, mushrooms, asparagus, etc. (*Howard and Herbold, p. 440. Williams, pp. 598–599.*)

**39 b** Myasthenia gravis is classified as an autoimmune neuromuscular disease. The most common initial symptom is ptosis and diplopia. (*Luckmann and Sorensen, p. 504. Moidel, Giblin, and Wagner, p. 938. Price and Wilson, p. 619.*)

**40 a** The Tensilon test is a diagnostic test that is used to confirm the diagnosis of myasthenia gravis. In this test an intravenous dose of endrophonium chloride is given to the patient. If the patient has an increase in muscle strength, the diagnosis of myasthenia gravis is confirmed. (*Bergersen, p. 376. Price and Wilson, p. 621. Rodman and Smith, p. 274.*)

**41 c** Anticholinesterase medications are used to treat myasthenia gravis. It is believed that these medications inactivate the cholinesterase liberated at the motor end plate. As a result, the activity of acetylcholine is prolonged and muscle weakness is relieved. An example of an anticholinesterase medication is neostigmine. (*Bergersen, p. 134.*)

**42 c** Mestinon is an anticholinesterase medication used to treat myasthenia gravis. The main advantage of the drug is its longer action, which enables the patient to take the drug at bedtime and sleep undisturbed. In addition the drug causes less stimulation of the gastrointestinal tract, hence, less side effects. The generic name is pyridostigmine bromide. (*Bergersen, pp. 135–136. Rodman and Smith, p. 274.*)

**43 b** Atropine is the antidote used for an overdose of an anticholinesterase medication. Patients with myasthenia gravis take anticholinesterase medications to relieve the symptoms. They should be watched closely for symptoms of overdosage. (*Bergersen, p. 135. Price and Wilson, p. 621.*)

**44 a** Respiratory distress is the major symptom of myasthenia crisis. Suction, tracheostomy, and assisted ventilation are usually indicated in myasthenia crisis. (*Moidel, Giblin, and Wagner, p. 943. Price and Wilson, p. 621.*)

**45 b** In planning a program of activities for the patient with myasthenia gravis, the patient should be told that his or her muscle strength is best when the medication has reached its peak activity. Important activities should be planned to coincide with this peak activity. Muscle strength is greatly diminished after exercise and in the evening. (*Luckmann and Sorensen, p. 504. Moidel, Giblin, and Wagner, p. 938.*)

**46 d** The basal ganglia are a part of the extrapyramidal tract and play a major role in coordination, especially the automatic associated movements of the body. Parkinson's disease is caused by degeneration of the basal ganglia of the extrapyramidal tract. (*Langley, Telford, and Christensen, p. 361. Luckmann and Sorensen, p. 499. Moidel, Giblin, and Wagner, p. 893.*)

**47 c** Parkinson's disease is a degenerative disease of the extrapyramidal tract. The basal ganglia are primarily involved. It is believed that there is a decrease of dopamine secretion in the corpus striatum of the basal ganglia. There seems to be evidence that dopamine plays a role in inhibiting the motor pathways that control gross intentional body movements. (*Jones, Dunbar, and Jirovec, p. 1244. Price and Wilson, p. 619.*)

**48 a** Symptoms of Parkinson's disease include "pill-rolling" tremors and cogwheel muscle rigidity. The pill-rolling tremor is a rhythmic movement of the thumb against the finger. The cogwheel muscle rigidity is a jerking rigidity that occurs when the muscles of the extremities are moved or stretched by the examiner. (*Luckmann and Sorensen, p. 499. Price and Wilson, p. 615.*)

**49 a** The gait that characterizes Parkinson's disease is referred to as "shuffling." The body is held rigid, while the trunk and head are bent forward. The patient takes short, quick, propulsive steps and often has difficulty stopping. (*Luckmann and Sorensen, p. 499. Moidel, Giblin, and Wagner, p. 893. Shafer et al., p. 889.*)

**50 d**  Side effects of levodopa include increased sex drive and priapism. The nurse should recognize that the erection of the penis is a drug-induced effect and should attempt to help the patient recognize it as such. (*Asperheim and Eisenhauer, p. 269. Rodman and Smith, p. 141.*).

**51 b**  The patient receiving levodopa should be told that any rapid change of position can cause postural hypotension. Bananas, ripe cheese, and chianti wine contain monoamine oxidase inhibitors, which increase the effects of levodopa. Pyridoxine and antihypertensive and antianxiety drugs decrease the effects of levodopa. (*Asperheim and Eisenhauer, p. 271. Bergersen, p. 378.*)

**52 a**  A harmless side effect of levodopa is red urine. It is not an indication to discontinue the medication. (*Fischback, p. 68.*)

**53 b**  Pyridoxine (vitamin $B_6$) interferes with the action of levodopa. Vitamin supplements containing pyridoxine should not be given to patients receiving levodopa. (*Bergersen, p. 378. Rodman and Smith, p. 142.*)

**54 c**  Emotional instability is one of the symptoms of multiple sclerosis. Unfortunately many persons have been labeled "neurotic" long before any overt symptoms of multiple sclerosis are evident. Family members and the patient need assistance in accepting the sudden, inappropriate emotional outbursts. (*Price and Wilson, pp. 617–618. Shafer et al., p. 888.*)

**55 d**  "Charcot's triad" refers to a group of symptoms that occur in multiple sclerosis if there is damage to the cerebellum. The triad of symptoms includes intention tremors, scanning speech, and nystagmus. (*Jones, Dunbar, and Jirovec, p. 1234. Luckmann and Sorensen, p. 506.*)

**56 c**  The person with intention tremors has oscillating tremors when attempts are made to grasp an object or hit a particular point; for example, peeling a boiled egg and threading a needle are extremely difficult. When the limbs are at rest, there are no tremors. (*Langley, Telford, and Christensen, p. 360. Vander, Sherman, and Luciano, p. 547.*)

**57 a** In multiple sclerosis the deep-tendon reflexes are hyperactive. Examples of deep-tendon reflexes are the biceps reflex, the triceps reflex, the brachioradialis reflex, the patellar reflex, and the ankle reflex. (*Jones, Dunbar, and Jirovec, p. 1100.*)

**58 b** A test to determine proprioreception sense and cerebellar function in the Romberg test. If the patient falls when asked to stand with the feet together and the eyes closed, then the Romberg test is positive. Patients with multiple sclerosis have a positive Romberg sign. (*Shafer et al., p. 859.*)

**59 b** Bulbar involvement can occur in the late stages of multiple sclerosis. The patient should be carefully observed for difficulties in chewing and swallowing. Proper positioning, suctioning, and assisting at mealtimes are other actions to be done by the nurse. (*Jones, Dunbar, and Jirovec, p. 1242.*)

**60 a** Mrs. Collins obviously is not ready to learn. Before attempts are made to teach Mrs. Collins how to care for the catheter, she must be convinced that she is able to perform the care and willing to see a need for learning. Physically she "feels too weak"; emotionally she may have a need to be dependent. (*Sierra-Franco, pp. 292, 307.*)

# UNIT 9

# Nursing care of the patient with an endocrine disorder

**OBJECTIVES**

To answer the following questions, the reader should be able to

1. Recognize the relationship of the nervous system to the endocrine system;
2. List the various hormones of the endocrine system;
3. Identify those systems that regulate hormone secretion;
4. Describe how the body adapts to disorders of endocrine function;
5. List the major signs and symptoms of select endocrine disorders;
6. Recognize the nurse's role in preparing the patient for select diagnostic tests;
7. Describe the nursing management of the patient with an endocrine disorder.

## QUESTIONS RELATED TO OBJECTIVES

*Instructions*: Choose the *one best* answer to the following questions.

1. The component of the central nervous system which plays an essential role in the control of hormone secretion is the
   a  Hypothalamus.
   b  Cerebellum.
   c  Medulla.
   d  Midbrain.

2. The hypothalamic releasing factors are hormones that control the release of hormones from the
   a  Adenohypophysis.
   b  Neurohypophysis.
   c  Target glands.
   d  Adrenal medulla.

3. "Tropic" hormones are released by the
   a  Hypothalamus.
   b  Adenohypophysis.
   c  Neurohypophysis.
   d  Autonomic nervous system.

4. An example of a negative-feedback control system is the action of
   a  Acetylcholine on glandular secretions.
   b  The vagus nerve on gastric secretions.
   c  Corticotropin-releasing hormone, corticotropin, and cortisol.
   d  The stretch recepton on the medulla.

5. The hormone that controls the activity of the thyroid gland is
   a  Thyroglobulin.
   b  Triiodothyronine.
   c  Thyrotropin.
   d  Thyroxine.

**6** The major glucocorticoid of the body is
  **a** Corticotropin.
  **b** Cortisone.
  **c** Hydrocortisone.
  **d** Corticosterone.

**7** Glucagon is a hormone of the pancreas that
  **a** Promotes the conversion of glycogen to glucose.
  **b** Inhibits the conversion of fat to glucose.
  **c** Promotes the intracellular transport of glucose.
  **d** Inhibits the conversion of protein into glucose.

**8** The secretion of parathyroid hormone is regulated by the
  **a** Hypothalamus.
  **b** Concentration of serum calcium.
  **c** Hypophysis.
  **d** Kidney.

**9** The secretion of aldosterone is controlled by the level of sodium concentration in the blood and by
  **a** The hypothalamus.
  **b** The neurohypophysis.
  **c** The renin-angiotensin system.
  **d** Cortisol secretions.

**10** Which of the following statements relating to somatotropin is true? Somatotropin
  **a** Is a hormone of the neurohypophysis.
  **b** Increases protein anabolism and fat metabolism.
  **c** Increases the rate of carbohydrate utilization and decreases blood sugar.
  **d** Inhibits the growth of long bones.

**11** An increased production of somatotropin in the adult causes
  **a** Acromegaly.
  **b** Simmond's disease.
  **c** Cushing's syndrome.
  **d** Gigantism.

**12** Choose the statement that best relates to the action of insulin on the body's cells.

　**a**　Insulin permits the entry of glucose into muscle cells.
　**b**　Insulin increases the transport of glucose into all types of cells.
　**c**　The cells of the brain are particularly sensitive to the action of insulin on the cell membrane.
　**d**　The epithelial cells of the gastrointestinal tract and the kidney tubules need insulin for the active transport of glucose.

**13** Grace McBride is a 46-year-old woman who has a family history of diabetes mellitus. She has no overt symptoms of diabetes but has abnormal blood-glucose tests. Mrs. McBride is classified as

　**a**　Prediabetic.
　**b**　Preclinical diabetic.
　**c**　Latent diabetic.
　**d**　Overt diabetic.

**14** Sylvia Rooney is a 51-year-old woman who is being admitted to the hospital for overt diabetes mellitus. Early symptoms of diabetes mellitus include

　**a**　Polyuria, loss of weight, and increased thirst.
　**b**　Headache, anuria, and edema.
　**c**　Increased appetite, weight gain, and hypertension.
　**d**　Dry skin, pruritus, and coma.

**15** Ms. Rooney was placed on tolbutamide. The nurse recognizes that tolbutamide

　**a**　Is a form of oral insulin.
　**b**　Can be used for adult-onset and juvenile diabetes.
　**c**　Is best tolerated when given with an antacid.
　**d**　Can cause an intolerance to alcohol.

**16** While teaching Ms. Rooney how to test her urine with Clinitest, the nurse pointed out that
  a  The tablets are normally speckled blue.
  b  If the tablet is added to urine, it goes through a "pass-through phenomenon" before the results can be read.
  c  A reaction occurs only in the presence of glucose.
  d  Large doses of vitamin C can cause a false positive reading.

**17** When using Clinitest to measure the urine for glucose, the nurse should be aware that certain drugs can alter the results. Drugs that give a false positive reaction include
  a  Cephalosporin, tetracycline, and chloramphenicol.
  b  Levodopa, methyldopa, and Coumarin derivatives.
  c  Atropine, scopalamine, and Pro-banthine.
  d  Aspirin, Mercuhydrin, and monamine oxidase inhibitors.

**18** Diabetic coma is an example of
  a  Respiratory acidosis.
  b  Respiratory alkalosis.
  c  Metabolic acidosis.
  d  Metabolic alkalosis.

**19** From the following statements, choose the one that best relates to the pathophysiology of diabetic ketoacidosis.
  a  The kidneys attempt to adapt to ketoacidosis by secreting a more alkaline urine.
  b  Sodium bicarbonate combines with acetoacetic acid which depletes the body's supply of alkaline reserve.
  c  Ketoacidosis interferes with the transport of fluids from the intracellular compartment, which results in retention of fluid in the tissue spaces.
  d  Ketone bodies accumulate as a direct result of the complete oxidation of fats as a source of energy.

**20** Signs and symptoms of diabetic ketoacidosis include
   **a** Convulsions, acetic acid odor to breath, and vomiting.
   **b** Diaphoresis, hypotension, and blurred vision.
   **c** Hunger, headache, and flushed skin.
   **d** Decreased skin turgor, fruity odor to breath, and abdominal pain.

**21** In an attempt to adapt to the ketoacidosis, the respirations become deep and rapid. This is called
   **a** "Cheyne-Stokes respiration."
   **b** "Kussmaul breathing."
   **c** "Sterterous breathing."
   **d** "Biot's respiration."

**22** The type of insulin that is given intravenously to treat diabetic coma is
   **a** Crystalline zinc insulin.
   **b** Protamine zinc insulin.
   **c** NPH insulin.
   **d** Lente insulin.

**23** From the following list of insulins, choose the one whose duration of action is similar to that of NPH insulin
   **a** Protamine zinc insulin.
   **b** Lente insulin.
   **c** Semilente.
   **d** Ultralente.

**24** The patient receives NPH insulin units 25 daily at 8 A.M. Hypoglycemia can most likely occur
   **a** Before breakfast.
   **b** From 10 A.M. to lunchtime.
   **c** From 3 P.M. to dinnertime.
   **d** From midnight to 3 A.M.

25 Choose the statement that best applies to the nurse's role in administering insulin.
   a  Insulin should be stored at room temperature in a dark place.
   b  If blood-sugar studies are being done, insulin administration should not be omitted.
   c  Insulin is administered by intramuscular injection.
   d  If the patient vomits after eating, the physician should be notified.

26 Signs and symptoms of insulin shock include
   a  Thirst, double vision, and fruity odor to the breath.
   b  Diaphoresis, hunger, and nervousness.
   c  Rapid respirations, dry skin, and loss of consciousness.
   d  Hypotension, decreased tissue turgor, and double vision.

27 Frank Kennedy is a patient with diabetes who is receiving ultralente insulin. While making rounds at 3 A.M., the nurse noticed that the patient was asleep but diaphoretic. The bedclothes were damp. The nurse
   a  Awakened him, checked his temperature, and changed the bed linens.
   b  Placed a dry flannel blanket over him, but did not awaken him since he had been complaining of insomnia.
   c  Awakened him, and gave him a glass of orange juice after determining that his urine was negative for sugar and acetone.
   d  Let him sleep, slowed down the infusion, placed a dry blanket on him, and checked him in 1 half hour.

28 The doctor ordered ultralente insulin units 25. The vial on hand was ultralente insulin units 100. Since there was no units 100 insulin syringe available on the unit, the nurse used a tuberculin syringe and administered
   a  0.25 minims.
   b  2.5 minims.
   c  4 minims.
   d  40 minims.

**29** While the nurse is reviewing the diabetic exchange list with Mr. Kennedy, he states, "I hate string beans, tomatoes, and broccoli!" The nurse explained that he could make the following substitutions:

- **a** Peas, winter squash, and spinach.
- **b** Lentils, carrots, and cucumbers
- **c** Corn, turnips, and brussels sprouts.
- **d** Asparagus, eggplant, and mushrooms.

**30** Mr. Kennedy is allowed on bread exchange at dinner. This means that he could substitute one slice of bread for

- **a** ½ a small banana.
- **b** A ½-in wedge of apple pie.
- **c** A 1-in wedge of avocado.
- **d** ½ cup of lima beans.

**31** Jennie Ann Hellmer is a 28-year-old woman admitted to the hospital with hyperthyroidism. She refuses to assist with her care and states that she "is in the hospital for a rest." You would

- **a** Conform to her request since it is important that she have emotional as well as physical rest.
- **b** Explain to Ms. Hellmer that it is important that she not become dependent and insist that she bathe herself.
- **c** Report the incident to the supervisor, since it is not usual to give complete care to patients who can care for themselves.
- **d** Leave a basin of water on the overbed table and tell Ms. Hellmer that you will be back in 20 minutes.

**32** In assessing the results of the diagnostic tests done on Ms. Hellmer, the nurse would expect a

  **a** Low serum concentration of protein-bound iodine (PBI), high serum cholesterol, and decreased radioactive iodine uptake.
  **b** High serum concentration of protein-bound iodine, low serum cholesterol, and increased radioactive iodine uptake.
  **c** Low serum concentration of protein-bound iodine, normal serum cholesterol, and increased radioactive iodine uptake.
  **d** Normal serum concentration of protein-bound iodine, elevated serum cholesterol, and increased radioactive iodine uptake.

**33** Physical assessment of the patient with hyperthyroidism reveals the following:

  **a** Hypotension, constipation, and loss of weight.
  **b** Tremors, amenorrhea, and hypophagia.
  **c** Widening pulse pressure, palpitations, and exophthalmos.
  **d** Increased appetite, arthralgia and bradycardia.

**34** Ms. Hellmer has an intolerance to heat. The nurse recognizes that the patient will

  **a** Have diaphoresis, so removes the rubber bed sheet.
  **b** Feel cold, so adds extra blankets.
  **c** Have a lowered body temperature and prefers a warm room temperature.
  **d** Feel more comfortable if she wears woolen socks to bed.

**35** Toxic effects of propylthiouracil include

  **a** Tachycardia, vertigo, and visual disturbances.
  **b** Hypertension, headache, and insomnia.
  **c** Leukopenia, sore throat, and fever.
  **d** Tremor, weight loss, and chest pain.

**36** Signs and symptoms of thyroid crisis include
  **a** Coma, hypothermia, and respiratory acidosis.
  **b** Paranoia, delusions, and depression.
  **c** Decreased blood pressure, edema, and anuria.
  **d** Elevated temperature, tachycardia, and delirium.

**37** The antithyroid preparation that can be given intravenously to treat severe thyroid crisis is
  **a** Propylthiouracil.
  **b** Sodium iodide.
  **c** Methimazole.
  **d** Aqueous iodine solution.

**38** When preparing the patient for the radioiodinated triiodothyronine test, the nurse recognizes that
  **a** Food and fluid are withheld for 8 hours prior to the exam.
  **b** Shellfish and iodized salt are not permitted for 72 hours prior to the exam.
  **c** A tracer dose of radioactive iodine is given to the patient intravenously.
  **d** A sample of the patient's blood is the only requirement for the test.

**39** Which of the following agents causes an elevation in the serum concentration of PBI?
  **a** Dilantin and reserpine.
  **b** Aspirin and cortisone.
  **c** Isoniazid and para-aminosalicylic acid.
  **d** Barbiturates and oral contraceptives.

**40** An example of an autoimmune disorder that causes hypothyroidism is
  **a** Grave's disease.
  **b** Hashimoto's disease.
  **c** Cretinism.
  **d** Endemic goiter.

**41** In hypothyroidism, the decreased metabolism decreases the amount of oxygen utilized by the cells. The body adapts by
   a   Decreasing cardiac output and lowering blood pressure.
   b   Increasing the number of red blood cells, causing secondary polycythemia.
   c   Increasing renal blood flow and urinary output.
   d   Decreasing capillary permeability and increasing bruising.

**42** In caring for the patient with myxedema, the nurse recognizes that
   a   An increase of urinary output occurs if the patient is placed on thyroid-hormone therapy.
   b   The use of hypnotics is recommended to alleviate the associated insomnia.
   c   The patient cannot tolerate a warm environment.
   d   Hormone-replacement therapy will be continued until the thyroid gland starts producing additional thyroxine.

**43** An example of a thyroid preparation used to treat hypothyroidism is
   a   Propylthiouracil.
   b   Methimazole.
   c   Sodium iodide.
   d   Sodium levothyroxine.

**44** Which of the following groups of drugs is enhanced by sodium levothyroxine (Synthroid)?
   a   Cardiotonics.
   b   Anticoagulants.
   c   Hypnotics.
   d   Narcotics.

**45** The thyroid preparation that has proven to be useful in treating patients who develop coma from myxedema or overtreatment of hyperthyroidism is
 a  Sodium levothyroxine (Synthroid).
 b  Sodium liothyronine (Cytomel).
 c  Thyroid extract.
 d  Thyroglobulin (Proloid).

**46** Symptoms of overdosage from thyroid preparations include
 a  Tachycardia, tremors, and nervousness.
 b  Soreness over thyroid area, skin rash, and jaundice.
 c  Lymphadenopathy, fever, and leukopenia.
 d  Sluggishness, weight gain, and dry skin.

**47** While teaching the patient with endemic goiter, the nurse pointed out that
 a  Endemic goiter can be prevented by use of iodized salt.
 b  It is caused by faulty iodine metabolism.
 c  It is caused by overtreatment of hyperthyroidism.
 d  Pregnancy is the primary factor in precipitating an acute attack.

**48** Atrophy or destruction of the adrenal cortex, which produces hyposecretion of adrenocortical hormones, is
 a  Pheochromocytoma.
 b  Cushing's syndrome.
 c  Addison's disease.
 d  Aldosteronism.

**49** Clarence Jones has been admitted to the hospital with Addison's disease. While taking a nursing history the nurse would expect to find the following:
 a  Fatigue, hypotension, and hyperpigmentation of the skin and mucous membrane.
 b  Hypertension, headache, and widening of the pulse pressure.
 c  Edema, anuria, and dizziness.
 d  Buffalo hump, acne, and moonface.

**50** While collecting data to make a nursing diagnosis on Mr. Jones, the nurse reviewed several results of diagnostic tests. In Addison's disease, the nurse would expect to find

  **a** Decreased fasting blood sugar, increased serum sodium, and decreased serum potassium.

  **b** Normal fasting blood sugar, increased serum sodium, and decreased serum potassium.

  **c** Increased fasting blood sugar, decreased serum sodium, and increased serum potassium.

  **d** Decreased fasting blood sugar, decreased serum sodium, and increased serum potassium.

**51** While preparing Mr. Jones for an 8-hour corticotropin test, the nurse

  **a** Collects a control 24-hour urine specimen prior to the intravenous administration of corticotropin, and a second 24-hour urine specimen is collected after the administration of corticotropin.

  **b** Withholds food and fluids for 8 hours prior to the administration of the test dose of corticotropin.

  **c** Tells the patient that the only requirement is a sampling of blood to measure the corticotropin level.

  **d** Tells the patient that radioactive corticotropin is injected IV before a sampling of blood and urine is taken.

**52** While helping Mr. Jones plan a program of care in preparation for discharge, the nurse tells him that

  **a** The corticosteroids will have to be withdrawn gradually when the laboratory tests come back normal.

  **b** He will be on corticosteroid-replacement therapy for the rest of his life.

  **c** Prolonged corticosteroid therapy causes atrophy of the adrenal cortex.

  **d** The corticosteroids will be discontinued within 12 to 18 months.

**53** Florinef is the trade name for fludrocortisone acetate, a synthetic corticosteroid used to treat Addison's disease. Choose the statement that best applies to Florinef. It is

    **a** Given because it has potent mineralocorticoid properties.
    **b** Inactivated when given orally.
    **c** Used in place of hydrocortisone.
    **d** Readily converted to hydrocortisone when absorbed by the stomach.

**54** In Addison's disease, there is also impaired secretion of the androgens. This is manifested by

    **a** Gynecomastia in men.
    **b** Decreased axillary and pubic hair in women.
    **c** Hirsutism in women.
    **d** High-pitched voice in men.

**55** Toxic symptoms of mineralocorticoid therapy include

    **a** Polyuria and pulmonary congestion.
    **b** Edema and hypertension.
    **c** Postural hypotension and tachycardia.
    **d** Cardiac arrhythmias and hyperkalemia.

**56** Which of the following statements relating to Addisonian crisis is true? Addisonian crisis

    **a** Can be brought on by overtreatment with the adrenocorticosteroids.
    **b** Is precipitated by infection, physical trauma, and psychological stress.
    **c** Causes hyperglycemia, which leads to fluid and electrolyte imbalance.
    **d** Is treated by relieving the severe hypertension and fluid retention.

**57** Which of the following corticosteroid preparations can be used intravenously to treat Addisonian crisis?

    **a** Cortisone acetate.
    **b** Corticotropin injection.
    **c** Desoxycorticosterone acetate.
    **d** Hydrocortisone sodium succinate.

## ANSWERS, EXPLANATIONS, AND REFERENCES

**1 a** The link between the central nervous system and the endocrine system is the hypothalamus. The hypothalamus plays an important role in controlling the secretion of hormones by secreting substances called "releasing factors." (*Langley, Telford, and Christensen, p. 717. Vander, Sherman, and Luciano, p. 173.*)

**2 a** The hypothalamus secretes substances called "hypothalmic releasing factors" into the hypothalamopituitary portal vessels. These hormones control the release of hormones from the adenohypophysis (the anterior lobe of the pituitary gland). (*Vander, Sherman, and Luciano, pp. 182–183.*)

**3 b** Tropic hormones are the hormones secreted by the adenohypophysis. Examples of tropic hormones are thyroid-stimulating hormones, adrenocorticotropic hormone, gonadotropic hormone, growth hormone, and prolactin. All but growth hormone control the secretion of the target organs. The target organs are the thyroid, the cortex of the adrenal gland, the ovaries, the testes, and the breast. Although growth hormone (somatotropin) is a tropic hormone, it does not have a specific target organ. It exerts metabolic effects on many tissues and organs. (*Vander, Sherman, and Luciano, pp. 180–181.*)

**4 c** The body has many systems for regulating hormone secretion. An example of a negative-feedback control system is the interaction of corticotropin-releasing factor, corticotropin, and cortisol. To clarify this a little, if the blood level of cortisol is decreased, the hypothalamus is stimulated to secrete corticotropin-releasing factors (CRF). The CRF in turn stimulates the adenohypophysis to release corticotropin (ACTH). The corticotropin then stimulates the adrenal cortex to secrete cortisol and the serum level increases. The mechanism also functions as the serum level of cortisol increases. This time the hypothalamus is inhibited. Less CRF is released, less corticotropin is released by the adenohypophysis, and finally less cortisol is secreted. This negative-feedback mechanism functions to keep the cortisol serum level within normal limits. (*Price and Wilson, p. 653.*)

**5 c** Thyrotropin (TSH) is a hormone secreted by the adenohypophysis which controls the activity of the thyroid gland. The synthesis of the thyroid hormones, the ability to take up and concentrate iodine, and the rate of release of the thyroid hormones are all aspects of thyroid activity controlled by thyrotropin. (*Langley, Telford, and Christensen, p. 727.*)

**6 c** The major glucocorticoid of the body is hydrocortisone. The other name for hydrocortisone is cortisol. The glucocorticoids play a role in the metabolism of fats, proteins, and carbohydrates. In addition, the glucocorticoids play a major role in the body's response to prolonged stress. (*Langley, Telford, and Christensen, p. 736.*)

**7 a** Glucagon is a hormone produced by the alpha cells of the pancreas and elevates blood sugar by promoting the conversion of glycogen to glucose. This action occurs when the glucose levels are decreased. In severe hypoglycemia, preparations of glucagon can be administered intravenously to raise the blood sugar level. (*Langley, Telford, and Christensen, p. 740.*)

**8 b** The parathyroid glands secrete parathyroid hormone when there is a decrease in the level of calcium ions in the serum. By the same token, an increased level of serum calcium suppresses the secretion of parathyroid hormone. The parathyroid is one of the few endocrine glands that are not controlled by the pituitary gland. Parathyroid hormones act on the intestines, the kidney, and the bones. (*Langley, Telford, and Christensen, p. 732.*)

**9 c** Another mechanism that exerts an influence on aldosterone secretion is the renin-angiotensin system. If blood flow to the kidney is impaired, renin is secreted. Renin works directly on angiotensinogen to convert it to angiotensin. Not only does angiotensin elevate blood pressure, but it also stimulates the adrenocortex to secrete aldosterone. (*Langley, Telford, and Christensen, p. 492, p. 736.*)

**10 b** Somatotropin (growth hormone) is a hormone secreted by the adenohypophysis. In addition to stimulating growth, somatotropin increases protein anabolism and fat catabolism and inhibits the rate of carbohydrate utilization. Somatotropin facilitates the transportation of amino acids through the cell membrane. As a result the amino acids are available for conversion into tissue proteins. The decreased rate of carbohydrate utilization causes an increased blood sugar level. (*Langley, Telford, and Christensen, p. 718.*)

**11 a** Hypersecreting tumors of the anterior pituitary gland can cause an increased production of somatotropin. In the adult, the increased levels of somatotropin causes acromegaly. This is manifest by large hands, feet, protruding jaw, thickened lips, and enlarged tongue. The internal organs become enlarged. (*Shafer et al., p. 767.*)

**12 a** Insulin is necessary for the entry of glucose in muscle cells and fat cells. In the absence of insulin, these cells are literally "bathed" in glucose from the extracellular compartment, but the glucose is unable to pass through the cell membrane. Insulin is not necessary for the active transport of glucose into the brain cells and into the epithelial cells of the kidney tubules and gastrointestinal tract. (*Guyton, p. 917. Luckmann and Sorensen, p. 1311. Vander, Sherman, and Luciano, p. 399.*)

**13 c** Diabetes mellitus can be divided into four stages: prediabetic, preclinical, latent, and overt. The prediabetic has normal blood-glucose tests with no overt symptoms but a family history of diabetes. In preclinical diabetes, there are no overt symptoms but the blood-glucose tests are abnormal during stressful periods. The person with latent diabetes has no overt symptoms but has abnormal blood-glucose tests. Overt diabetes is the fourth stage of diabetes. The blood-glucose tests are abnormal and the person has overt symptoms. (*Jones, Dunbar, and Jirovec, p. 670. Luckmann and Sorensen, p. 1320.*)

**14 a** Early symptoms of diabetes mellitus include polyuria, increased thirst, and loss of weight. These symptoms occur as the body attempts to adapt to hyperglycemia and glycosuria. As the blood sugar increases, the kidneys excrete the excess sugar via the urine. A large quantity of water is lost as the excess sugar is excreted, resulting in polyuria and increased thirst. Loss of weight occurs because the body loses calories via the urine and then utilizes stored fats and, ultimately, stored proteins as a source of energy. (*Jones, Dunbar, and Jirovec, p. 667. Luckmann and Sorensen, p. 1315.*)

**15 d** Tolbutamide is an oral antidiabetic agent that stimulates the pancreas to secrete insulin. Because of this action, it can be used only for those patients who have some functioning pancreatic cells. It cannot be used in severe or juvenile diabetics. Patients should be cautioned that use of the medication can produce an intolerance to alcohol. (*Asperheim and Eisenhauer, p. 352. Bergersen, p. 583. Rodman and Smith, p. 485.*)

**16 d** When one is teaching the patient how to test the urine with Clinitest, the patient should be told that aspirin and large doses of vitamin C can give false positive results. The patient should also be aware that the tablets are normally light blue. Any discoloration or the appearance of dark speckles could mean that the tablets have lost their potency. If the urine contains more than 2% glucose, a pass-through phenomenon can occur. The test should be repeated using 2 gtt of urine and 10 gtt of water instead of 5 gtt of urine and 10 gtt of water. (*Jones, Dunbar, and Jirovec, p. 678. Luckmann and Sorensen, p. 1320.*)

**17 a** Clinitest is a substance commonly used to measure the amount of glucose in the urine. The nurse should be aware that antibiotics such as cephalosporin, tetracycline, and chloramphenicol can alter the results of the test. If the patient is receiving any of these drugs, the nurse can use Tes-tape or Clinistix to test the urine. (*Jones, Dunbar, and Jirovec, p. 679.*)

**18 c** Diabetic coma, or diabetic ketoacidosis, is a form of metabolic acidosis caused by an accumulation of ketone bodies, namely, acetoacetic acid, beta-hydroxybutyric acid, and acetone. These ketone bodies are metabolically produced and create metabolic acidosis. (*Luckmann and Sorensen, p. 226. Shafer et al., p. 117.*)

**19 b** Because the cells cannot utilize carbohydrate as a source of energy, fats are mobilized from the adipose tissue and utilized as a source of energy. Since the demand of the cells for energy exceeds the rate of fat metabolism, the fats cannot be completely oxidized. As a result, the intermediary products of fat metabolism, namely, acetoacetic acid, acetone, and beta-hydroxybutyric acid, tend to accumulate in the body. The sodium bicarbonate buffers combine with acetoacetic acid in an effort to maintain the normal pH of the blood. However, these acids accumulate faster than what the buffer system can handle. As a result, the hydrogen-ion concentration of the blood increases, the pH falls, and the patient develops ketoacidosis. (*Jones, Dunbar, and Jirovec, p. 687. Luckmann and Sorensen, p. 1335.*)

**20 d** Hyperglycemia and glycosuria ultimately lead to the fluid and electrolyte imbalance and dehydration associated with diabetic ketoacidosis. Abdominal pain is caused by sodium depletion; decreased skin turgor is caused by dehydration; and the fruity odor of the breath is caused by the excess acetone being blown off by the lungs. (*Jones, Dunbar, and Jirovec, p. 687. Luckmann and Sorensen, p. 1335.*)

**21 b** In the body's attempt to adapt to diabetic ketoacidosis, the respirations become deep and rapid. This rids the body of excess carbon dioxide and water and excess acetone. These respirations are referred to as "Kussmaul respirations" or as "air hunger." The decreased pH of the blood stimulates the respiratory center of the brain. (*Luckmann and Sorensen, pp. 1335–1337.*)

**22 a** Although all insulins are given subcutaneously, not all insulins can be given intravenously. Crystalline zinc insulin is a preparation that can be given intravenously and therefore can be given to treat diabetic coma. (*Bergersen, p. 580.*)

**23 b**  The official name of lente insulin is insulin zinc suspension. It is classified as an intermediate-acting insulin. The time of onset, peak of action, and duration of action are similar to those of NPH insulin. (*Bergersen, pp. 579–580.*)

**24 c**  If the patient receives a dose of NPH insulin at 8 A.M., the peak action occurs 8 to 12 hours after administration. This means that hypoglycemia can most likely occur from 3 P.M. to dinnertime. (*Bergersen, p. 580.*)

**25 d**  If the patient has received a dose of insulin, it is important that the intake of carbohydrate be adequate to prevent insulin shock. The physician should be notified if the patient refuses to eat or vomits after eating. (*Bergersen, p. 348.*)

**26 b**  Symptoms of insulin shock include diaphoresis, hunger, and nervousness. Other symptoms include cold, clammy skin; tremors; and double vision. Patients suffering from these symptoms should receive treatment immediately to prevent damage to the nervous system from prolonged hypoglycemia. (*Asperheim and Eisenhauer, p. 346. Rodman and Smith, p. 484.*)

**27 c**  Ultralente is a long-acting insulin whose peak of action occurs between 12 and 16 hours after administration. Hypoglycemia occurs most frequently during the night or early morning hours. If the nurse discovers that the patient has diaphoresis while asleep, the patient should be awakened and the urine tested for sugar and acetone. If both are negative, then a soluble form of carbohydrate should be given orally. (*Bergersen, p. 581.*)

**28 c**  To prepare 25 units of ultralente insulin from a vial of lente insulin units 100, the nurse would administer 4 minims of lente insulin units 100. (*Saxton, Ercolano, and Walter, pp. 46–47.*)

$$\frac{\text{Desired 25 units}}{\text{Have 100 units}} = \frac{\text{Desired } x \text{ minims}}{\text{Have 16 minims}}$$

$$100x = 400$$

$$x = 4 \text{ minims}$$

**29 d** String beans, tomatoes, and broccoli are on *List 2, Vegetable Exchanges*, of the American Diabetic Association Exchange List. One-half cup of asparagus, mushrooms, or eggplant is equivalent to $\frac{1}{2}$ cup of string beans, broccoli, or tomatoes. Other substitutions or exchanges include cauliflower, brussels sprouts, etc. (*Howard and Herbold, p. 431. Jones, Dunbar, and Jirovec, p. 674. Krause and Hunscher, p. 403.*)

**30 d** According to the American Diabetic Association Exchange List, one slice of bread can be exchanged for $\frac{1}{2}$ cup of lima beans. Other exchanges for one slice of bread include $\frac{1}{2}$ English muffin, $\frac{1}{2}$ hamburger bun, $\frac{1}{2}$ cup of peas, and 1 small white potato. (*Howard and Herbold, p. 432. Jones, Dunbar, and Jirovec, p. 675. Krause and Hunscher, p. 404.*)

**31 a** Maintaining physical and emotional rest is an important objective of nursing care for Ms. Hellmer. The patient is hyperirritable and hyperexcitable and becomes easily upset. In order to achieve the objectives of care, the nurse should conform to her request. (*Beland, p. 221. Jones, Dunbar, and Jirovec, p. 715.*)

**32 b** Diagnostic tests used to diagnose disorders of thyroid function include serum protein-bound iodine, serum cholesterol, and radioactive iodine uptake. In hyperthyroidism, there is a high serum concentration of protein-bound iodine, low serum cholesterol, and an increased radioactive iodine uptake. (*Beland, p. 216.*)

**33 c** Hyperthyroidism is manifest by widening pulse pressure, palpitations, and exophthalmos. Other symptoms include tachycardia, hypertension, amenorrhea, loss of weight, increased appetite, nervousness, and diarrhea. (*Beland, p. 219.*)

**34 a** The increased metabolic rate that characterizes hyperthyroidism causes the patient to have an intolerance to heat. The body adapts to this by increased diaphoresis, which is an attempt to keep the body cool. Rubber bed sheets or plastic mattress covers should be removed because they tend to increase diaphoresis even more.

If the mattesss is covered with plastic ticking, it is a good idea to cover the entire mattress with a mattress cover or a bath blanket. (*Beland, p. 221. Luckmann and Sorensen, p. 1358.*)

**35 c** Propylthiouracil is an antithyroid drug used to treat hyperthyroidism. Symptoms of hyperthyroidism are relieved because the drug interferes with the synthesis of thyroid hormone. This in turn results in decreased levels of thyroid hormone in the body. Toxic symptoms include leukopenia, agranulocytosis, sore throat, and fever. Skin rash and lymphadenopathy are other symptoms of toxicity. (*Bergersen, p. 564.*)

**36 d** Thyroid crisis is a very serious complication of hyperthyroidism. It can be precipitated by infection, emotional stress, and trauma. Signs and symptoms include high fever, tachycardia, delirium, and severe dehydration. If not treated, the patient can die from heart failure. (*Jones, Dunbar, and Jirovec, p. 714. Luckmann and Sorensen, p. 1358. Shafer et al., p. 742.*)

**37 d** Sodium iodine is an antithyroid preparation that can be given intravenously to treat severe thyroid crisis. (*Bergersen, p. 560.*)

**38 d** The radioiodinated triiodothyronine test is a diagnostic test used to measure the ability of the serum proteins to bind with triiodothyronine. Since the level of circulating triiodothyronine is high is hyperthyroidism, the binding ability is high. There is no special preparation of the patient for this test. The only requirement is a sampling of the patient's blood for laboratory study. (*Beland, p. 216.*)

**39 d** The nurse should be aware that certain medications can destroy the results of the serum concentration of protein-bound iodine in the blood. Agents that cause a false increased concentration include the barbiturates, oral contraceptives, estrogens, lithium, etc. Aspirin, Dilantin, reserpine, PAS, isoniazid, etc., produce a false low PBI. (*Luckmann and Sorensen, p. 1347.*)

**40 b** Hashimoto's disease is an autoimmune disorder of the thyroid gland that causes hypothyroidism. (*Jones, Dunbar, and Jirovec, p. 698.*)

**41 a** The decreased metabolic rate that occurs in hypothyroidism results in a decreased utilization of oxygen by the tissue cells. This is manifest by decreased cardiac output, bradycardia, decreased blood pressure, decreased red-blood-cell production, and increased capillary permeability. *(Jones, Dunbar, and Jirovec, pp. 699–701.)*

**42 a** In caring for the patient with myxedema, the nurse should expect an increase of urinary output when the patient is started on thyroid-hormone therapy. The patient should be weighed daily and intake and output carefully monitored. An assessment of puffiness and edema should also be made. *(Jones, Dunbar, and Jirovec, p. 705. Luckmann and Sorensen, p. 1355.)*

**43 d** Sodium levothyroxine (Synthroid) is a thyroid preparation used to treat hypothyroidism. The usual oral dose ranges from 100 to 400 mg daily. *(Bergersen, p. 559.)*

**44 b** Sodium levothyroxine (Synthroid) is a thyroid preparation that enhances the action of oral anticoagulants such as Dicumarol (bishyroxycoumarin) and Coumadin (warfarin sodium). *(Bergersen, p. 559.)*

**45 b** Sodium liothyronine (Cytomel) is a rapidly acting thyroid preparation that can be used intravenously to treat myxedemic coma. The main advantages for intravenous use are its faster onset and short duration of action. *(Bergersen, p. 559.)*

**46 a** Symptoms of overdosage from thyroid preparations are similar to those seen in hyperthyroidism. They include loss of weight, insomnia, nervousness, tachycardia, tremors, dyspnea, chest pain, palpitation, and diaphoresis. *(Bergersen, p. 558.)*

**47 a** While teaching the patient with endemic goiter, the nurse should point out that it can be prevented by use of iodized salt in the daily diet. Endemic goiter is a form of simple goiter that occurs in those geographic areas that have a deficiency of iodine in the water and the soil. *(Luckmann and Sorensen, p. 1351.)*

**48 c** Addison's disease is a disorder of the adrenal gland caused by atrophy or destruction of the adrenal cortex.

As a result, there is hyposecretion of the mineralocorticoids, glucocorticoids, and androgens. (*Jones, Dunbar, and Jirovec, p. 717. Shafer et al., p. 762.*)

**49 a** The symptoms of Addison's disease, or adrenocortical insufficiency, result from a deficiency of the mineralocorticoids and glucocorticoids. As a result of the deficiencies, the patient will complain of weakness and fatigue, loss of weight, nausea, and vomiting. The skin and mucous membrane become hyperpigmented. The patient also has hypotension, which becomes more severe if the patient moves or changes position suddenly. (*Jones, Dunbar, and Jirovec, p. 717. Shafer et al., p. 762.*)

**50 d** In Addison's disease, there is a decreased secretion of the glucocorticoids and mineralocorticoids. As a result there is a decreased fasting blood sugar, a decrease of the serum sodium, and an increase of the serum potassium. (*Jones, Dunbar, and Jirovec, p. 702. Shafer et al., p. 762.*)

**51 a** The 8-hour corticotropin test is a specific diagnostic test used to determine adrenocortical function. Corticotropin is given intravenously over an 8-hour period. Prior to the administration of the corticotropin, a control 24-hour urine specimen is collected and measured for corticosteroid levels. After the intravenous administration of corticotropin, another 24-hour urine specimen is collected and measured for corticocosteroid levels. Normally there should be an increased level. In Addison's disease there is no increase. (*Jones, Dunbar, and Jirovec, p. 723. Luckmann and Sorensen, p. 1372.*)

**52 b** Patients with Addison's disease must recognize that corticosteroid-replacement therapy must be continued for the rest of their lives. They should also recognize the importance of taking medications daily without fail. Physical and emotional stress can increase the body's need for the corticosteroids. With the advice of the physician, the patient will have to adjust the dosage accordingly. (*Jones, Dunbar, and Jirovec, p. 725. Luckmann and Sorensen, p. 1372. Shafer et al., p. 763.*)

**53 a** Florinef is used to treat Addison's disease because of its mineralocorticoid properties. It promotes sodium retention and potassium excretion by working directly on the kidney tubules. It is used in conjunction with the glucocorticoids. (*Asperheim and Eisenhauer, p. 366.*)

**54 b** The adrenal cortex normally produces weak androgens in both the male and the female. In Addison's disease there is a decreased secretion of androgens. As a result there is decreased axillary and pubic hair in women. Usually no effects are seen in the male since the testes are the major source of androgens. (*Jones, Dunbar, and Jirovec, p. 720. Luckmann and Sorensen, p. 1371.*)

**55 b** Mineralocorticoids are used to treat acute and chronic adrenal insufficiency. Patients should be carefully observed for toxic symptoms and side effects. The most common are edema, hypertension, and hypokalemia. (*Asperheim and Eisenhauer, p. 366. Bergersen, pp. 570–572. Jones, Dunbar, and Jirovec, p. 724.*)

**56 b** Addisonian crisis is an acute adrenocortica insufficiency that can be precipitated by infection, physical trauma, and emotional stress. It can also be brought on by sudden withdrawal of prescribed adrenocorticosteroids. The nurse should recognize that when it occurs, it is a true emergency. If treatment is not initiated promptly, death can occur from circulatory collapse. (*Jones, Dunbar, and Jirovec, p. 725. Shafer et al., p. 763.*)

**57 d** Hydrocortisone sodium succinate is the soluble form of hydrocortisone and can be used intravenously. Corticotropin is not used to treat Addisonian crisis since it is not effective if there is no functioning adrenal cortex. (*Bergersen, p. 570.*)

# UNIT 10
# Nursing care of the patient with a gastrointestinal disorder

**OBJECTIVES**

To answer the questions in this unit, the reader should be able to

1. Identify the functions of the gastrointestinal tract;
2. List the various secretions of the gastrointestinal tract;
3. Describe how the body adapts to disorders of the gastrointestinal tract;
4. List the major signs and symptoms of gastrointestinal disorders;
5. Recognize the nurse's role in caring for patients having select diagnostic tests performed;
6. Describe the nursing management of the patient with a gastrointestinal disorder;

## QUESTIONS RELATED TO OBJECTIVES

*Instructions*: Choose the *one best* answer to the following questions.

1. The most important function of the stomach is
   a. Digestion of fats, proteins, and carbohydrates.
   b. Regulation of the rate at which chyme enters the small intestine.
   c. Absorption of water-soluble vitamins.
   d. Absorption of the end products of digestion.

2. Most digestion and absorption of food occur in the
   a. Stomach.
   b. Small intestine.
   c. Ileum.
   d. Cecum.

3. Choose the most correct answer.
   a. About 200 mL of saliva is produced per day.
   b. Approximately 2 L of hydrochloric acid is secreted per day.
   c. The pancreas secretes about 300 mL of sodium bicarbonate per day.
   d. Approximately 100 mL of bile is manufactured per day.

4. The cells of the stomach that secrete hydrochloric acid are the
   a. Neck cells.
   b. Parietal cells.
   c. Chief cells.
   d. Beta cells.

5. The nerve that innervates the stomach and increases gastric secretions and gastric motility is the
   a. Phrenic nerve.
   b. Vagus nerve.
   c. Splanchnic nerve.
   d. Accessory nerve.

**6** The three major hormones of the gastrointestinal tract are
  **a** Enterokinase, lecithin, and histamine.
  **b** Hydrochloric acid, sodium bicarbonate, and bile.
  **c** Gastrin, secretin, and cholecystokinin.
  **d** Trypsin, amylase, and lipase.

**7** Choose the statement that best relates to the function of the large intestine.
  **a** The large intestine secretes enzymes essential for the terminal digestion of proteins.
  **b** Vitamin K can be synthesized by the action of the bacterial flora of the large intestine.
  **c** Most absorption of water occurs in the large intestine.
  **d** The secretions of the large intestine have an acid reaction.

**8** Choose the statement that best describes cardiospasm. "Cardiospasm" is
  **a** A disorder of the esophagus that results in hypermotility of the esophagus.
  **b** Caused by hypertrophy of the cardiac sphincter.
  **c** A neuromuscular disorder of the esophagus causing aperistalsis.
  **d** A disorder of the cardiac sphincter causing rapid emptying of the stomach.

**9** A symptom commonly seen in patients with achalasia is
  **a** Dysphagia.
  **b** Hematemesis.
  **c** Vomiting.
  **d** Melena.

**10** Patti John is a patient in the medical clinic who has been told that she has a hiatus hernia. While doing patient teaching, the nurse told her that the symptoms can be relieved by sleeping
   **a** In a supine position with her head turned to the side.
   **b** On her left side.
   **c** In a prone position with her head turned to the side.
   **d** With the head of the bed elevated.

**11** Choose the statement that best relates to hiatus hernia.
   **a** Surgery is the treatment of choice.
   **b** Anticholineric drugs are recommended for relief of symptoms.
   **c** Dilation of the esophagus with mercury-tipped bougies is the most effective treatment.
   **d** Small, frequent feedings and antacids is the recommended treatment.

**12** A gastroscope is being done on your patient. After the procedure the nurse
   **a** Tested the gag reflex before allowing the patient to take anything by mouth.
   **b** Monitored the pulse and blood pressure $q \frac{1}{2}$ h until stable.
   **c** Applied a small pillow to the left upper quadrant for 1 hour.
   **d** Administered cleansing enemas.

**13** In preparing the patient for an upper GI series, the nurse explained to the patient that
   **a** Foods and fluids will be withheld for 8 to 10 hours prior to the examination.
   **b** Cleansing enemas will be administered on the morning of the examination.
   **c** Barium will be administered via the rectum.
   **d** Radiopaque tablets will be administered the night before the exam.

**14** A gastric analysis was done on the patient to confirm the diagnosis of duodenal ulcer. You would expect the following results:
   **a** Increased acid secretions.
   **b** Normal acid secretions.
   **c** Decreased acid secretions.
   **d** Absent acid secretions.

**15** The pain of a duodenal ulcer is characteristically
   **a** Relieved by ingestion of food.
   **b** Intensified by ingestion of food.
   **c** Most severe upon awakening and before breakfast.
   **d** Aggravated by eating foods high in hidden fats.

**16** The incidence of duodenal ulcer is highest in persons who have which of the following blood types?
   **a** A.
   **b** B.
   **c** O.
   **d** AB.

**17** From the following statements choose the one that is most correct.
   **a** Duodenal ulcers can be a premalignant lesion.
   **b** Hydrochloric acid production is increased in persons with gastric and duodenal ulcers.
   **c** Nocturnal pain is common in gastric ulcers as well as duodenal ulcers.
   **d** Psychological stress is a factor contributing to the development of duodenal ulcers.

**18** Jim Murray has been admitted with an acute duodenal ulcer. The doctor's orders include cimetidine 300 mg qid; Maalox 15 mL 1 hour after meals and hs; Valium 10 mg hs. It is 2 A.M. and Mr. Murray complains of pain in the midepigastric region. The nurse would
   a  Offer him a glass of milk.
   b  Notify the physician and ask for a medication for pain.
   c  Give him 10 mg of Valium.
   d  Ask him if he would like to discuss what is bothering him.

**19** While teaching Mr. Murray in preparation for discharge, the nurse pointed out that
   a  The use of fats in the diet should be avoided.
   b  Three regular meals per day must be adhered to strictly.
   c  A bland diet should be adhered to strictly.
   d  A more liberalized individual diet is currently being recommended.

**20** Choose the statement that best relates to the action of cimetidine (Tagamet). Cimetidine is a
   a  Cholinergic blocking agent that acts directly on the vagus nerve.
   b  Tranquilizer that specifically decreases nocturnal acid secretion.
   c  Synthetic hydrogen receptor antagonist that inhibits acid output.
   d  Systemic antacid that neutralizes gastric acid secretions.

**21** Choose the statement that best applies to the use of antacids in treating peptic ulcer.
   a  Sodium bicarbonate is a systemic antacid that has a prolonged buffering effect on hydrochloric acid.
   b  The main disadvantage of aluminum hydroxide is the production of constipation and fecal impaction.
   c  Local antacids in tablet form are as effective as the liquids.
   d  Local antacids are not as likely to produce systemic alkalosis.

**22** Examples of anticholinergic medications that are used to treat disorders of the gastrointestinal tract include
  **a** Propantheline bromide (Pro-banthine) and methscopalamine bromide (Pamine).
  **b** Dicyclomine (Bentyl) and prochlorperazine (Compazine).
  **c** Carbachol (Doryl) and bethanecol chloride (Urecholine).
  **d** Tridihexethyl chloride (Pathilon) and diazepam (Valium).

**23** Toxic effects of the anticholinergic drugs include
  **a** Nausea, vomiting, and diarrhea.
  **b** Dryness of the mouth, urinary retention, and tachycardia.
  **c** Leukopenia, drowsiness, and circumoral flush.
  **d** Mental confusion, skin rash, and blurred vision.

**24** Patients with ulcers should be cautioned about the use of
  **a** Aspirin, corticosteroids, and phenylbutazone.
  **b** Anticoagulants, acetaminophen, and aspirin.
  **c** Sodium bicarbonate, vasodilators, and aspirin.
  **d** Anticholinergics, decongestants, and aspirin.

**25** A characteristic sign of a perforated ulcer is
  **a** Persistent projectile vomiting.
  **b** Hematemesis and melena.
  **c** Sudden, severe pain aggravated by movement.
  **d** Abdominal distention.

**26** Choose the statement that best applies to the treatment of bleeding peptic ulcers.
  **a** A Sengstaken-Blakemore tube is inserted to control bleeding.
  **b** The insertion of nasogastric tubes is contraindicated since they tend to renew bleeding.
  **c** Gastric lavage with iced saline is used to control bleeding.
  **d** Large doses of vitamin K are given to hasten clot formation.

**27** While caring for the patient receiving continuous gastric hypothermia, the nurse should recognize that
  **a** Woolen blankets should not be used since they counteract the effects of gastric hypothermia.
  **b** Arrhythmias can develop because the cooling solution comes in such close proximity to the heart as it passes into the stomach.
  **c** Cooling blankets are placed under and over the patient in an attempt to control bleeding.
  **d** Special care to the skin should be done to prevent tissue breakdown.

**28** Gastrointestinal bleeding is an example of
  **a** Vasogenic shock.
  **b** Cardiogenic shock.
  **c** Neurogenic shock.
  **d** Hypovolemic shock.

**29** The doctor ordered Sodium Luminal 100 mg q4h around the clock. The ampule was labeled "Sodium Luminal 130 mg—to dilute add 1 mL of sterile water." To administer 100 mg, the nurse administered
  **a** 0.3 mL.
  **b** 0.8 mL.
  **c** 1.0 mL.
  **d** 1.3 mL.

**30** From the following list, choose the generic name for Sodium Luminal.
  **a** Pentobarbital sodium.
  **b** Secobarbital sodium.
  **c** Phenobarbital sodium.
  **d** Sodium amytal.

## NURSING CARE OF THE PATIENT WITH A GASTROINTESTINAL DISORDER

**31** Maryjane Crosthwaite is a 26-year-old woman who has had a nasogastric tube attached to low suction. She complains of nausea and of "feeling full." The nurse recognizes that
   **a** This is a common sensation experienced by patients with a nasogastric tube.
   **b** Administration of an antiemetic IM will relieve the sensation.
   **c** This could be an indication of an impatent tube.
   **d** Taking a local antacid by mouth will relieve the full feeling and the nausea.

**32** Patients on prolonged gastric suction are likely to develop
   **a** Metabolic alkalosis.
   **b** Metabolic acidosis.
   **c** Respiratory alkalosis.
   **d** Respiratory acidosis.

**33** Patients with diverticulitis are cautioned to avoid constipation and to take daily dose of a bulk-increasing cathartic such as
   **a** Mineral oil.
   **b** Metamucil.
   **c** Magnesium hydroxide.
   **d** Magnesium citrate.

**34** While caring for the patient who is having a Cantor inserted, the nurse should recognize that the
   **a** Tube should extend over the nose and be anchored to the forehead once it enters the duodenum.
   **b** Patient should be positioned on the right side until the tube has passed through the pylorus.
   **c** Tube should be advanced about 4 in. every 15 minutes until it reaches the desired site.
   **d** Tube should be irrigated with normal saline every 30 minutes until it is time to attach it to low suction.

**35** Eleanor Curtin is a 45-year-old woman who has been admitted to the hospital with a diagnosis of an intestinal obstruction. A Cantor tube has been inserted and attached to suction. The Cantor tube is a
  a  Double-lumen intestinal tube.
  b  Single-lumen stomach tube.
  c  Single-lumen intestinal tube.
  d  Double-lumen stomach tube.

**36** Patients with prolonged intestinal-tube suction should be observed for
  a  Metabolic acidosis.
  b  Metabolic alkalosis.
  c  Respiratory acidosis.
  d  Respiratory alkalosis.

**37** A barium enema was ordered for Ms. Curtin. The nurse told her that
  a  She would have to take radiopaque tablets the night before the examination.
  b  There was no special preparation for the examination.
  c  She would be given cleansing enemas prior to the examination.
  d  She would have to drink a glassful of barium so that the intestines could be visualized.

**38** While doing a nursing history on the patient being admitted with chronic ulcerative colitis, the nurse would expect the patient to describe the stool as
  a  Crimson-colored.
  b  Black and tarry.
  c  Containing blood and mucus.
  d  Greenish black.

**39** The doctor wrote an order for a guaiac test. This test is done on a stool specimen to determine the presence of
   a  Bacteria.
   b  Mucus.
   c  Blood.
   d  Ova and parasites.

**40** Barbara is an 18-year-old patient who is receiving salicylazosulfapyridine (Azulfidine) for an acute exacerbation of ulcerative colitis and complains of orange-yellow urine. The nurse recognizes that this
   a  Is a symptom of overdosage and withholds the medication.
   b  Is unrelated to Azulfidine and asks Barbara if she has eaten anything unusual.
   c  Occurs with Azulfidine if the urine is alkaline.
   d  Is probably due to an increased intake of carrots.

**41** Choose the group of foods that is best tolerated by patients with ulcerative colitis.
   a  Shredded wheat with bananas and milk.
   b  Solf-boiled egg, toast, and tea.
   c  Pancakes, orange slices, and hot chocolate.
   d  Bran muffins, coffee, and grapefruit.

**42** Prednisone is a medication used to treat ulcerative colitis. Prednisone is
   a  An anticholinergic agent.
   b  An antibiotic.
   c  A sulfonamide.
   d  A corticosteroid.

**43** A medication that is used to control diarrhea is
   a  Tigan.
   b  Dramamine.
   c  Lomotil.
   d  Titralac.

**44** From the following list, choose the vein that is most commonly used for the administration of total parenteral nutrition (hyperalimentation).
  **a** Cephalic vein.
  **b** Brachial vein.
  **c** Subclavian vein.
  **d** Median cubital vein.

**45** While caring for the patient with hyperalimentation, the nurse recognized that
  **a** The flow rate should be speeded up if the hourly rate falls behind schedule.
  **b** IV medications can be piggybacked to the hyperalimentation line.
  **c** Blood samples can be withdrawn from the hyperalimentation line.
  **d** Hypoglycemia can develop if the administration of the hyperalimentation solution is suddenly discontinued.

**46** From the following list, choose the nursing action that best applies to the care of the patient receiving total parenteral nutrition.
  **a** Urine should be tested for glycosuria.
  **b** Blood pressure should be monitored hourly for the first 24 hours.
  **c** The dressing at the insertion site should be changed once on each shift.
  **d** Solutions can be prepared in advance and stored in the refrigerator until ready for use.

**47** Lipomul is a parenteral fat emulsion that can be given intravenously to treat severe nutritional disorders. Choose the statement that best applies.
  **a** Fat emulsions can be piggybacked to the primary IV.
  **b** Lipomul is a clear, colorless solution.
  **c** Side effects can occur as late as 3 weeks after the initial administration.
  **d** Vitamins and potassium chloride can be mixed with parenteral fat emulsions.

## ANSWERS, EXPLANATIONS, AND REFERENCES

**1 b** The most important function of the stomach is to regulate the rate at which chyme enters the small intestine. Actually very little digestion occurs in the stomach. (*Vander, Sherman, and Luciano, p. 363.*)

**2 b** Most digestion and absorption of food occur in the small intestine. By the time the digested food reaches the middle of the jejunum, most absorption has occurred. (*Vander, Sherman, and Luciano, p. 381.*)

**3 b** The parietal cells of the stomach produce about 2 liters of hydrochloric acid per day. The gastric secretions, composed mainly of hydrochloric acid (HCl), are essential to denature protein and to kill many types of bacteria. (*Langley, Telford, and Christensen, pp. 612–613. Vander, Sherman, and Luciano, p. 361.*)

**4 b** The cells of the stomach that secrete hydrochloric acid are the parietal cells. The chief cells secrete pepsin, and the neck cells secrete mucus. (*Vander, Sherman, and Luciano, p. 367.*)

**5 b** The vagus nerve of the parasympathetic nervous system innervates the stomach, the small intestine, and portions of the large intestines. Its main action in the stomach is to increase gastric secretions and gastric motility. (*Price and Wilson, p. 208. Vander, Sherman, and Luciano, p. 358.*)

**6 c** The three major hormones of the gastrointestinal tract are gastrin, secretin, and cholecystokinin. (*Vander, Sherman, and Luciano, p. 357.*)

**7 b** The normal bacterial flora of the large intestines are capable of synthesizing vitamin K from the constant putrefaction of proteins not digested in the small intestine. (*Price and Wilson, p. 242.*)

**8 c** Cardiospasm, or achalasia, is a disorder of the esophagus caused by degeneration of muscular innervation. The disruption of innervation results in aperistalsis of the esophagus and lack of stimulation to the cardiac sphincter. This results in an inability of food to enter the stomach and distention. (*Luckmann and Sorensen, p. 1080. Shafer et al., p. 659.*)

**9 a**  Dysphagia is a symptom experienced by many patients with achalasia. The patient describes the dysphagia as "food sticking" in the chest while food is being swallowed. Other symptoms include regurgitation of food, chest pain, etc. (*Beland, p. 776. Moidel, Giblin, and Wagner, p. 736. Shafer et al., p. 659.*)

**10 d**  To prevent nocturnal regurgitation and possible aspiration pneumonia, patients with hiatus hernia should be told to sleep with the head of the bed elevated. (*Luckmann and Sorensen, p. 1080. Shafer et al., p. 664.*)

**11 d**  Hiatus hernia is an outpouching of the stomach through the esophageal hiatus of the diaphragm. Regurgitation of stomach contents is the symptom that causes the patient to seek medical advice. Most persons with hiatus hernia respond well to medical treatment, which includes taking small, frequent meals; using antacids; sleeping with the head of the bed elevated, and avoiding sharp, forward bending. (*Luckmann and Sorensen, p. 1080.*)

**12 a**  A gastroscopy is a diagnostic procedure that can be done to visualize the inner lining of the stomach. It can be done by inserting a lighted instrument or a fibroscope into the stomach via the mouth and esophagus. A biopsy of the stomach can also be done after the instrument is inserted. Because a local anesthesia is used to facilitate passage of the "scope," the patient should not be allowed to have fluids until the gag reflex returns. (*Luckmann and Sorensen, p. 1057.*)

**13 a**  The upper GI series is an x-ray and fluoroscopic examination of the esophagus, stomach, and small intestines. The patient drinks a specified amount of barium, which allows the upper GI tract to be visualized. Withholding of foods and fluids for 8 to 10 hours prior to the examination is necessary for successful visualization. (*Shafer et al., p. 650.*)

**14 a**  In duodenal ulcer, the output of acid secretions is much higher than normal. The increased quantity of acid occurs between meals and during the night even though there is no gastric stimulation. (*Jones, Dunbar, and Jirovec, p. 587. Luckmann and Sorensen, p. 1086.*)

**15 a** The pain associated with a duodenal ulcer is characteristically relieved by the ingestion of food or, in some instances, by vomiting. Nocturnal pain is also characteristic of duodenal ulcers, as is the absence of pain upon awakening in the morning. (*Jones, Dunbar, and Jirovec, p. 586.*)

**16 c** Clinical studies have indicated that duodenal ulcers occur more frequently in persons with blood type O. (*Jones, Dunbar, and Jirovec, p. 585.*)

**17 d** Psychological stress is a factor linked to the development of duodenal ulcers. Although it is not the only factor, there seems to be a relationship between psychological stress and its stimulating effect on the vagus nerve, which in turn increases gastric acid secretions. (*Jones, Dunbar, and Jirovec, p. 584. Luckmann and Sorensen, p. 1086.*)

**18 a** Patients with a duodenal ulcer often experience pain at about 1 or 2 A.M. The pain is best relieved by the ingestion of food. Gastric secretions, which are increased during the night, enter the duodenum with a decreased pH. The high acidity of the secretions comes in direct contact with the ulcerated lining of the duodenum and causes the pain. (*Jones, Dunbar, and Jirovec, p. 586. Shafer et al., p. 666.*)

**19 d** The restrictive nature of the traditional bland diet for the management of peptic ulcers has currently been under attack. Success in the use of a more liberalized individual diet has been documented by various study groups. In spite of the controversy that exists, all groups agree that small frequent feedings are better tolerated by ulcer patients than are three meals per day. (*Jones, Dunbar, and Jirovec, p. 588. Williams, p. 536.*)

**20 c** Cimetidine is a synthetic hydrogen receptor antagonist that inhibits both daytime and nocturnal basal gastric acid secretion. The decreased acid output can result in complete healing of the ulcer. There are minimal side effects. The route of administration is oral or intravenous. (*Jones, Dunbar, and Jirovec, p. 589. Physicians Desk Reference, pp. 1578–1580.*)

**21 d** Local, or nonsystemic, antacids form insoluble salts when they come in contact with the hydrochloric acid in the stomach. These insoluble salts are not readily absorbed. As a result they have no effect on the pH of the blood and are not likely to produce systemic alkalosis. (*Bergersen, pp. 670–674.*)

**22 a** Pro-banthine and Pamine are examples of anticholinergic medications that work directly on smooth muscle to decrease muscle tone and peristalsis. As a result patients are relieved of the hypermotility and spasm associated with many gastrointestinal disorders. Bentyl and Pathilon are also anticholinergic medications. (*Asperheim and Eisenhauer, pp. 288–292. Bergensen, pp. 138–144.*)

**23 b** Anticholinergic agents inhibit the action of acetylcholine at the postganglionic nerve endings. Broadly speaking, anticholinergic agents relax smooth muscle, decrease secretions of exocrine glands, and cause the pupils of the eyes to dilate. Toxic effects include dryness of the mouth, urinary retention, tachycardia, circumoral flush, blurred vision, and constipation. (*Asperheim and Eisenhauer, p. 288. Bergensen, p. 140.*)

**24 a** Patients with peptic ulcers should be cautioned about using medications that are ulcerogenic. Among these drugs are aspirin, corticosteroids, and phenylbutazone. Many cold preparations contain aspirin, and the patients should be made aware of this. (*Jones, Dunbar, and Jirovec, pp. 584–585. Shafer et al., p. 668.*)

**25 c** Perforation is a serious complication of peptic ulcer that can be death producing if not corrected. Sudden onset of severe pain that is intensified by movement characteristically occurs with a perforation. The treatment is immediate surgery. (*Price and Wilson, p. 216. Shafer et al., p. 669.*)

**26 c** A common complication of peptic ulcers is bleeding. Gastric lavage with iced saline is a means used to control bleeding. It is believed that the iced saline causes local vasoconstriction, which in turn stops bleeding. (*Jones, Dunbar, and Jirovec, p. 592.*)

**27 b** The nurse should check the blood pressure and pulse and observe the patient very closely for arrhythmias. Patients receiving continuous gastric hypothermia are especially prone to arrhythmias. As the cooling solution passes into the stomach, it comes in close proximity to the heart and can cause arrhythmias. (*Henderson and Nite, p. 1665.*)

**28 d** Hemorrhage and gastrointestinal bleeding are examples of physiological stressors leading to hypovolemic shock. Typically, hypovolemic shock can be caused by any stressor that causes a loss of whole blood or of the plasma portion of the blood. Vomiting, diarrhea, burns, etc., are other causes of hypovolemic shock. (*Stroot, Lee, and Schaper, p. 167.*)

**29 b** To administer 100 mg of Sodium Luminal from an ampule labeled "Sodium Luminal Powder 130 mg," the nurse added 1 mL of sterile water to the ampul, withdrew 0.8 mL of the solution, discarded 0.2 mL, and administered 0.8 mL. To compute this arithmetically, you can set it up in the following manner:

$$\frac{\text{Desired}}{\text{Have}} = \frac{\text{Desired}}{\text{Have}}$$

$$\frac{100 \text{ mg}}{130 \text{ mg}} = \frac{x \text{ mL}}{1 \text{ mL}}$$

$$130x = 100$$

$$x = 0.76 \text{ or } 0.8 \text{ mL}$$

(*Saxton, Ercolano, and Walter, p. 42.*)

**30 c** The generic name for Sodium Luminal is phenobarbital sodium. The nurse should recognize that Sodium Luminal and Luminal cannot be used interchangeably. Luminal (phenobarbital) is given orally but not parenterally. The parenteral preparation is Sodium Luminal. (*Bergersen, p. 250.*)

**31 c** If the patient with a nasogastric tube attached to low suction complains of nausea, vomiting, or a feeling of fullness, it usually is an indication that the nasogastric tube is impatent. To maintain patency of the tube, irrigation of the tube with normal saline or injection of small amounts of air into the tubing is usually ordered by the physician. (Beland, p. 926. *Jones, Dunbar, and Jirovec, p. 591.*)

**32 a** Patients on prolonged gastric suction lose valuable fluids and electrolytes via the gastric tube. Although the body attempts to adapt to these losses, there comes a time when it can no longer compensate. As a result the pH of the blood rises and the patient develops metabolic alkalosis. (*Henderson and Nite, p. 1221.*)

**33 b** Metamucil is a bulk-increasing cathartic that swells in the presence of water to form a gel. As a result, it has a softening effect on fecal material and is not irritating to the bowel mucosa. It is important to mix the powder with water at the time of administration and then follow it with an additional glass of water. Metamucil is often recommended for patients with diverticulitis. (*Asperheim and Eisenhauer, p. 413. Bergersen, p. 685. Shafer et al., p. 684.*)

**34 b** A Cantor tube is an intestinal tube that is passed via the nose into the stomach through the pylorus and finally into the small intestine. Once the tube enters the stomach, the patient should be positioned on the right side to facilitate passage of the tube through the stomach. (*Henderson and Nite, p. 1218.*)

**35 c** A Cantor tube is a single-lumen intestinal tube used to remove gas and fluids from the intestinal tract when it is desirable to prevent or treat abdominal distention. (*Henderson and Nite, p. 1216.*)

**36 a** Patients on prolonged intestinal-tube suction lose valuable fluids and electrolytes. Although the body tries to adapt to the loss, eventually the plasma pH falls and the patient develops metabolic acidosis. (*Henderson and Nite, p. 1221.*)

**37 c** The preparation of the patient having a barium enema includes cleansing the lower bowel by administering cleansing enemas prior to the examination. (*Jones, Dunbar, and Jirovec, p. 615. Shafer et al., p. 650.*)

**38 c** In chronic ulcerative colitis the stool contains blood, mucus, and pus. (*Jones, Dunbar, and Jirovec, p. 618. Luckmann and Sorensen, p. 1100.*)

**39 c** The guaiac test is a diagnostic test done to determine the presence of blood in the stool. The nurse should be aware that a false positive reading can be caused by eating meat for 3 days before the specimen is collected. (*Luckmann and Sorensen, p. 1059.*)

**40 c** Salicylazosulfapyridine (Azulfidine) is a sulfonamide preparation that has antiinfective and analgesic action. It can be used as an adjunct to corticosteroid therapy in the treatment of ulcerative colitis. The patient and the nurse should be aware that the medication can cause the urine to be orange-yellow if the urine is alkaline. (*Asperheim and Eisenhauer, p. 186.*)

**41 b** Patients with ulcerative colitis are usually placed on a graduated low-residue diet. Foods that are not allowed include milk in any form, cereals containing bran or shredded wheat, raw fruits, etc. (*Williams, p. 540.*)

**42 d** Corticosteroids are used to treat ulcerative colitis. Their antiinflammatory effects help to relieve the symptoms. Prednisone is a corticosteroid commonly used. (*Jones, Dunbar, and Jirovec, p. 616.*)

**43 c** Lomotil is a combination of atropine, an anticholinergic agent, and diphenoxylate hydrochloride, an analgesic chemically related to meperidine. It is used to control diarrhea because of its effectiveness in decreasing intestinal motility. (*Asperheim and Eisenhauer, p. 421. Bergersen, p. 691.*)

**44 c** When administering total parenteral nutrition, the subclavian vein should be used rather than the smaller peripheral veins of the arm. The hypertonicity of the solution tends to cause inflammation and thrombus formation in the peripheral veins. (*Jones, Dunbar, and Jirovec, p. 571.*)

**45 d** While caring for the patient receiving total parenteral nutrition (hyperalimentation), the nurse should recognize that suddenly discontinuing the infusion can lead to hypoglycemia. Since hypertonic glucose solutions are administered, the resulting hyperglycemia causes an increased secretion of insulin. If the infusion rate is suddenly terminated, the increased insulin secretion results in hypoglycemia. To prevent this complication, it is best to taper off the infusions gradually over a 48-hour period. (*Luckmann and Sorensen, p. 1064. Jones, Dunbar, and Jirovec, p. 571.*)

**46 a** Hypertonic glucose solutions are used for total parenteral nutrition. Patients are prone to develop hyperglycemia and glycosuria. One should test the urine every 6 hours to detect glycosuria. (*Jones, Dunbar, and Jirovec, p. 571. Luckmann and Sorensen, p. 1064.*)

**47 c** Parenteral fat emulsions are sometimes used for patients with severe nutritional disorders because they provide an excellent source of calories. However, it must be understood that fat emulsions are not perfectly safe to administer, and the patients must be carefully observed for side effects when the infusion is initially started and as late as 3 weeks following the infusion. Anemia, blood clotting, and hemorrhage are the later reactions. (*Luckmann and Sorensen, p. 253.*)

# UNIT 11

# Nursing care of the patient with a hepatopancreatic disorder

To answer the questions in this unit, the reader should be able to

1. List the functions of the liver and the pancreas;
2. Trace the hepatic portal circulation;
3. Identify the structures of the biliary tract;
4. Recognize the commonalities of disorders of the liver, pancreas, and biliary tract;
5. Describe how the body adapts to physiological stressors leading to disorders of the liver and pancreas;
6. Identify the major signs and symptoms relating to disorders of the liver and pancreas;
7. Recognize the nurse's role in caring for patients with specific diagnostic tests and examinations;
8. Describe the nursing management of the patient with disorders of the liver and pancreas.

## QUESTIONS RELATED TO OBJECTIVES

*Instructions*: Choose the *one best* answer to the following questions.

1. Choose the statement which best applies to the function of the liver. The liver
   - **a** Plays a major role in converting glucose to lactic acid.
   - **b** Destroys red blood cells and converts the end product to unconjugated bilirubin.
   - **c** Manufactures prothrombin, fibrinogen, and other factors essential for coagulation.
   - **d** Stores ascorbic and folic acids.

2. That portion of the liver which plays an important role in removing bacteria from the blood is the
   - **a** Canaliculi.
   - **b** Parenchymal cells.
   - **c** Sinusoids.
   - **d** Kupfer cells.

3. Ammonia ($NH_3$) is converted to urea by the
   - **a** Large intestine.
   - **b** Kidneys.
   - **c** Liver.
   - **d** Muscles.

4. The liver manufactures approximately how much bile per day?
   - **a** 50 mL.
   - **b** 100 mL.
   - **c** 700 mL.
   - **d** 2000 mL.

**5** Choose the most correct statement relating to the hepatic portal circulation.
   **a** The portal vein drains directly into inferior vena cava.
   **b** Blood from the liver lobules drains into the portal vein.
   **c** Capillaries from the abdominal viscera drain into the hepatic vein.
   **d** The portal vein is the only vein of the body that is interposed between the capillary networks.

**6** The main function of the gallbladder is to
   **a** Manufacture and secrete bile.
   **b** Store and concentrate bile.
   **c** Regulate the metabolism of bile pigment.
   **d** Emulsify fats to fatty acids.

**7** The bile duct that empties into the duodenum is the
   **a** Hepatic duct.
   **b** Cystic duct.
   **c** Common duct.
   **d** Pancreatic duct.

**8** The sphincter that surrounds the bile duct as it enters the duodenum is the
   **a** Cardiac sphincter.
   **b** Pyloric sphincter.
   **c** Sphincter of Oddi.
   **d** External sphincter.

**9** The enzymes found in the pancreatic juice are
   **a** Rennin, lipase, and pepsinogen.
   **b** Enterokinase, sucrase, and maltase.
   **c** Trypsin, amylase, and lipase.
   **d** Pepsin, lactase, and lipase.

**10** The pancreatic duct cells secrete
  **a** Hydrochloric acid.
  **b** Sodium bicarbonate.
  **c** Enterokinase.
  **d** Succus entericus.

**11** The most common stressor contributing to the development of acute pancreatitis is
  **a** Emotional upheavals.
  **b** Alcoholism.
  **c** Obesity.
  **d** Vitamin deficiency.

**12** In acute pancreatitis, there is an elevation of the serum
  **a** Alkaline phosphatase.
  **b** Albumin.
  **c** Amylase.
  **d** Lactic dehydrogenase.

**13** In caring for the patient with acute pancreatitis, the relief of pain is a priority. Which of the following analgesics is contraindicated?
  **a** Propoxyphene (Darvon).
  **b** Pentazocine (Talwin).
  **c** Meperidine (Demerol).
  **d** Morphine.

**14** One objective in the treatment of acute pancreatitis is to reduce pancreatic secretions. This can be done by
  **a** Maintaining intermittent nasogastric suction and eliminating oral intake of food.
  **b** Performing a paracentesis and offering milk and cream hourly.
  **c** Administering hydrocortisone and performing peritoneal dialysis.
  **d** Ordering a low-fat, high-carbohydrate diet and insulin coverage.

15 Malabsorption of fats can occur in chronic pancreatitis. When this occurs the stool
   a  Is bulky, frothy, and voluminous.
   b  Is clay-colored and watery.
   c  Contains mucus, blood, and pus.
   d  Is greenish black.

16 To counteract the bleeding tendencies associated with obstructive jaundice, the physician ordered
   a  Vitamin $B_{12}$.
   b  Folic acid.
   c  Vitamin K.
   d  Pituitrin.

17 While caring for the patient with obstructive jaundice, the nurse should
   a  Place the patient on isolation.
   b  Use hot, soapy water to remove the accumulation of bile salts on the skin.
   c  Encourage the patient to eat green, leafy vegetables.
   d  Observe the urine and stool for signs of bleeding.

18 In assessing the patient with obstructive jaundice, the nurse would expect
   a  Clay-colored stools and light amber urine.
   b  Dark brown stools and dark urine.
   c  Clay-colored stools and dark urine.
   d  Dark brown stools and light amber urine.

19 Many persons with chronic gallbladder disease can remain symptom-free by adhering to a low-fat diet. Choose the group of food that is lowest in fat.
   a  Waffles with syrup, coffee with evaporated milk, and orange slices.
   b  Cornflakes with milk, sliced bananas, and coffee cake.
   c  Cream of wheat with brown sugar, toast with jelly, and grapefruit juice.
   d  Soft-boiled egg, toast with margarine, and hot chocolate.

**20** An oral cholecystogram was ordered for the patient with chronic cholecystitis. The nurse should recognize that
  **a** There is no special preparation for the test.
  **b** Vomiting and diarrhea can interfere with absorption of the radiopaque tablets.
  **c** The radiopaque tablets must be ingested 1 hour before the x-ray examination.
  **d** A high-fat diet must be eaten the night before the examination to assure visualization of the gallbladder.

**21** To reduce the danger of bleeding following a liver biopsy, the patient should be placed
  **a** In a Trendelenburg position.
  **b** On the right side.
  **c** In a semi-Fowler's position.
  **d** In a dorsal recumbent position.

**22** In the early stages of alcoholic portal cirrhosis, the diet recommended is
  **a** High-carbohydrate, low-protein.
  **b** High-carbohydrate, high-protein.
  **c** Low-carbohydrate, high-protein.
  **d** Low-carbohydrate, low-protein.

**23** In cirrhosis of the liver, the spider angioma, palmar erythema, and axillary alopecia are caused by
  **a** An excess of circulating estrogens.
  **b** A decrease of serum prothrombin.
  **c** An excess of circulating corticosteroids.
  **d** A decrease of serum testosterone.

24 The ascites and peripheral edema associated with cirrhosis of the liver are caused by
   a  Decreased serum albumin, hyperaldosteronism, and portal hypertension.
   b  Decreased serum globulins, hypoaldosteronism, and portal hypertension.
   c  Increased serum albumin, hyperaldosteronism, and sodium retention.
   d  Decreased serum albumin, hypoaldosteronism, and sodium retention.

25 A diuretic that is used to treat ascites in advanced cirrhosis by counteracting the effects of aldosterone on the kidney tubules is
   a  Spironolactone (Aldactone).
   b  Hydrochlorothiazide (Hydrodiuril).
   c  Mannitol (Osmitrol).
   d  Meralluride (Mercuhydrin).

26 Since the patient was not responding to diuretic therapy and a low-sodium diet, the doctor ordered a paracentesis. A "paracentesis" is the
   a  Removal of fluid from the peritoneal cavity.
   b  Removal of fluid from the thoracic cavity.
   c  Measurement of pressure in the portal vein.
   d  Inflow and outflow of fluid from the abdominal cavity.

27 A diagnostic test used to measure the total serum bilirubin is the
   a  Cephalin flocculation test.
   b  Thymol turbidity test.
   c  Hippuric acid test.
   d  Quantitative van den Bergh test.

**28** The patient with jaundice secondary to cirrhosis of the liver will probably have
   **a** Elevated total serum bilirubin, no urine bilirubin, and dark brown stool.
   **b** Elevated total serum bilirubin, increased urine bilirubin, and light brown stool.
   **c** Normal total serum bilirubin, increased urine bilirubin, and clay-colored stool.
   **d** Elevated total serum bilirubin, no urine bilirubin, and clay-colored stool.

**29** Clayton Smith was admitted to the hospital with a diagnosis of primary carcinoma of the liver. Because of the severe ascites, a paracentesis was done by the physician. The nurse would expect the ascitic fluid to be
   **a** Amber-colored.
   **b** Bile-colored.
   **c** Bloody.
   **d** Colorless.

**30** While preparing Mr. Smith for a paracentesis, the nurse recognized that he should be told that
   **a** It is a noninvasive procedure and will cause no pain.
   **b** It is essential to void before beginning the procedure.
   **c** Rapid removal of the fluid causes the least discomfort and danger to the patient.
   **d** He will be expected to lie in a knee-chest position during the procedure.

**31** The parenteral replacement fluid used to counteract the hypovolemia and shock associated with paracentesis is
   **a** Normal saline.
   **b** 5% glucose in water.
   **c** Salt-poor serum albumin.
   **d** Blood.

**32** Hypoprothrombinemia can occur in severe liver damage. Patients should be observed carefully for
  **a** Bleeding tendencies.
  **b** Peripheral edema.
  **c** Steatorrhea.
  **d** Signs of infection.

**33** Choose the group of drugs that would be toxic to the patient with severe liver damage.
  **a** Corticosteroids.
  **b** Anticholinergics.
  **c** Antibiotics.
  **d** Narcotics.

**34** William White is a 65-year-old man who was admitted to the medical intensive care unit (ICU) for bleeding esophageal varices. A Sengstaken-Blakemore tube was inserted to control bleeding. The nurse
  **a** Encouraged him to swallow his saliva to prevent aspiration.
  **b** Attached the tube marked "gastric balloon" to low intermittent suction.
  **c** Checked the manometer attached to the esophageal and gastric balloons for variations in the prescribed pressure.
  **d** Deflated the esophageal and gastric balloons every hour for 5 minutes.

**35** The greatest danger from rupture or sudden deflation of the gastric balloon of the Sengstaken-Blakemore tube is that
  **a** The entire tube may move up and obstruct the patient's airway.
  **b** Pressure is exerted on the nares and causes necrosis of the nares.
  **c** Tissue damage occurs in the esophagus, resulting in tracheoesophageal fistulae.
  **d** Ulceration of the gastric mucosa occurs, with erosion of the coronary vein of the stomach.

**36** One of the objectives in the treatment of bleeding esophageal varices is to lower portal venous pressure. This can be temporarily achieved by the administration of

  **a** Hydrocortisone (Solu-cortef).
  **b** Cimetidine (Tagamet).
  **c** Metaraminol bitartrate (Aramine).
  **d** Vasopressin (Pitressin).

**37** While preparing the patient with esophageal varices for discharge, the nurse included his wife in the teaching program. The nurse emphasized to his wife that

  **a** A small glass of port wine before meals will relieve the anorexia.
  **b** Any change in his behavior or handwriting should be reported to the physician.
  **c** Protein must be completely eliminated from his diet.
  **d** Aspirin can be safely given to relieve pain.

**38** A common physiological stressor contributing to hepatic encephalopathy in persons with impaired liver function is

  **a** Gastrointestinal bleeding.
  **b** Nausea and vomiting.
  **c** Diarrhea and tenesmus.
  **d** Anorexia and weight loss.

**39** In addition to increased serum ammonia levels, which of the following diagnostic tests confirms the diagnosis of hepatic encephalopathy?

  **a** Electroencephalogram.
  **b** Brain scan.
  **c** Angiogram.
  **d** Echogram.

**40** The peculiar flapping tremors seen in hepatic encephalopathy is referred to as
  **a** "Apraxia."
  **b** "Aphasia."
  **c** "Aphagia."
  **d** "Asterixis."

**41** If signs of impending hepatic coma develop, the daily protein intake should
  **a** Be completely eliminated until the liver regenerates.
  **b** Not exceed 30 g.
  **c** Range between 45 and 60 g.
  **d** Range between 75 and 100 g.

**42** An antibiotic used in hepatic coma to inhibit the growth of bacterial flora in the large intestine is
  **a** Tetracycline.
  **b** Amphotericin.
  **c** Neomycin.
  **d** Cephalexin.

**43** An example of an ammonia detoxicant used in the treatment of hepatic coma is
  **a** Sodium citrate.
  **b** Arginine hydrochloride.
  **c** Ethacrynic acid.
  **d** Lactic acid.

**44** Choose the statement that best applies to the action of lactulose in the treatment of hepatic coma. Lactulose is
  **a** An antibiotic that destroys the bacterial flora of the large intestine.
  **b** An ammonia detoxicant that accelerates the synthesis of urea from ammonia.
  **c** A synthetic disaccharide that lowers the pH of the stool and decreases ammonia production in the intestine.
  **d** An ammonia detoxicant that combines with free ammonia to form glutamine.

## ANSWERS, EXPLANATIONS, AND REFERENCES

**1 c** One of the major functions of the liver is to manufacture prothrombin, fibrinogen, and other factors essential for the coagulation of blood. (*Langley, Telford, and Christensen, p. 638.*)

**2 d** The Kupfer cells of the liver play a vital role in filtering blood as it flows through the liver. These cells phagocytize bacteria in the blood; thus hepatic blood is practically bacteria-free. (*Langley, Telford, and Christensen, p. 513.*)

**3 c** Ammonia ($NH_3$), an end product of protein metabolism, is converted to urea by the liver. Once it is synthesized, it is excreted by the kidneys via the urine. (*Vander, Sherman, and Luciano, p. 88, p. 392.*)

**4 c** Bile is synthesized and secreted by the liver at a rate of 250 to 1000 mL per day. On the average, about 700 mL is secreted per day. (*Langley, Telford, and Christensen, p. 617.*)

**5 d** Veins ordinarily transport blood from capillaries to the vena cava and finally the heart. The portal vein is unique in that it carries blood from the capillaries draining the stomach, intestines, spleen, and pancreas to the capillaries of the liver (liver sinusoids). (*Langley, Telford, and Christensen, p. 456. Price and Wilson, p. 259.*)

**6 b** The main function of the gallbladder is to store and concentrate bile. The liver manufactures bile, and it is then transported to the gallbladder via the hepatic bile duct and the cystic duct. In the gallbladder, water and salts are absorbed from the bile via the lymphatics and blood vessels. As a result, the bile stored in the liver is about 10 times more concentrated than hepatic bile. (*Price and Wilson, p. 262.*)

**7 c** The common bile duct empties into the duodenum. The hepatic bile duct, which transports bile from the liver, and the cystic duct, which transports bile from the gallbladder, join to form the common bile duct. (*Langley, Telford, and Christensen, p. 617.*)

**8 c** The sphincter of Oddi is a band of smooth muscle that surrounds the bile duct as it enters the duodenum. (*Vander, Sherman, and Luciano, p. 376.*)

**9 c** The pancreas secretes a digestive juice that contains trypsin, amylase, and lipase. These enzymes are very potent and are essential for the digestion of protein, fats, and carbohydrates. (*Langley, Telford, and Christensen, p. 615.*)

**10 b** The pancreatic duct cells secrete sodium bicarbonate into the pancreatic juices. Sodium bicarbonate, which has an alkaline pH, progressively neutralizes the acid pH of the intestinal contents so it is almost neutral by the time it reaches the ileum. (*Langley, Telford, and Christensen, p. 615.*)

**11 b** The most common stressor contributing to the development of acute pancreatitis is alcoholism. Other stressors include physical trauma, certain drugs, viral infection, and obstruction of the biliary tract. (*Jones, Dunbar, and Jirovec, p. 604.*)

**12 c** Obstructions or inflammations of the pancreas impair the flow of amylase into the intestinal tract. As a result there is an elevation of amylase in the blood, especially during the first 24 to 72 hours of the disease. The normal serum amylase is 60 to 100 units per 100 mL. (*Price and Wilson, p. 265.*)

**13 d** Morphine is an analgesic that is contraindicated for the relief of pain associated with acute pancreatitis. It is believed that morphine increases spasm of the sphincter of Oddi. (*Jones, Dunbar, and Jirovec, p. 606. Luckmann and Sorensen, p. 1140.*)

**14 a** An objective in the treatment of acute pancreatitis is to reduce pancreatic secretions. This can be accomplished by eliminating oral intake of food and maintaining intermittent nasogastric suction. Although some sources recommend the use of anticholinergic drugs, other sources question their use. (*Jones, Dunbar, and Jirovec, p. 607. Luckmann and Sorensen, p. 1140.*)

**15 a** Late in the course of chronic pancreatitis, faulty absorption of fat can occur. The stool is bulky, frothy, and voluminous because of an excess fat content. "Steatorrhea" is the term used to describe the characteristic stool. (*Moidel, Giblin, and Wagner, p. 720.*)

**16 c** In obstructive jaundice, bile is unable to enter the duodenum to emulsify fats. As a result, vitamin K, a fat-soluble vitamin, cannot be absorbed and a deficiency of prothrombin develops. To counteract the resulting bleeding tendencies that can develop, the doctor may order vitamin K parenterally. (*Beland, p. 556. Jones, Dunbar, and Jirovec, p. 602.*)

**17 d** In caring for patients with obstructive jaundice, they should be observed for signs of gastrointestinal bleeding, hematuria, or bleeding from any other body orifices. (*Jones, Dunbar, and Jirovec, p. 602. Moidel, Giblin, and Wagner, pp. 357–358.*)

**18 c** When the hepatic or the common bile duct becomes obstructed, bilirubin (a constituent of bile) cannot enter the duodenum. As a result the stool becomes clay-colored. The excess bilirubin is reabsorbed into blood and excreted by the kidneys, giving the urine a dark color. (*Jones, Dunbar, and Jirovec, p. 599. Shafer et al., p. 705.*)

**19 c** The group of food that is the lowest is cream of wheat with brown sugar, toast with jelly, and grapefruit juice. All the other groups contain foods high in fat: waffles, evaporated milk, milk, coffee cake, eggs, hot chocolate, margarine. (*Robinson and Lawler, pp. 534–535. Williams, p. 551.*)

**20 b** One type of x-ray examination used to visualize the gallbladder is an oral cholecystogram. In order for the gallbladder to appear on the x-ray, the patient must take radiopaque tablets the night before the examination is scheduled. In some patients the drug can cause vomiting and diarrhea. If this happens the physician should be notified, since vomiting and diarrhea can interfere with absorption of the radiopaque dye. (*Jones, Dunbar, and Jirovec, p. 598.*)

**21 b** Liver biopsy is done on patients to confirm the extent of liver damage. Since the liver is such a vascular organ, bleeding during and after the procedure is potentially hazardous. The patients should be told to lie on their right side to reduce the danger of bleeding. (*Jones, Dunbar, and Jirovec, p. 647. Luckmann and Sorensen, p. 1121. Shafer et al., p. 710.*)

**22 b** In the early stages of alcoholic portal cirrhosis, it is essential for the patient to maintain optimum nutrition. To prevent further damage to the liver, the patient is advised to eat a high-carbohydrate, high-protein diet for liver regeneration to occur. (*Howard and Herbold, pp. 375–376. Jones, Dunbar, and Jirovec, p. 647.*)

**23 a** The steroids, namely, the glucocorticosteroids, the mineral corticosteroids, and the sex hormones, are normally destroyed by the liver. In severe liver damage, as in cirrhosis, the liver's ability to destroy the steroids is impaired. The spider angioma, palmar erythema, axillary alopecia, gynecomastia, and testicular atrophy are all caused by an elevation of the circulating estrogens. (*Jones, Dunbar, and Jirovec, p. 641. Price and Wilson, p. 273.*)

**24 a** The ascites and peripheral edema associated with cirrhosis of the liver are caused by decreased levels of serum albumin, hyperaldosteronism, and portal hypertension. In cirrhosis of the liver, normally functioning liver tissue is gradually replaced with fibrous tissue, which cannot perform the many functions of the liver. As a result, pressure in the portal vein increases, the liver cannot adequately synthesize albumin from amino acids, and aldosterone cannot be detoxified. (*Beland, p. 734. Luckmann and Sorensen, p. 1125.*)

**25 a** Spironolactone (Aldactone) is a diuretic that counteracts the effects of aldosterone on the kidney tubules. Since the increased serum levels of aldosterone contribute to ascites and peripheral edema in advanced cirrhosis, Aldactone is especially useful. (*Bergersen, p. 450.*)

**26 a** When ascites becomes so severe that it interferes with breathing and cannot be controlled with diuretic therapy and sodium restriction, a paracentesis may be ordered. A paracentesis is the removal of fluid from the peritoneal cavity. *(Beland, p.734.)*

**27 d** A test used to measure the total serum bilirubin is the quantitative van den Bergh test. The test can differentiate between protein-bound (unconjugated) bilirubin and soluble (conjugated) bilirubin. Normal values for total serum bilirubin range from 0.1 to 1 mg/100 mL. *(Shafer et al., p. 705.)*

**28 b** In cirrhosis of the liver there is an elevation of the total serum bilirubin, an increase in the urine bilirubin, and light brown stool. The jaundice is caused by faulty hepatic function. *(Shafer et al., p. 710.)*

**29 c** In carcinoma of the liver, the ascitic fluid is bloody and contains malignant cells. *(Jones, Dunbar, and Jirovec, p. 661.)*

**30 b** To prevent inadvertently puncturing the urinary bladder during the paracentesis, it is essential to have the patient void prior to the introduction of the cannula into the peritoneal cavity. If the patient is unable to void, the physician writes an order for a urinary catheterization. *(Beland, p. 734.)*

**31 c** When a paracentesis is done for ascites, the fluid removed is high in protein. Salt-poor serum albumin can be administered to prevent the shock and hypovolemia that can occur from the loss of fluid and protein. *(Shafer et al., p. 721.)*

**32 a** Patients with severe liver damage cannot manufacture adequate amounts of prothrombin, in addition to other factors necessary for blood clotting. As a result, these patients are particularly prone to bleeding tendencies. Both the patient and the nurse should be made aware of the implications of this problem. *(Luckmann and Sorensen, p. 1127.)*

**33 d** Narcotics are particularly toxic to the patient with severe liver damage. Since the detoxification function of the liver is impaired, there tends to be an accumulation of these drugs in the body, leading to toxic symptoms. *(Jones, Dunbar, and Jirovec, p. 651. Shafer et al., p. 712.)*

**34 c** Patients with a Sengstaken-Blakemore tube usually have a manometer attached to the esophageal and gastric balloons so that the nurse or physician can detect any variation in the prescribed balloon pressure. The nurse should notify the physician of any variations so that the necessary corrections can be made. (*Luckmann and Sorensen, p. 1128.*)

**35 a** While caring for the patient with a Sengstaken-Blakemore tube, the nurse must carefully monitor the pressure in the esophageal and gastric balloons. The nurse should be aware that if the gastric balloon suddenly ruptures or is deflated, that the entire tube can move up into the oropharynx and occlude the patient's airway. To prevent death from asphyxiation, the esophageal balloon must quickly be deflated and the tube removed. (*Shafer et al., p. 722.*)

**36 d** One of the objectives in the treatment of bleeding esophageal varices is to lower portal venous pressure. This can be temporarily achieved by the administration of vasopressin infusions. It is believed that vasopressin decreases esophageal bleeding by reducing splanchnic blood and reducing portal pressure. (*Harrison, p. 1612. Luckmann and Sorensen, p. 1129.*)

**37 b** Bleeding esophageal varices can lead to hepatic coma because of the increased ammonia production by the intestinal bacteria in the protein-rich blood. If the patient is being discharged, the family should be told to notify the physician if there are any changes in behavior, speech, or handwriting. (*Jones, Dunbar, and Jirovec, p. 651.*)

**38 a** Gastrointestinal bleeding is the most common cause of hepatic encephalopathy in the patient with impaired liver function. As the blood passes along the intestines, there is bacterial breakdown of the protein portion of the blood. Ammonia, the end product of this bacterial breakdown, enters the circulation via the portal vein. Under normal conditions, the liver would be able to convert the excess ammonia to urea; however, since there is so much damage to the liver, the serum ammonia level rises, causing cerebral intoxication. (*Price and Wilson, pp. 276–277.*)

**39 a** Patients with hepatic encephalopathy have increased serum ammonia levels and changes in the electroencephalogram. Both these findings can occur before any overt symptoms appear. (*Luckmann and Sorensen, p. 1128.*)

**40 d** The flapping tremors seen in hepatic encephalopathy are referred to as "asterixis." Asterixis is a manifestation of impaired cerebral metabolism. (*Price and Wilson, p. 278.*)

**41 b** In patients with impending hepatic coma, protein intake should not exceed 30 g per day. High-protein diets are contraindicated because of the increased production of ammonia being formed from the deaminization of amino acids. Although in some instances protein is completely eliminated, this cannot be done for prolonged periods of time. (*Beland, p. 735. Moidel, Giblin, and Wagner, p. 712. Robinson and Lawler, p. 472.*)

**42 c** Neomycin is an antibiotic that is poorly absorbed from the gastrointestinal tract when given orally. As a result, it is used in hepatic coma to inhibit the growth of bacterial flora in the large intestine and to subsequently reduce the amount of ammonia formed. (*Luckmann and Sorensen, p. 1129. Shafer et al., p. 724.*)

**43 b** Arginine hydrochloride is an ammonia detoxicant used in the treatment of hepatic coma. The blood ammonia content is reduced because the arginine hydrochloride accelerates urea formation from ammonia. (*Asperheim and Eisenhauer, p. 455.*)

**44 c** Lactulose is a synthetic disaccharide that alters the bacterial flora in the colon by lowering the pH of the stool. As a result there is decreased ammonia production and absorption in the intestine. (*Jones, Dunbar, and Jirovec, p. 651. Luckmann and Sorensen, p. 1129. Shafer et al., p. 725.*)

# UNIT 12

# Nursing care of the patient with a cardiovascular disorder

**OBJECTIVES**

To answer the questions in this unit, the reader should be able to

1. Identify the anatomical structures of the heart;
2. Recognize how the heart adapts to damage or injury;
3. List the signs and symptoms of select cardiovascular disorders;
4. Recognize the nurse's role in administering the various medications used to treat cardiovascular disorders;
5. Describe the nurse's role in the care of patients with cardiovascular disorders.

## QUESTIONS RELATED TO OBJECTIVES

*Instructions*: Choose the *one best* answer to the following questions.

1. The volume of blood ejected by each ventricle per minute is called the
   a  "Stroke volume."
   b  "Ejection fraction."
   c  "Cardiac output."
   d  "End systolic volume."

2. The heart chamber that has the thickest wall to allow for its greater workload is the
   a  Right atrium.
   b  Right ventricle.
   c  Left atrium.
   d  Left ventricle.

3. The force of blood that is exerted against the walls of an artery when the heart is at rest is referred to as
   a  "Arterial blood pressure."
   b  "Systolic blood pressure."
   c  "Diastolic blood pressure."
   d  "Pulse pressure."

4. The inherent rhythm of cardiac muscle varies in different parts of the heart. The inherent rhythm of the ventricles is
   a  70 to 80 beats per minute.
   b  60 to 65 beats per minute.
   c  30 to 40 beats per minute.
   d  15 to 25 beats per minute.

5. The motor nerve responsible for inhibiting the rate of the heart is the
   a  Sympathetic accelerator nerve.
   b  Vagus nerve.
   c  Inferior cardiac nerve.
   d  Phrenic nerve.

**6** Normally the pulse pressure should not exceed
   **a** 20 mmHg.
   **b** 40 mmHg.
   **c** 70 mmHg.
   **d** 90 mmHg.

**7** The pacemaker of the heart is located in the
   **a** Vagus nerve.
   **b** Vasomotor center of the brain.
   **c** Sinoatrial node.
   **d** Bundle of His.

**8** The normal pathway of the conduction system is
   **a** SA node → bundle of His → AV node → bundle branches → Purkinje fibers.
   **b** AV node → SA node → bundle of His → bundle branches → Purkinje fibers.
   **c** SA node → AV node → bundle of His → bundle branches → Purkinje fibers.
   **d** SA node → AV node → Bachman's bundle → bundle branches → Purkinje fibers.

**9** Robert Rooney is a 51-year-old patient who is being treated with quinidine for atrial fibrillation. The nurse should
   **a** Monitor the blood pressure before giving the medication.
   **b** Administer it sublingually.
   **c** Check the partial thromboplastin time (PTT) before administering it.
   **d** Check his apical pulse before administration.

**10** The patient with premature ventricular contractions should be told which factors stimulate their development. From the following, choose the factors the patient should be made aware of:
   **a** Smoking, eating large meals, psychological stress, and caffeine.
   **b** Obesity, psychological stress, smoking, and genetic predisposition.
   **c** Water hardness, eating large meals, physical activity, and caffeine.
   **d** Coffee drinking, smoking, hyperlipidemia, and physical activity.

**11** Choose the drugs that are most frequently administered IV to treat the patient with premature ventricular contractions.
   **a** Digitalis and isoproterenol (Isuprel).
   **b** Aminophylline and quinidine.
   **c** Epinephrine and ephedrine.
   **d** Lidocaine (Xylocaine) and procainamide (Pronestyl).

**12** The patient with a complete heart block has a ventricular rate of
   **a** Below 40 beats per minute.
   **b** 60 to 100 beats per minute.
   **c** 120 to 200 beats per minute.
   **d** Over 200 beats per minute.

**13** Anthony Miccio has had a permanent pacemaker inserted for a complete heart block. A discharge teaching plan for him would include explaining to him that
   **a** Sexual activity is contraindicated.
   **b** Microwave ovens, power lawn mowers, and electric razors can cause pacemaker dysfunction.
   **c** Swimming and showering are contraindicated.
   **d** Palpitations are a normal occurrence and should not cause alarm.

14 Life-threatening arrhythmias that must be treated promptly include
   a  Atrial fibrillation and premature ventricular contractions.
   b  Atrial tachycardia and bundle branch block.
   c  Ventricular tachycardia and ventricular fibrillation.
   d  First-degree heart block and ventricular fibrillation.

15 A procedure that is used to correct ventricular fibrillation is
   a  Cardioversion.
   b  Defibrillation.
   c  Implantation of an epicardial pacemaker.
   d  Insertion of a temporary transvenous pacemaker.

16 After establishing unresponsiveness, the first step in cardiopulmonary resuscitation (CPR) is to
   a  Clear the airway by tilting the head backward and hyperextending the neck.
   b  Clear the mouth and pharynx with a sweeping motion of the fingers.
   c  Inflate the lungs four times by forcibly blowing air into the patient's mouth.
   d  Compress the heart by exerting a forceful downward pressure on the lower portion of the sternum.

17 Once the brain has been deprived of oxygen, irreversible brain damage can develop. The maximum period of time that the brain can be deprived of oxygen is
   a  1 to 2 minutes.
   b  2 to 4 minutes.
   c  4 to 6 minutes.
   d  6 to 10 minutes.

18 When performing cardiac compression in the adult, the nurse depresses the sternum
   a  $\frac{1}{2}$ to $\frac{3}{4}$ in.
   b  $\frac{3}{4}$ to 1 in.
   c  1 to $1\frac{1}{2}$ in.
   d  $1\frac{1}{2}$ to 2 in.

**19** When performing cardiopulmonary resuscitation with one rescuer, the ratio of heart compressions to lung inflations is
   **a** 5:1.
   **b** 10:1.
   **c** 15:2.
   **d** 20:3.

**20** When performing cardiopulmonary resuscitation with two rescuers, the ratio of cardiac compressions to lung inflations is
   **a** 5:1.
   **b** 7:1.
   **c** 10:1.
   **d** 15:2.

**21** From the following list, choose the one statement that is most correct.
   **a** The precardial thump should be used in all types of cardiac arrest.
   **b** Downward pressure is exerted on the tip of the xiphoid when performing cardiac compression.
   **c** The initial ventilatory maneuver is two quick, full breaths.
   **d** External cardiac compression must always be accompanied by artificial ventilation.

**22** From the following statements, choose the one that *best* applies to bacterial endocarditis.
   **a** Bacterial endocarditis characteristically involves the three layers of the heart.
   **b** Bacterial endocarditis is an autoimmune response that affects the endocardium.
   **c** Aschoff's bodies are the characteristic lesions that invade the endocardium.
   **d** The characteristic lesion is a friable vegetation that forms on the valves of the heart.

**23** The antibiotic that is most effective in treating bacterial endocarditis is
   a  Penicillin.
   b  Cephalosporin.
   c  Tetracycline.
   d  Chloromycetin.

**24** Guanethidine sulfate (Ismelin) is a medication commonly used to
   a  Reduce hypertension.
   b  Correct cardiac arrhythmias.
   c  Reduce spasm of the coronary artery.
   d  Impair clot formation.

**25** Patients on antihypertensive therapy who experience postural hypotension should be told that
   a  Omitting the medication for 24 hours will relieve it.
   b  Standing perfectly still when this occurs will restore normotension.
   c  Taking a hot bath immediately upon arising will divert the blood to the heart and brain.
   d  Rising slowly from a lying or a sitting position helps to prevent this from occurring.

**26** Sophie Boos was placed on a mild sodium-restricted diet (2 to 3 g) for hypertension. While doing dietary teaching you emphasized to Ms. Boos that
   a  Luncheon meats, frankfurters, and bacon can be used as desired.
   b  Salt can be used lightly in cooking.
   c  Bouillon, cheese, and crackers can be used liberally as snack foods.
   d  Flavoring aids such as catsup, prepared mustard, and relishes can be used liberally.

**27** Atherosclerosis has been named the most common cause of coronary artery disease. From the following statements, choose the one that is most correct.
  **a** Men and women are equally susceptible to atherosclerosis throughout the life cycle.
  **b** Whites are more prone to atherosclerosis than are blacks.
  **c** There is no correlation between psychological stress and the development of atherosclerosis.
  **d** Persons with hypertension are more susceptible to atherosclerosis than are those persons with normotension.

**28** Nitroglycerin is a medication used to treat angina pectoris. The nurse should instruct the patient to
  **a** Sit or lie down when taking the medication sublingually.
  **b** Notify the physician if the pain is not relieved within 10 minutes after taking one dose.
  **c** Check the radial pulse before taking the medication.
  **d** Take the drug for severe pain only because it is habit-forming.

**29** Choose the statement that best describes the chest pain associated with acute myocardial infarction. The pain is severe and
  **a** Is relieved by nitroglycerin.
  **b** Is relieved by rest.
  **c** Can radiate to the jaw, neck, or teeth.
  **d** Is intermittent and of short duration.

**30** The electrocardiogram becomes a valuable tool to aid in the diagnosis of myocardial infarction. In myocardial infarction there is
  **a** Absence of a P wave.
  **b** Widening of the QRS complex.
  **c** Inversion of the T wave.
  **d** Shortening of the PR interval.

**31** From the following list choose the enzyme that is the most cardiospecific and the earliest to be released into the circulation following a myocardial infarction.
  **a** Lactic dehydrogenase (LDH).
  **b** Serum glutamicoxaloacetic transaminase (SGOT).
  **c** Serum glutamicpyruvic transaminase (SGPT).
  **d** Creatine phosphokinase (CPK).

**32** Choose the statement that best relates to the nursing care of the patient with a myocardial infarction.
  **a** Place the patient in a Trendelenberg position.
  **b** Report to the physician a CVP reading below 3 cm $H_2O$.
  **c** Notify the physician if the urinary output is 30 mL for 3 consecutive hours.
  **d** Take rectal temps every 4 hours.

**33** Choose the statement that best applies to the administration of heparin.
  **a** After subcutaneous injection, the injection site should be massaged gently to prevent bleeding under the skin.
  **b** Oral anticoagulants should never be given while the patient is receiving heparin.
  **c** Daily prothrombin times are done to determine the effectiveness of therapy.
  **d** It is important to give heparin promptly at the specified time to maintain optimum anticoagulation.

**34** The antidote for heparin is
  **a** Calcium gluconate.
  **b** Vitamin K.
  **c** Protamine sulfate.
  **d** Aramine.

**35** Daily dosage of heparin is based on the results of the
  **a** Prothrombin time.
  **b** Platelet count.
  **c** Lee-White coagulation time.
  **d** Coomb's test.

**36** While preparing Mr. Richards for discharge, the nurse told him to keep all his appointments for periodic blood tests. Which of the following blood tests will the physician want done if the patient is on oral anticoagulants?
    **a** Platelet count.
    **b** Coagulation time.
    **c** Bleeding time.
    **d** Prothrombin time.

**37** Mr. Richards was placed on a low-cholesterol diet. Choose the group of foods that is lowest in cholesterol.
    **a** Cheese omelet and cucumber salad.
    **b** Lobster Newburg and tossed salad.
    **c** Liver and onions with tomato salad.
    **d** Broiled flounder and bean salad.

**38** A falling blood pressure and a narrowing pulse pressure are a sign of dysfunction of the
    **a** Left ventricle.
    **b** Right ventricle.
    **c** Conduction system of the heart.
    **d** Coronary arteries.

**39** One of the first symptoms experienced by the patient with left-sided heart failure is
    **a** Engorgement of the neck veins.
    **b** Orthopnea.
    **c** Ankle edema.
    **d** Dyspnea on exertion.

**40** Irene Peoble was admitted to the hospital with pulmonary edema secondary to left-sided heart failure. The physician ordered rotating tourniquets. Choose the most correct statement.
   **a** Tourniquets are initially applied to the upper portion of all four extremities.
   **b** If the distal pulses are palpable, the tourniquets should be applied more tightly.
   **c** Every 30 minutes the tourniquets are rotated in a clockwise direction.
   **d** When the treatment is discontinued, remove one tourniquet every 15 minutes.

**41** Aminophylline 250 mg was being given IV to Mrs. Peoble to relieve the pulmonary edema. The nurse should be aware that
   **a** It can cause sloughing of tissue at the injection site.
   **b** The patient will experience a burning sensation while it is being administered.
   **c** Severe hypotension can occur if it is given too rapidly.
   **d** It must never be piggybacked to the primary intravenous infusion.

**42** The physician ordered oxygen via nasal catheter to relieve the dyspnea associated with pulmonary edema. Choose the statement that best applies to this method of oxygen administration.
   **a** It is less irritating to the nasal mucosa than other methods of oxygen administration.
   **b** The usual flow rate is 8 to 10 L per minute.
   **c** The approximate distance the catheter should be inserted is the distance from the tip of the nose to the earlobe.
   **d** If the nasal catheter is properly lubricated prior to insertion, a humidifier is not needed.

**43** The normal range for central venous pressure is between
  **a** 0 to 5 cm of water.
  **b** 5 to 10 cm of water.
  **c** 12 to 20 cm of water.
  **d** 20 to 25 cm of water.

**44** The central venous pressure is elevated in
  **a** Congestive heart failure.
  **b** Cardiogenic shock.
  **c** Hemorrhage.
  **d** Dehydration.

**45** To determine the patency of the central venous pressure line, the nurse adjusts the stopcock so that fluid from the manometer flows into the vein. The fluid in the manometer should
  **a** Remain at a fixed level.
  **b** Fluctuate synchronously with the patient's respiration.
  **c** Fall freely when the patient coughs.
  **d** Rise sharply to 30 cm.

**46** Engorgement of the jugular veins in the neck is a sign of
  **a** Congestive heart failure.
  **b** Myocardial infarction.
  **c** Hypertension.
  **d** Circulatory collapse.

**47** From the following groups of diuretics, choose the ones referred to as "powerful" or "potent" diuretics.
  **a** Ethacrynic acid (Edecrin) and furosemide (Lasix).
  **b** Chlorothiazide (Diuril) and acetazolamide (Diamox).
  **c** Hydrochlorothiazide (Hydrodiuril) and meralluride (Mercuhydrin).
  **d** Spironolactone (Aldactone) and urea (Urevert).

**48** Symptoms of digitalis toxicity include
  **a** Bigeminal pulse, blurred vision, and anorexia.
  **b** Hematuria, anorexia, and epistaxis.
  **c** Cystitis, nausea and vomiting, and diarrhea.
  **d** Polyuria, asterixis, and pulse deficit.

**49** Which of the following fluid and electrolyte imbalances makes the patient most vulnerable to digitalis toxicity?
  **a** Hypokalemia.
  **b** Hyponatremia.
  **c** Hypocalcemia.
  **d** Hypoproteinemia.

**50** The doctor prescribed Lanoxin 0.25 mg po. From the following list choose the one that is the same as Lanoxin.
  **a** Digoxin.
  **b** Digitoxin.
  **c** Gitalin.
  **d** Lanatoside.

**51** A low-sodium diet was ordered for Mrs. Peoble. From the following list of cereals choose the one that is *lowest* in sodium.
  **a** Quick-cooking farina.
  **b** 40 percent bran flakes.
  **c** Corn flakes.
  **d** Puffed rice.

**52** From the following list of frozen vegetables, choose the one that is *lowest* in sodium.
  **a** Asparagus.
  **b** Spinach.
  **c** Peas.
  **d** Lima beans.

**53** Which of the following observations by the nurse would be an indication of successful dietary and diuretic treatment of congestive heart failure?
   **a** Fullness of the neck veins.
   **b** Decreased urinary output.
   **c** Increased venous pressure.
   **d** Weight loss.

**54** Laurence O'Neil is a 47-year-old patient who has peripheral vascular disease. He complains of pain in the calf muscles which is brought on by exercise and relieved by rest. This type of pain is referred to as
   **a** "Ischemic pain."
   **b** "Intermittent claudication."
   **c** "Homan's sign."
   **d** "Leriche syndrome."

**55** Which of the following intensifies the symptoms of Raynaud's disease?
   **a** Smoking.
   **b** High-cholesterol diet.
   **c** Alcohol.
   **d** Warm climates.

**56** Choose the statement that best applies to the nursing care of patients with peripheral vascular disease.
   **a** Hot foot soaks should be used to increase circulation.
   **b** Exercise should be encouraged in the patient with leg ulcers to improve circulation.
   **c** Meticulous care of the feet is a vital part of nursing care.
   **d** The knee gatch of the bed should be used to elevate the legs.

## ANSWERS, EXPLANATIONS, AND REFERENCES

**1 c**  The volume of blood ejected per minute by each ventricle is called the "cardiac output." The cardiac output averages about 5 L per minute. (*Price and Wilson, p. 307.*)

**2 d**  The muscle of the left ventricle is thicker than the muscle in the other chambers of the heart so that blood can be pumped through the systemic circulation at a higher pressure. (*Langley, Telford, and Christensen, p. 404. Phibbs, p. 9.*)

**3 c**  Diastolic blood pressure is the force of blood exerted against the wall of an artery when the heart is at rest. (*Jones, Dunbar, and Jirovec, p. 758.*)

**4 c**  Cardiac muscle is unique in that it has an inherent rhythm of its own. This means that cardiac muscle has the ability to establish a fundamental rhythm of its own if its innervation is severed or eliminated in any manner. If the impulses to the ventricles are not received, they can establish a rate of 30 to 40 beats per minute. (*Vander, Sherman, and Luciano, p. 237.*)

**5 b**  The autonomic nervous system innervates the heart muscle so that the heart rate can either be increased or decreased. The vagus nerve, a motor nerve of the parasympathetic nervous system, sends impulses to the heart, which decreases its rate. (*Langley, Telford, and Christensen, p. 405.*)

**6 b**  Pulse pressure is the difference between the systolic and diastolic blood pressure. Normally it should not exceed 40 mmHg. (*Jones, Dunbar, and Jirovec, p. 758.*)

**7 c**  The pacemaker of the heart is a mass of specialized nervous tissue located in the sinoatrial node of the heart. Cardiac impulses are normally initiated in the SA node and then transmitted over both atria to the AV node. (*Jones, Dunbar, and Jirovec, pp. 749–750.*)

**8 c**  The conduction system of the heart transmits impulses through the myocardium, which stimulates muscle contractions. The normal pathway of the conduction system is the SA node → AV node → bundle of His → bundle branches → Purkinje fibers. (*Jones, Dunbar, and Jirovec, pp. 749–750. Price and Wilson, p. 295.*)

**9 d** Quinidine is used to treat atrial fibrillation. One of the effects of quinidine is to slow the rate at which abnormal impulses arise in the atria. However, this action can depress conduction too much. The nurse should check the apical pulse before administering quinidine to detect any unusual arrhythmias. (*Asperheim and Eisenhauer, p. 310. Rodman and Smith, p. 356.*)

**10 a** The patient should be aware of those factors that contribute to the development of premature ventricular contractions. Smoking, caffeine, large meals, and psychological stress predispose the individual to premature beats. Coffee, tea, cola drinks, and cocoa contain caffeine and therefore should be avoided. (*Jones, Dunbar, and Jirovec, p. 856.*)

**11 d** Patients having infrequent premature ventricular contractions usually need no treatment. When they occur more frequently (six per more per minute) the arrhythmia becomes more severe and is treated with antiarrhythmic drugs. The drugs most frequently used are lidocaine and procainamide. (*Jones, Dunbar, and Jirovec, p. 857. Luckmann and Sorensen, p. 650. Shafer et al., p. 349.*)

**12 a** In complete heart block, the impulses that originate in the SA node are not transmitted to the ventricles. As a result the ventricles establish their own rate. This rate is usually below 40 beats per minute. If complete heart block is not treated, it can cause death. (*Jones, Dunbar, and Jirovec, p. 850. Luckmann and Sorensen, p. 647. Shafer et al., p. 347.*)

**13 b** A discharge teaching plan should include telling the patient that some types of electric equipment can cause pacemaker dysfunction. Electric razors, snowmobiles, power lawn mowers, microwave ovens, etc., can create a problem. (*Hamilton, p. 135. Jones, Dunbar, and Jirovec, p. 863.*)

**14 c** Life-threatening arrhythmias that must be treated immediately to prevent death are ventricular tachycardia and ventricular fibrillation. In these cases seconds, not minutes, count. (*Jones, Dunbar, and Jirovec, p. 857. Luckmann and Sorensen, p. 650.*)

**15 b** Defibrillation is a form of precordial shock used to correct ventricular fibrillation. A high-voltage electric current is delivered to the heart and actually stops it from beating. The heart is completely depolarized, which enables the SA node to take over and restore normal rhythm. (*Luckmann and Sorensen, p. 650. Massachusetts General Hospital, p. 245.*)

**16 a** The first step in cardiopulmonary resuscitation is to clear the airway by tilting the head backward and hyperextending the neck. (*Journal of the American Medical Association, p. 841.*)

**17 c** If the brain is deprived of oxygen for more than 4 to 6 minutes, irreversible brain damage can occur. To prevent this from happening, cardiopulmonary resuscitation should be initiated within 4 to 6 minutes following the cardiac arrest. (*Jones, Dunbar, and Jirovec, p. 658.*)

**18 d** When performing cardiac compressions in the adult, the sternum is depressed approximately 1½ to 2 in. (*Journal of the American Medical Association, p. 845.*)

**19 c** When performing CPR with one rescuer, the ratio of cardiac compressions to lung inflation is 15:2. (*Journal of the American Medical Association, p. 846.*)

**20 a** When performing CPR with two rescuers, the ratio of cardiac compressions to lung inflation is 5:1. (*Journal of the American Medical Association, p. 845.*)

**21 d** Artificial ventilation must always be done when external cardiac compression is used. Cardiac compression produces some oxygenation but not enough for adequate oxygenation. (*Journal of the American Medical Association, p. 845.*)

**22 d** Bacterial endocarditis is a severe infection that involves the endocardium of the heart. It can often develop following acute infections of the tonsils, teeth, or gums.

The characteristic lesions are colonies of friable bacterial vegetation on the valves of the heart. (*Jones, Dunbar, and Jirovec, p. 604. Luckmann and Sorensen, pp. 689–690.*)

**23 a** Penicillin is the antibiotic that is most effective in treating bacterial endocarditis. Although other antibiotics can be used if the patient has severe allergies to penicillin, they are not as effective and the incidence of a relapse is much higher. (*Luckmann and Sorensen, p. 692.*)

**24 a** Guanethidine sulfate is an antihypertensive agent currently being used to treat many different forms of hypertension. It is believed that guanethidine produces its effects by depleting norepinephrine from the heart and other peripheral organs. (*Bergersen, p. 176.*)

**25 d** The patient who is on antihypertensive therapy and experiences postural hypotension should be told to rise slowly from a lying or a sitting position. Doing this allows the vascular system to adjust to the change of position. The patient should be told to avoid taking hot baths and standing still for any prolonged period of time. When postural hypotension does occur, the patient should lie flat. (*Bergersen, p. 184. Rodman and Smith, p. 325.*)

**26 b** On a mild sodium-restricted diet, the patient can be told that salt may be used in cooking but salting food at the table should be omitted. Salt-preserved and highly salted foods and flavoring aids should be omitted. (*Robinson and Lawler, pp. 546–547.*)

**27 d** Persons with hypertension are more susceptible to atherosclerosis than those persons with normal blood pressure. The higher the blood pressure the greater is the risk of developing vascular changes. (*Price and Wilson, p. 338.*)

**28 a** Nitroglycerin is a vasodilator used to treat angina pectoris because it increases blood flow to the myocardium. When the drug is taken sublingually, the blood pressure can drop within a very few minutes. Because of this, the patient should be advised to sit or lie down when taking the medication. (*Bergersen, p. 170. Rodman and Smith, pp. 372–373.*)

**29 c** The pain associated with acute myocardial infarction is severe and prolonged. Typically the pain occurs in the anterior portion of the chest and can radiate to the arm, neck, teeth, and jaw and is not relieved by nitroglycerin or rest. (*Jones, Dunbar, and Jirovec, pp. 684–685. Luckmann and Sorensen, p. 670.*)

**30 c** One of the changes that occurs on the electrocardiogram is an inversion of the T wave. Inversion of the T wave and elevation of the S-T segment indicate injury and ischemia. (*Jones, Dunbar, and Jirovec, p. 887.*)

**31 d** Enzyme studies have become an important aspect of diagnosing an acute myocardial infarction. Following tissue necrosis, enzymes are released into the circulation. Creatinine phosphokinase (CPK) is released within 6 hours following myocardial infarction and is, therefore, the earliest enzyme to appear. Because CPK is only found in cardiac and skeletal muscle and the brain, it is more cardiospecific than SGOT. (*Jones, Dunbar, and Jirovec, pp. 886–887. Barber, Stokes, and Billings, p. 900. Moidel, Giblin, and Wagner, p. 531.*)

**32 b** While caring for the patient with a myocardial infarction, the physician should be notified if the central venous pressue (CVP) falls below 3 cm $H_2O$. A low CVP reading could indicate shock and circulatory failure. (*Luckmann and Sorensen, pp. 640–641.*)

**33 d** Heparin is an anticoagulant that is inactivated when taken by mouth. The preferred method of administration is intravenous. Because of its rapid onset and short duration of action, it is important that heparin be given promptly at the time specified to maintain an optimum and consistent degree of anticoagulation. (*Asperheim and Eisenhauer, p. 328.*)

**34 c** The antidote for heparin is protamine sulfate. If bleeding occurs in patients receiving heparin, the protamine sulfate neutralizes the excess circulating heparin. (*Rodman and Smith, p. 399.*)

**35 c** The daily dose of heparin is determined by the results of the Lee-White coagulation time. This test measures all the factors involved in the coagulation time. The normal range is 9 to 12 minutes. (*Falconer, Sheridan, et al., p. 317.*)

**36 d** Patients on oral anticoagulants should have regular prothrombin times done to prevent any serious bleeding complications. It is believed that the oral anticoagulants interfere with the manufacture of prothrombin in the liver. (*Asperheim and Eisenhauer, p. 329. Bergersen, p. 202. Rodman and Smith, p. 399.*)

**37 d** Foods high in cholesterol include eggs, shellfish (lobster, crab, shrimp) and organ meats (liver, brains, kidneys, etc.). Fish is comparatively lower in cholesterol. (*Robinson and Lawler, pp. 670–673.*)

**38 a** A falling blood pressure and a narrowing pulse pressure are signs of left-ventricular dysfunction. If arterial blood pressure falls, a compensatory vasoconstriction occurs. As a result the pulse pressure is reduced or narrowed. A narrow pulse pressure indicates a low stroke volume, high peripheral resistance, or both. (*Price and Wilson, p. 317.*)

**39 d** Dyspnea on exertion is one of the first symptoms experienced by the patient with left-sided heart failure. The lung becomes congested as the left ventricle becomes unable to adequately pump blood into the systemic circulation. As the lungs become more engorged, the dyspnea advances to orthopnea. (*Jones, Dunbar, and Jirovec, p. 620. Luckmann and Sorensen, p. 613.*)

**40 d** Rotating tourniquets are used in pulmonary edema to reduce the workload of the heart by decreasing venous return. Initially, the tourniquets are applied to three extremities at a time. Every 15 minutes a tourniquet is removed from one extremity and applied to the extremity with no tourniquet on it. Care should be exercised so that no one extremity is occluded for more than 45 minutes at a time. When the treatment is discontinued, remove one tourniquet at a time to permit the heart to adjust to the increased venous return. (*Jones, Dunbar, and Jirovec, p. 834. Shafer et al., pp. 361–362.*)

**41 c** Aminophylline (theophylline) is a bronchodilator used to relieve the congestion of the bronchioles associated with pulmonary edema. If aminophylline is given too rapidly IV, it can cause severe hypotension. (*Jones, Dunbar, and Jirovec, p. 834.*)

**42 c** To approximate the distance the catheter should be inserted, measure the distance from the tip of the nose to the earlobe. This point is then marked on the catheter with a small piece of tape. (*Henderson and Nite, p. 1093.*)

**43 b** The normal range for central venous pressure is between 5 and 10 cm of water. (*Hamilton, p. 9. Luckmann and Sorensen, p. 621.*)

**44 a** The central venous pressure is elevated in congestive heart failure. Since the heart no longer serves as an adequate pump, the pressure in the right atrium rises as the venous system becomes engorged from inadequate emptying. (*Hamilton, p. 11. Luckmann and Sorensen, p. 621.*)

**45 b** To determine the patency of the central venous pressure line, the fluid in the manometer should fluctuate synchronously with the patient's respirations. The fluid should also rise with coughing and straining. If the fluid remains at a fixed level or fluctuates sluggishly, it could mean that the tip of the catheter is occluded with a blood clot or wedged in the wall of the vessel. (*Hamilton, p. 9.*)

**46 a** Engorgement of the jugular veins of the neck is a sign of congestive heart failure. The nurse can determine this by elevating the head of the bed so that the patient is sitting at a 45° angle. If the patient has congestive heart failure, the veins will remain engorged. (*Luckmann and Sorensen, p. 621.*)

**47 a** Furosemide (Lasix) and ethacrynic acid (Edecrin) are referred to as "powerful" or "potent" diuretics. Their rapid onset in producing diuresis when given intravenously makes them particularly useful in treating edema associated with congestive heart failure and acute pulmonary edema. (*Asperheim and Eisenhauer, p. 450. Bergersen, p. 445. Rodman and Smith, p. 335.*)

**48 a** Bigeminal pulse, anorexia, and blurred vision are symptoms of digitalis toxicity. These symptoms should be reported to the physician. (*Rodman and Smith, p. 348.*)

**49 a** Hypokalemia (potassium deficit) is a common cause of digitalis toxicity. The effect of digitalis on the myocardium is increased as the serum level of potassium decreases. Patients who are taking diuretics along with digitalis preparations are particularly vulnerable to potassium deficit and digitalis toxicity. (*Asperheim and Eisenhauer, p. 308. Bergersen, p. 160.*)

**50 a** The proprietary name for Lanoxin is digoxin. Caution should be exercised by the nurse so that digoxin and digitoxin are not confused. Because of the many errors that have been made, many hospitals prefer using the name Lanoxin instead of digoxin. (*Bergersen, p. 159. Rodman and Smith, p. 344.*)

**51 d** A 100-g serving of puffed rice contains 2 mg of sodium. All the others listed are high in sodium and are therefore not allowed on a low-sodium diet. (*Robinson and Lawler, pp. 642–657. Williams, pp. 660–672.*)

**52 a** A 100-g portion of frozen asparagus contains 1 mg of sodium. Frozen spinach contains 52 mg, frozen peas contain 115 mg, and lima beans contain 129 mg. (*Williams, pp. 660–672.*)

**53 d** Weight loss is an observation that indicates that dietary and diuretic treatment has been successful. Other indications of successful therapy are increased urinary output, decreased venous pressure, absence of neck vein engorgement, and decrease in pitting edema. (*Luckmann and Sorensen, p. 640.*)

**54 b** The pain that occurs in the calf muscle with exercise and that disappears with rest is called "intermittent claudication." The pain is caused by impaired arterial circulation to the contracting muscle. The ischemia and a build-up of lactic acid cause painful spasm of the muscle. (*Jones, Dunbar, and Jirovec, p. 982. Luckmann and Sorensen, p. 806.*)

**55 a** Raynaud's disease affects the arterioles of the extremities. Smoking intensifies the symptoms since the nicotine causes vasoconstriction, which further damages the arterioles of the extremities. (*Luckmann and Sorensen, p. 818.*)

**56 c** Foot care is an important part of the nursing care of patients with peripheral vascular disease. Because of the impaired circulation, minor foot problems can become gangrenous in spite of the best treatment. Preventive care should be practiced by the patient and the nurse. (*Luckmann and Sorensen, p. 810.*)

# UNIT 13
# Nursing care of the patient with a respiratory disorder

**OBJECTIVES**

To answer the questions in this unit, the reader should be able to

1. Identify the structures and the functions of the respiratory system;
2. Describe how the body adapts to damage or injury to the respiratory system;
3. List the signs and symptoms of respiratory disorders;
4. Describe the nursing management of the patient with a respiratory disorder.

## QUESTIONS RELATED TO OBJECTIVES

*Instructions*: Choose the *one best* answer to the following questions.

1. The exchange of oxygen and carbon dioxide within the lungs occurs in the
   a  Bronchiole.
   b  Alveoli.
   c  Pulmonary venule.
   d  Pulmonary arteriole.

2. During normal respirations, the pressure in the intraplural space
   a  Is below atmospheric pressure.
   b  Exceeds atmospheric pressure.
   c  Is equal to atmospheric pressure.
   d  Varies between being below and being above atmospheric pressure.

3. During expiration, the intrapulmonic pressure
   a  Is equal to atmospheric pressure and there is no exchange of air.
   b  Is less than atmospheric pressure and air flows out of the lung.
   c  Is greater than atmospheric pressure and air flows out of the lung.
   d  Is less than atmospheric pressure and air flows into the lung.

4. The substance that reduces the surface tension of the water molecules in the alveoli and thus permits the lung to expand is
   a  Acetylcholine.
   b  Carbonic anhydrase.
   c  Epinephrine.
   d  Surfactant.

**5** The chemical composition of the blood has a major influence on the respiratory center in the brain. Choose those concentrations that stimulate respirations.
  **a** Decreased pH, increased carbon dioxide, and decreased oxygen.
  **b** Decreased pH, decreased carbon dioxide, and increased oxygen.
  **c** Increased pH, decreased carbon dioxide, and increased oxygen.
  **d** Increased pH, increased carbon dioxide, and decreased oxygen.

**6** The normal arterial $P_{CO_2}$ (partial pressure of carbon dioxide) in the arterial circulation is approximately
  **a** 25 to 35 mmHg.
  **b** 35 to 45 mmHg.
  **c** 55 to 65 mmHg.
  **d** 65 to 75 mmHg.

**7** The normal arterial $P_{O_2}$ (partial pressure of oxygen) in the arterial circulation is approximately
  **a** 40 to 50 mmHg.
  **b** 60 to 70 mmHg.
  **c** 80 to 90 mmHg.
  **d** 90 to 100 mmHg.

**8** As an individual ascends to a higher altitude, the body adapts by
  **a** Decreasing ventilation.
  **b** Decreasing cardiac output.
  **c** Increasing production of erythrocytes.
  **d** Increasing urinary output.

**9** Ethan Elber, a 54-year-old man, was admitted to the hospital with emphysema. Symptoms of emphysema include
  **a** Dyspnea on exertion, nonproductive cough, and wheezing on inspiration.
  **b** Dyspnea at rest, productive cough, and thoracic respirations.
  **c** Diaphragmatic respirations, hemoptysis, and purulent sputum.
  **d** Shortness of breath, "barrel" chest, and difficulty in exhaling.

**10** Serum electrophoresis was being done on Mr. Elber, the patient with chronic obstructive pulmonary disease (COPD). In COPD, this test usually shows a deficiency of
  **a** Albumin.
  **b** Gamma globulin.
  **c** Beta globulin.
  **d** Alpha$_1$ antitrypsin.

**11** Mr. Elber is receiving intermittent positive pressure breathing (IPPB) with 1:200 isoproterenol (Isuprel) 0.5 mL tid × 15 minutes. Isuprel is being used to
  **a** Relieve bronchial spasm and loosen bronchial secretions.
  **b** Prevent cardiac arrhythmias and increase cardiac output.
  **c** Suppress cough and dry up secretions.
  **d** Prevent respiratory infections.

**12** During the IPPB therapy, the nurse told Mr. Elber to
  **a** Lie flat in bed.
  **b** Breath deeply through the nose during the procedure.
  **c** Add the medication to the humidifier container.
  **d** Exhale completely before attaching himself to the machine.

**13** While preparing Mr. Elber for discharge, the nurse told him to
- **a** Jog daily to improve alveolar ventilation.
- **b** Drink extra fluids to help liquefy lung secretions.
- **c** Take antibiotics at the first sign of an infection.
- **d** Plan his activities so that the ones that require the most energy are done immediately upon arising.

**14** Breathing retraining should be included in a teaching program for the patient with COPD. The patient should be instructed to
- **a** Inhale deeply through the mouth and exhale slowly through the nose.
- **b** Take deep breaths through the nose and exhale forcefully through the nose.
- **c** Inhale slowly through the mouth and exhale forcefully through pursed lips.
- **d** Inhale slowly through the nose and exhale slowly through pursed lips.

**15** As a result of pulmonary hypertension and hypoxia, the patient with chronic obstructive pulmonary disease developed right-sided ventricular hypertrophy. This physiological adaptation is called
- **a** "Mitral insufficiency."
- **b** "Hypertensive heart disease."
- **c** "Cor pulmonale."
- **d** "Pulmonary stenosis."

**16** In chronic respiratory insufficiency secondary to chronic obstructive pulmonary disease, the recommended oxygen concentration is
- **a** 25 to 35 percent at 1 to 2 L per minute.
- **b** 35 to 45 percent at 6 to 8 L per minute.
- **c** 45 to 55 percent at 8 to 10 L per minute.
- **d** 55 to 65 percent at 10 to 12 L per minute.

**17** In administering oxygen to the patient with COPD, the nurse should observe for carbon dioxide narcosis. Symptoms include

   **a** Nasal congestion, cough, and cyanosis.
   **b** Flushed skin, shallow breathing, and falling blood pressure.
   **c** Ringing in ears, shortness of breath, and tetany.
   **d** Syncope, petit mal seizures, and Cheyne-Stokes respirations.

**18** Which of the following tests should be done to determine the effects of oxygen therapy?

   **a** Blood-gas studies.
   **b** Red blood count and hemoglobin.
   **c** Hematocrit.
   **d** Carbon dioxide combining power.

**19** Intermittent positive pressure breathing is contraindicated in those patients who have

   **a** Atelectasis.
   **b** Pneumonthorax.
   **c** Respiratory insufficiency.
   **d** Respiratory paralysis.

**20** Early signs of mild hypoxia include

   **a** Hypertension, tachycardia, and hyperventilation.
   **b** Bradycardia, pulse deficit, and cyanosis.
   **c** Decreased respirations, hypotension, and chest pains.
   **d** Dyspnea, widening pulse pressure, and bigeminal pulse.

**21** Early symptoms of acute respiratory failure include

   **a** Drowsiness, mental confusion, and cynosis.
   **b** Restlessness, anxiety, and headache.
   **c** Ringing in the ears, diaphoresis, and syncope.
   **d** Blurred vision, vertigo, and somnolence.

**22** Physiological adaptations to respiratory acidosis include
   **a** Excessive retention of carbon dioxide and carbonic acid and decreased arterial pH.
   **b** Deficit of carbon dioxide and carbonic acid and increased arterial pH.
   **c** Excessive retention of bicarbonate and decreased arterial pH.
   **d** Deficit of bicarbonate and increased arterial pH.

**23** While performing endotracheal suctioning, the nurse recognizes that
   **a** Continuous suctioning for 15 to 30 seconds can produce cardiac arrest.
   **b** Tracheal suctioning is a "clean" procedure rather than a sterile procedure.
   **c** The same catheter can be used for nasal and oral suctioning.
   **d** A closed-tip catheter is the most effective type.

**24** Humidification is essential when delivering oxygen to the patient with an endotracheal tube. The nurse should recognize that
   **a** The humidifier reservoir should be refilled daily with tap water.
   **b** Condensed water that collects in the delivery tubing can be returned to the humidifier reservoir.
   **c** The delivery tubing should be disconnected from the patient before the nurse empties the accumulated condensed water.
   **d** The water that collects in the slack loops of tubing helps to humidify the oxygen.

**25** "Atelectasis" can best be defined as
  **a** Chronic dilatation of the bronchioles, causing profuse purulent discharge.
  **b** A collection of air in the pleural cavity, causing collapse of a lung.
  **c** Airlessness of a portion of the lung, causing collapse of the affected tissue.
  **d** Destruction of the alveoli, causing narrowing of the bronchial airway.

**26** A bronchoscopy was done on Anne Kramer to remove a mucus plug from the bronchus. Following the bronchoscopy, the nurse should
  **a** Notify the physician if the patient complains of hoarseness.
  **b** Withhold fluids and food until the gag reflex returns.
  **c** Observe the patient for a delayed reaction to the radiopaque dye.
  **d** Encourage the patient to swallow the large amounts of sputum that are produced.

**27** Tetracycline (Achromycin) is frequently ordered for the patient with a respiratory infection. This medication should be administered
  **a** With milk.
  **b** With an antacid.
  **c** With meals.
  **d** On an empty stomach.

**28** Symptoms of bronchiectasis include
  **a** Dyspnea, cyanosis, and orthopnea.
  **b** Pain on inspiration, dry cough, and elevated temperature.
  **c** Barrel chest, productive cough, and paradoxical respirations.
  **d** Chronic productive cough, purulent sputum, and fetid breath.

**29** Postural drainage was ordered for the patient with bronchiectasis. Choose the statement that best applies to postural drainage.
  **a** Postural drainage can decrease the need for deep tracheobronchial secretions.
  **b** Breathing exercises should not be done with the patient in the postural drainage position.
  **c** When performing postural drainage on more than one lobe, the lower lobes should be drained first.
  **d** Postural drainage is most effective if done after meals.

## ANSWERS, EXPLANATIONS, AND REFERENCES

**1 b** The alveoli are tiny blind sacs that are the actual sites for the exchange of oxygen and carbon dioxide in the lungs. (*Vander, Sherman, and Luciano, p. 284.*)

**2 a** The pressure in the pleural space (the intrapleural pressure) is normally below atmospheric pressure. During normal respirations the pressure varies from −4 to about −6 mmHg. (*Langley, Telford, and Christensen, p. 538.*)

**3 c** During aspiration, the intrapulmonic pressure exceeds atmospheric pressure and air moves out of the lung. (*Langley, Telford, and Christensen, p. 538.*)

**4 d** Surfactant is a substance produced by the alveolar cells. Its primary purpose is to reduce the surface tension of the water molecules and to prevent the lungs from collapsing. (*Langley, Telford, and Christensen, p. 538. Vander, Sherman, and Luciano, p. 295.*)

**5 a** The chemical composition of the blood has a major influence on the respiratory center in the brain. A decreased pH, an increased carbon dioxide concentration, and a decreased oxygen concentration stimulate respirations. (*Langley, Telford, and Christensen, pp. 562–564.*)

**6 b** The normal arterial $P_{CO_2}$ is approximately 35 to 45 mmHg. The average is about 40 mmHg. (*Bushnell, p. 326. Hamilton, p. 166.*)

**7 d** The normal arterial $P_{O_2}$ is approximately 90 to 100 mmHg. The average is about 94 mmHg. (*Bushnell, p. 326. Hamilton, p. 158.*)

**8 c** As the individual ascends to a higher altitude, the body must adapt to the decreased oxygen supply. Initially the body responds by increasing ventilation and cardiac output. Red-blood-cell production is stimulated by the decreased oxygen supply. (*Vander, Sherman, and Luciano, p. 316.*)

**9 d** Symptoms of emphysema include shortness of breath, difficulty exhaling, and barrel chest. The barrel chest develops as a result of pulmonary overdistention and air trapping. (*Luckmann and Sorensen, p. 994.*)

**10 d** If a serum electrophoresis is done on the patient with chronic obstructive pulmonary disease, it shows a deficiency of alpha$_1$-antitrypsin. (*Jones, Dunbar, and Jirovec, p. 1019.*)

**11 a** Isoproteronol (Isuprel) is an andrenergic agent that is used in emphysema to relieve bronchial spasm and loosen bronchial secretions. (*Falconer et al., p. 247.*)

**12 d** IPPB can be utilized to administer medications when the local effect on the lungs is desired. To be most effective the patient should be sitting upright and exhale completely before being attached to the machine. Once the mouthpiece is in place, the patient should be instructed to breathe slowly and deeply to trigger the respirator. In some instances a nose clip may be necessary. (*Bushnell, p. 119. Luckmann and Sorensen, p. 929.*)

**13 b** As a means of liquefying lung secretions, the patient should be encouraged to drink extra fluids. (*Jones, Dunbar, and Jirovec, p. 1021. Shafer et al., p. 567.*)

**14 d** Breathing exercises should be taught to the patient to prevent airway collapse. Pursed-lip breathing is recommended. The patient should be instructed to inhale slowly through the nose, then to exhale slowly through pursed lips. (*Jones, Dunbar, and Jirover, p. 1030. Shafer et al., p. 568.*)

**15 c** Damage to the alveoli results in damage to the pulmonary capillary bed located in the alveoli. As a result there is a chronic hypoxia and a chronic hypercapnia. The body's adaptation to the reduction of space in the pulmonary capillary bed is pulmonary hypertension. This eventually leads to right-sided heart failure, or cor pulmonale. (*Luckmann and Sorensen, p. 993*.)

**16 a** In chronic respiratory insufficiency secondary to chronic obstructive pulmonary disease, low concentrations of oxygen (25 to 35 percent) at a flow rate of 1 to 2 L per minute is recommended. High concentrations of oxygen depress the respiratory center in the brain, and respirations are depressed. However, alveolar hypoventilation becomes more severe resulting in carbon dioxide narcosis. (*Barber et al., p. 838. Luckmann and Sorensen, p. 918. Shafer et al., p. 591*.)

**17 b** If the patient with chronic obstructive pulmonary disease is receiving oxygen, the nurse should carefully observe the patient for carbon dioxide narcosis. Signs and symptoms include flushed skin, shallow breathing, and falling blood pressure. (*Barber et al., p. 830. Luckmann and Sorensen, p. 230*.)

**18 a** To determine the effectiveness of oxygen therapy, blood-gas studies should be taken. (*Jones, Dunbar, and Jirovec, p. 1019. Luckmann and Sorensen, p. 920*.)

**19 b** IPPB is contraindicated in those patients who have pulmonary bleeding, pneumothorax, active tuberculosis, and hyperventilation. (*Luckmann and Sorensen, p. 924*.)

**20 a** The nurse should be aware of the early signs of mild hypoxia so that proper treatment can be initiated. Early signs include hypertension, tachycardia, and increased respiration. (*Luckmann and Sorensen, p. 894*.)

**21 b** Early symptoms of acute respiratory failure include anxiety, headache, and restlessness. The nurse should carefully observe the patient for these symptoms and notify the physician so that therapy can be initiated. (*Luckmann and Sorensen, p. 899*.)

22 a  In respiratory acidosis there is an excessive retention of carbon dioxide and carbonic acid and a decreased arterial pH. (*Luckmann and Sorensen, p. 229.*)

23 a  Prolonged suctioning can produce cardiac arrest. Therefore, continuous suctioning for 15 to 30 seconds should not be done. (*Bushnell, p. 198. Luckmann and Sorensen, p. 932.*)

24 c  While caring for the patient who has an endotracheal tube or a tracheostomy, it is important that the inspired oxygen be humidified. Condensed water tends to accumulate in the slack loops of tubing. Before attempting to empty the tubing of the water, the nurse should first disconnect the tubing so that the excess water does not drain into the respiratory tract. (*Bushnell, p. 199.*)

25 c  "Atelectasis" is airlessness of a portion of a lung, causing that portion of the lung to collapse. The main cause of atelectasis is obstruction of the bronchus by secretions, mucus plugs, bronchospasm, etc. (*Luckmann and Sorensen, p. 942.*)

26 b  Following a bronchoscopy, the nurse should withhold food or fluids until the gag reflex returns. Prior to the procedure, a local topical anesthesia that inhibits the cough and swallowing reflex is administered. (*Luckmann and Sorensen, p. 864. Shafer et al., p. 552.*)

27 c  Tetracycline is an antibiotic that should be given with meals to reduce nausea and vomiting. Patients taking this medication should be told that foods high in calcium (milk and milk products) impair its absorption in the GI tract. (*Asperheim and Eisenhauer, p. 173. Bergersen, p. 477. Jones, Dunbar, and Jirovec, p. 1022.*)

28 d  Symptoms of bronchiectasis include chronic productive cough, purulent sputum, and fetid breath. The bronchial walls lose their elasticity and become permanently dilated. As a result, secretions cannot be adequately re-

moved and are prone to infection. (*Luckmann and Sorensen, p. 945.*)

**29 a** Postural drainage is a therapeutic procedure that is used to remove retained secretions from the lung. If done properly, postural drainage can decrease the need for deep tracheobronchial suction. (*Bushnell, p. 193. Luckmann and Sorensen, p. 910.*)

# UNIT 14

# Nursing care of the patient with a renal disorder

## OBJECTIVES

To answer the questions in this unit, the reader should be able to

1. Identify the components of the nephron;
2. Trace the renal blood flow;
3. List the major functions of the kidney;
4. Describe how the body adapts to renal disorders;
5. List the major signs and symptoms of specific renal disorders;
6. Recognize the nurse's role in caring for patients having specific diagnostic tests;
7. Describe the nursing management of the patient with a renal disorder;
8. Describe the care of the patient having dialysis treatment.

## QUESTIONS RELATED TO OBJECTIVES

*Instructions*: Choose the *one best* answer to the following questions.

1. The functional unit of the kidney is
   a   The glomerulus.
   b   The renal tubule.
   c   Bowman's capsule.
   d   The nephron.

2. The network of capillaries that is a component of the nephron is called
   a   "The glomerulus."
   b   "The afferent arterioles."
   c   "The efferent arterioles."
   d   "Bowman's capsule."

3. Choose the statement that best applies to vascular supply of the kidney.
   a   The peritubular capillaries lie within Bowman's capsule.
   b   The interlobular arterioles terminate in the glomeruli and re-form into interlobular venules.
   c   The afferent arterioles terminate in the glomeruli, then re-form into the efferent venule.
   d   The afferent arterioles terminate in the glomerular capillaries and re-form into the efferent arterioles.

4. Choose the statement that is most correct.
   a   The filtrate that passes through the glomerulus into Bowman's capsule is essentially protein-free.
   b   The pressure in the glomerular capillary is equivalent to about 12 mmHg.
   c   The normal glomerular filtration rate is approximately 30 mL per minute.
   d   When the glomerular filtrate enters Bowman's capsule it is more concentrated than plasma.

5 The portion of the nephron responsible for selective reabsorption is
   a The glomerulus.
   b Bowman's capsule.
   c The proximal tubule.
   d The distal tubule.

6 Secretion of hydrogen ions and potassium ions occurs in the
   a Glomerulus.
   b Loop of Henle.
   c Descending tubule.
   d Distal tubule.

7 The substance produced by the kidney which plays an important role in stimulating red-blood-cell production in the bone marrow is
   a Insulin.
   b Renin.
   c Erythropoietin.
   d Folic acid.

8 Normal blood urea nitrogen (BUN) ranges from
   a 0.8 to 1.4 mg/100 mL.
   b 5 to 25 mg/100 mL.
   c 50 to 75 mg/100 mL.
   d 80 to 120 mg/100 mL.

9 If fluid intake is normal, the normal specific gravity of urine is approximately
   a 1.001 to 1.010.
   b 1.016 to 1.022.
   c 1.030 to 1.042.
   d 1.040 to 1.050.

**10** While reading the patient's chart, the nurse notices that the patient has oliguria with a fixed specific gravity of urine of 1.010. This means that the patient
   **a** Is dehydrated and needs more fluids.
   **b** Is adapting adequately to decreased fluid intake.
   **c** Has hypervolemia and fluid intake should be decreased.
   **d** Has severe renal failure.

**11** Kidney-function tests that are indirect measurements of glomerular function include the
   **a** Phenolsulfonphthalein (PSP) test, intravenous pyelogram, and sodium excretion tests.
   **b** Urine concentration tests, specific gravity, and renal angiograms.
   **c** Serum creatinine, blood urea nitrogen, and renal clearance tests.
   **d** Urine dilution tests, renal biopsy, and x-rays.

**12** While preparing the patient for an intravenous pyelogram (IVP) the nurse
   **a** Told the patient that the only requirement for the test is an intravenous injection of a radiopaque substance.
   **b** Recognized that the test should not be performed on patients with a known sensitivity to iodine.
   **c** Told the patient to report to the physician any sensations of warmth or a salty taste in the mouth.
   **d** Told the patient that a catheter is threaded into the femoral artery.

**13** Aftercare of the patient having a renal biopsy includes
   **a** Keeping the patient NPO for 24 hours after the biopsy.
   **b** Positioning the patient on the right side for 8 hours.
   **c** Encouraging the patient to cough and deep-breathe during and after the procedure.
   **d** Maintaining the patient on bed rest for 24 hours after the biopsy.

**14** To collect a clean voided specimen for culture on a female patient, the nurse
  **a** Cleansed the meatus and the surrounding area using a fresh sterile cleansing sponge for each downward stroke.
  **b** Collected the specimen as soon as the urinary stream was initiated.
  **c** Used a clean, dry receptacle to collect the urine.
  **d** Used a sterile catheter to collect the urine.

**15** Nancy Murray is a 21-year-old college student who has been admitted to the hospital with a diagnosis of acute glomerulonephritis. While doing a nursing history, the nurse would expect that Nancy would complain of
  **a** Edema and increased urinary output.
  **b** Loss of weight and increased urinary output.
  **c** Edema and decreased urinary output.
  **d** Loss of weight and decreased urinary output.

**16** Choose the statement that best applies to acute glomerulonephritis. Acute glomerulonephritis
  **a** Is an ascending infection from the lower urinary tract.
  **b** Is generally preceded by an upper respiratory streptococcal infection.
  **c** Is associated with renal calculi.
  **d** Is most commonly caused by fecal contamination into the urethra.

**17** In acute glomerulonephritis there is inflammation of the glomeruli of both kidneys. As a result, urinary findings include
  **a** Proteinuria and hematuria.
  **b** Bacteriuria and hematuria.
  **c** Pyuria and albuminuria.
  **d** Bacteriuria and pyuria.

**18** The most common microbiological organism causing infections of the urinary tract is
   **a** *Proteus vulgaris.*
   **b** *Streptococcus.*
   **c** *Enterococcus.*
   **d** *Escherichia coli.*

**19** Typical urinary findings seen in acute pyelonephritis include
   **a** Myoglobinuria and white-cell casts.
   **b** Pyuria and bacteriuria.
   **c** Hematuria and albuminuria.
   **d** Proteinuria and red-cell casts.

**20** While caring for Lisa, a patient with acute pyelonephritis, the nurse should recognize that
   **a** All urine will have to be strained and measured.
   **b** Antibiotic therapy will be discontinued as soon as the urine culture is negative.
   **c** Weekly catheterized urine and cultures will be ordered.
   **d** Forcing fluids is an important part of the care.

**21** Lisa is receiving Azo-Gantrisin. The nurse explained to Lisa that
   **a** It should be administered with an antacid to enhance the rate of absorption.
   **b** Fluids should be restricted to assure maximum effect in the kidneys.
   **c** It gives the urine an orange-red color and she should not become alarmed when this happens.
   **d** It is a combination of a sulfonamide and an antibiotic that has more sustained action.

**22** Cephalexin monohydrate (Keflex) is another medication used to treat urinary tract infections. The nurse should recognize that Keflex
  **a** Can be administered only parenterally.
  **b** Should not be given with meals since it decreases absorption.
  **c** Causes a false positive reaction for glucose when testing the urine with Clinitest tablets.
  **d** Is a sulfonamide with bacteriostatic and bacteriocidal actions.

**23** Choose the statement that should be included in a teaching program for a patient with cystitis.
  **a** Fluids should be restricted to reduce the work load of the urinary tract.
  **b** The bladder should be emptied regularly to avoid bladder stasis.
  **c** Sexual activity is not related to the high incidence of cystitis in women.
  **d** Men do not respond well to treatment because the male urethra is longer than the female.

**24** The earliest sign of acute renal failure is
  **a** Widening pulse pressure.
  **b** Postural hypotension.
  **c** Decreased urinary output.
  **d** Uremic frost.

**25** Choose the statement that best applies to the care of the patient during the oliguric phase of acute renal failure.
  **a** Fluids should be encouraged during this period so that the tubules can become unplugged.
  **b** Increased urinary output is an ominous sign because of the resulting hypovolemia.
  **c** The patient should be observed for hypokalemia because of the damage to the renal tubules.
  **d** Vital signs should be monitored since an increase in the depth and rate of respirations could be a sign of metabolic acidosis.

26 During the oliguric phase of acute renal failure, many substances normally excreted in the urine are retained in the blood. The retention of which of the following will most likely cause serious cardiac arrhythmias?
   a  Sulfate.
   b  Phosphate.
   c  Magnesium.
   d  Potassium.

27 In acute renal failure, if hyperkalemia is severe, ion-exchange resins can be administered. An example of an ion-exchange resin used to lower potassium levels is
   a  Cholestyramine resin (Cuemid).
   b  Sodium polystyrene sulfonate (Kayexalate).
   c  Carbacrylamine resin (Carbo-resin).
   d  Acetazolamide (Diamox).

28 The anemia associated with renal failure is due to a deficiency of
   a  Iron.
   b  Erythropoietin.
   c  Folic acid.
   d  Vitamin $B_{12}$.

29 Because of the decrease in platelet production associated with renal failure, the patient should be observed very closely for
   a  Shortness of breath on exertion.
   b  Blood reactions when receiving blood transfusions.
   c  Spontaneous gastrointestinal bleeding.
   d  Signs and symptoms of vitamin K deficiency.

30 In chronic renal failure, the damage to the kidneys causes impaired excretion of hydrogen ions and impaired manufacture of bicarbonate. As a result, the patient develops
   a  Respiratory acidosis.
   b  Respiratory alkalosis.
   c  Metabolic acidosis.
   d  Metabolic alkalosis.

# NURSING CARE OF THE PATIENT WITH A RENAL DISORDER

**31** While planning nursing care for the patient with chronic renal failure, the nurse recognizes that
   **a** Hypotension frequently accompanies chronic renal failure.
   **b** Hypokalemia occurs in chronic renal failure because of tubular destruction.
   **c** In chronic renal failure, the patient's resistance to infection is lowered.
   **d** Hypercalcemia develops because of increased absorption from the intestines.

**32** Choose the group of symptoms related to the end stage of renal failure (uremia).
   **a** Edema, hypertension, and convulsions.
   **b** Hypertension, polyuria, and pruritus.
   **c** Pruritus, hypotension, and headache.
   **d** Oliguria, convulsions, and alkalosis.

**33** In caring for the patient on peritoneal dialysis, the nurse recognizes that
   **a** The outflow fluid is blood-tinged during the entire exchange.
   **b** The patient is placed on NPO for the entire procedure.
   **c** The dialysate is refrigerated until ready for use.
   **d** Vital signs should be monitored since hypotension can occur as the blood volume is reduced.

**34** During the inflow phase of peritoneal dialysis, the patient complained of abdominal discomfort and a "feeling of fullness." The nurse
   **a** Notified the physician and requested an analgesic for pain.
   **b** Decreased the rate of administration of the dialysate solution.
   **c** Lowered the head of the bed so that the fluid would be more evenly dispersed.
   **d** Removed the peritoneal catheter and notified the physician.

**35** When the inflow phase of peritoneal dialysis was completed, the nurse
   **a** Kept the inflow tube open, opened the outflow tube, and let it drain by gravity.
   **b** Clamped the inflow tube, opened the outflow tube, and attached it to low suction.
   **c** Clamped the inflow tube, allowed the fluid to remain in the cavity for 30 to 60 minutes, then opened the outflow tube to gravity drainage.
   **d** Clamped the inflow tube, opened the outflow tube, and allowed it to drain by gravity.

**36** While doing dietary teaching for the patient with chronic renal failure who is on a controlled protein, sodium, and potassium diet, the nurse pointed out that
   **a** Saltwater fish contains more sodium than freshwater fish does.
   **b** Foods containing essential proteins are omitted.
   **c** The use of butter, margarine, oils, and heavy cream is restricted.
   **d** Foods cooked in large quantities of water lose some of their potassium to the cooking liquid.

**37** The Giordano-Giovanetti diet is sometimes prescribed in the terminal stage of renal disease. Choose the statement that best applies.
   **a** Almost the entire daily protein allowance is derived from one egg and $6\frac{1}{2}$ oz of milk.
   **b** Meat and fish are used as a source of high-biological-value protein.
   **c** Legumes are used in place of animal protein.
   **d** No protein is allowed on the diet.

**38** The following statements apply to the procedures used to gain access to the patient's bloodstream during hemodialysis. Choose the most correct statement.
   **a** The problem of clotting is the main disadvantage of the internal arteriovenous fistula.
   **b** If the connecting tube of the external arteriovenous shunt becomes separated, fatal blood loss can occur.
   **c** Each time the patient goes on hemodialysis, a venipuncture is required for the external arteriovenous shunt.
   **d** Daily dressing changes are required for an internal arteriovenous fistula.

**39** The patient for whom you are caring has an external arteriovenous shunt for hemodialysis. The nurse should notify the physician if
   **a** The flow of blood can be felt in the external cannula.
   **b** Audible bruit is heard with a stethoscope in the venous portion of the cannula.
   **c** Blood flow can be observed through the cannula.
   **d** The fluid flowing through the cannula is straw-colored.

**40** Decreasing blood flow through the arteriovenous shunt or fistula can result in clotting. All the following can cause clotting *except*
   **a** Taking blood pressure on the arm that has the shunt or fistula.
   **b** Phlebitis from venipunctures of the involved vein.
   **c** Infection of the shunt or fistula.
   **d** Activity during the hemodialysis treatment.

**41** Disequilibrium syndrome can occur during the hemodialysis treatment. The symptoms that occur are due to
   **a** Heparinization needed to prevent blood from clotting.
   **b** Rapid removal of urea nitrogen and electrolytes from the blood in relation to their removal from the brain.
   **c** Hypokalemia developing as the potassium is being diffused from the blood.
   **d** The administration of incorrect dialysate solution during the treatment.

**42** Signs and symptoms of disequilibrium syndrome include
   a  Confusion, nausea and vomiting, and convulsions.
   b  Bleeding from body orifices, shock, and apprehension.
   c  Hypertension, edema, and headache.
   d  Rapid respirations, coma, and bradycardia.

## ANSWERS, EXPLANATIONS, AND REFERENCES

**1 d**  The functional unit of the kidney is the nephron. The glomerulus and the renal tubule are its two major components. (*Langley, Telford, and Christensen, p. 670.*)

**2 a**  The network of capillaries that is a major component of the nephron is called the "glomerulus." (*Langley, Telford, and Christensen, p. 670.*)

**3 d**  As blood enters the kidney via the renal artery, it ultimately subdivides into afferent arterioles. These arterioles enter the glomerulus, which are tufts of capillaries enclosed in Bowman's capsule. Instead of these capillaries forming venules, as they do elsewhere in the body, the glomerular capillaries form efferent arterioles. The efferent areterioles subdivide again into the peritubular capillaries. This entire process is a unique feature of the kidneys. (*Langley, Telford, and Christensen, p. 670. Vander, Sherman, and Luciano, p. 322.*)

**4 a**  As blood filters from the glomerular capillaries into Bowman's capsule, it is essentially protein-free. The capillaries are permeable to water and solutes of small molecular size but impermeable to the plasma proteins (large molecules). The filtrate contains everything plasma does, with the exception of proteins. (*Langley, Telford, and Christensen, p. 679. Vander, Sherman, and Luciano, p. 325.*)

**5 c**  Selective reabsorption of potassium, sodium, glucose, amino acids, etc., takes place in the proximal tubules. Actually, of the 125 mL of glomerular filtrate that passes through the proximal tubules, about 100 mL is reabsorbed. As the remaining 25 mL continues through the distal tubules, more reabsorption takes place, so that by the time the filtrate reaches the kidney pelvis, 1 mL remains. (*Langley, Telford, and Christensen, p. 681.*)

**6 d** The distal tubules of the nephron secrete a variety of substances, such as potassium, hydrogen, and ammonia. Foreign substances, such as medication and drugs, are also secreted through the distal tubules. (*Beland, p. 479. Stroot, Lee, and Schaper, p. 123. Vander, Sherman, and Luciano, p. 353.*)

**7 c** Erythropoietin, a substance produced by the kidney, plays an important role in stimulating red-blood-cell production in the marrow. If the supply of oxygen is decreased, the kidneys release erythropoietin into the blood. It is then transported to the bone marrow, where it stimulates red-blood-cell production. As a result of the increase in RBCs, more oxygen is transported to the cells. (*Langley, Telford, and Christensen, p. 379, Price and Wilson, p. 492.*)

**8 b** The normal range for blood urea nitrogen is 5 to 25 mg/100 mL. Elevations usually indicate impaired renal function. (*Beland, p. 527.*)

**9 b** The specific gravity of urine varies from 1.016 to 1.022 when fluid intake is normal. This figure will vary slightly. (*Henderson and Nite, p. 497.*)

**10 d** Throughout a 24-hour period, the specific gravity of urine varies. Fluid intake alters the specific gravity of urine. Normally the specific gravity of urine is higher as the urine becomes more concentrated. If the urine is dilute, the specific gravity is lower. Increasing fluid intake decreases the specific gravity of urine. If a patient has oliguria and a fixed specific gravity of about 1.010, this indicates severe renal failure. (*Beland, p. 527.*)

**11 c** Kidney-function tests that are indirect measurements of glomerular function include serum creatinine, blood urea nitrogen, and renal clearance tests. (*Moidel, Giblin, and Wagner, p. 654. Shafer et al., p. 427.*)

**12 b** While preparing the patient for an IVP, the nurse should recognize that the test is not done on patients who are sensitive to iodine. A reaction to the dye would be manifest by tachycardia, diaphoresis, respiratory distress, and urticaria. (*Luckmann and Sorensen, p. 721. Shafer et al., p. 431.*)

**13 d** Most physicians recommend that the patient who has had a renal biopsy should be kept on bed rest for 24 hours. If there is any visible blood in the urine, the patient should be observed carefully and encouraged to stay in bed. (*Jones, Dunbar, and Jirovec, p. 510. Moidel, Giblin, and Wagner, p. 658. Shafer et al., p. 434.*)

**14 a** A voided specimen can be used for culture if asepsis is maintained to collect the specimen. A sterile urine-collection receptacle, sterile cotton balls or sponges, and an antiseptic cleansing solution are used. When cleansing the urinary meatus and surrounding area of the female patient, one hand is used to separate the labia. The other hand is used to cleanse the area. A fresh, sterile cleansing sponge is used for each downward stroke and then is discarded. (*Shafer et al., p. 427.*)

**15 c** Symptoms of acute glomerulonephritis include edema and decreased urinary output. These symptoms probably occur because the glomerular filtration rate is depressed, causing decreased excretion of water, sodium, and nitrogenous waste products. Increased aldosterone also influences the retention of sodium and water. (*Price and Wilson, pp. 525–526.*)

**16 b** Acute glomerulonephritis is often preceded by an upper respiratory streptococcal infection. Most authorities feel that the inflammation that develops in the glomeruli of the kidney is caused by an autoimmune response to streptococcal toxins. (*Barber, Stokes, and Billings, p. 744. Jones, Dunbar, and Jirovec, p. 516.*)

**17 a** Inflammation of the glomerulus, as seen in acute glomerulonephritis, causes the basement membrane of the capillaries to become more permeable to the filtration of proteins and red blood cells. As a result, the urinary findings include proteinuria and hematuria. (*Jones, Dunbar, and Jirovec, p. 516. Luckmann and Sorensen, p. 728. Moidel, Giblin, and Wagner, p. 653.*)

**18 d** The most common microbiological organism causing infections of the urinary tract is the *Escherichia coli* (*E. coli*). The others listed can cause infections, but to a lesser degree. (*Barber, Stokes, and Billings, p. 732. Jones, Dunbar, and Jirovec, p. 518. Moidel, Giblin, and Wagner, p. 662.*)

**19 b** Typical urinary findings in acute pyelonephritis include bacteriuria and pyuria. The urine may have a foul smell and appear cloudy. (*Luckmann and Sorensen, p. 725. Moidel, Giblin, and Wagner, p. 653, p. 663. Shafer et al., p. 453.*)

**20 d** The nurse should recognize that forcing fluids is an important aspect of care for the patient with acute pyelonephritis. The more dilute the urine, the less burning it will cause on urination. Furthermore, the extra fluids will help to reduce the temperature, flush out the bacteria in the urinary tract, and decrease the workload of the kidneys. (*Jones, Dunbar, and Jirovec, p. 520. Luckmann and Sorensen, p. 725.*)

**21 c** Azo-Gantrisin is a combination of sulfisoxizole and phenazopyridine hydrocholride (Pyridium). The sulfisoxizole provides bacteriostatic action, and Pyridium has analgesic action on the inflamed mucosa. Pyridium causes the urine to become orange-red. (*Bergersen, p. 471.*)

**22 c** Cephalexin monohydrate (Keflex) is a semisynthetic cephalosporin antibiotic that is especially useful in treating urinary tract infections. It can be given orally and may be given with meals. The nurse should recognize that the cephalosporins (Keflex, Keflin, Kefzol) can cause a false positive reaction for glucose when the urine is tested with Clinitest tablets or Benedict's solution. Tes-tape or Combistix can be substituted. (*Asperheim and Eisenhauer, p. 180.*)

**23 b** In planning a teaching program for the patient with cystitis, the nurse should point out that bladder stasis should be avoided because the overdistention of the bladder from retention makes it more vulnerable to infection. Patients should be told to empty the bladder regularly. (*Barber, Stokes, and Billings. p. 732.*)

**24 c** The earliest sign of impending renal failure is a decrease in the urinary output. The nurse must be alert to decrease in urinary output and notify the physician once that assessment has been made. (*Luckmann and Sorensen, p. 731. Stroot, Lee, and Schaper, p. 123.*)

**25 d** During the oliguric phase of renal failure, urinary output is severely reduced. As a result, there is an accumulation of metabolically produced acids in the blood. As the pH decreases, the respiratory center in the brain is stimulated. This increase in the depth and rate of respirations can be detected while the nurse is monitoring vital signs. (*Jones, Dunbar, and Jirovec, p. 500.*)

**26 d** Hyperkalemia (increased serum potassium) can develop during the oliguric phase of acute renal failure. If this occurs, patients should be carefully observed for serious cardiac arrhythmias that can lead to cardiac arrest. (*Jones, Dunbar, and Jirovec, p. 498. Stroot, Lee, and Schaper, p. 128.*)

**27 b** Kayexalate is a substance that can be used in the treatment of hyperkalemia. They are given orally and work in the gastrointestinal tract by exchanging sodium ions for potassium ions. As a result potassium is excreted in the feces. (*Asperheim and Eisenhauer, p. 461. Shafer et al., p. 465.*)

**28 b** Erythropoietin is normally manufactured by the kidney. In renal failure, there is a deficiency of this substance. As a result the patient becomes anemic. (*Jones, Dunbar, and Jirovec, p. 501. Moidel, Giblin, and Wagner, p. 673.*)

**29 c** Patients with renal failure have a decreased production of platelets. There are many theories concerning the cause of this defect. The important point to remember is that patients have bleeding problems associated with the decrease in platelets. They should be observed for spontaneous bleeding in the gastrointestinal tract. (*Jones, Dunbar, and Jirovec, p. 501. Moidel, Giblin, and Wagner, p. 673.*)

**30 c** One of the functions of the kidney is to maintain the acid-base balance. If the pH of the blood is too acid, the kidney tubules are capable of secreting the excess hydrogen ions into the urine or of reabsorbing more bicarbonate. In chronic renal failure, the damaged kidney is unable to maintain this function. As a result the patient is more prone to develop metabolic acidosis since the excretion of acid and reabsorption of bicarbonate are impaired. (*Moidel, Giblin, and Wagner, p. 672. Shafer et al., p. 470.*)

**31 c** Patients with chronic renal failure are more susceptible to infections. Because of this, the nurse should take precautions to prevent infections and to teach the patient concerning methods of preventing infections. (*Jones, Dunbar, and Jirovec, p. 512. Shafer et al., p. 473.*)

**32 a** In the end stage of chronic renal failure (uremia), many systems of the body are involved. Edema results from the retention of sodium; hypertension probably results from increased extracellular fluid and increase in renin. Convulsions result as the nephrotoxins accumulate. (*Jones, Dunbar, and Jirovec, pp. 507–508, Luckmann and Sorensen, p. 730. Moidel, Giblin, and Wagner, pp. 668–674.*)

**33 d** The nurse caring for the patient on peritoneal dialysis should monitor the vital signs at frequent intervals. As the blood volume is reduced, the blood pressure is lowered. Severe hypotension should be reported to the physician. (*Luckmann and Sorensen, p. 734. Shafer et al., p. 479.*)

**34 b** Abdominal discomfort and a feeling of fullness are complaints that some patients have during the inflow phase of peritoneal dialysis. This can be minimized by warming the dialyzing fluid before administration or by decreasing the rate of administration of the inflow fluid. The physician should be notified if the pain persists. (*Henderson and Nite, p. 1290. Jones, Dunbar, and Jirovec, p. 1290.*)

**35 c** To assure that the transfer of solutes and water (dialysis) will occur across the peritoneal membrane, the dialysate should remain in the peritoneal cavity for 30 to 60 minutes before one opens the outflow tube to gravity drainage. (*Henderson and Nite, p. 1291. Jones, Dunbar, and Jirovec, p. 504. Moidel, Giblin, and Wagner, p. 684.*)

**36 d** When teaching the patient who is on a controlled protein, sodium, and potassium diet, the nurse should be aware of some of the factors that modify preparation of food. For example, cutting food into small pieces before cooking reduces the potassium content. In addition, using large amount of water to cook the food reduces the potassium content. (*Robinson and Lawler, pp. 558–559.*)

**37 a** The Giordano-Giovanetti diet can be used in the terminal stages of renal diseases as a means of reducing the BUN. High-biologic-value proteins, such as eggs and milk, contain essential amino acids. Other protein-containing foods are sharply restricted. One egg and $6\frac{1}{2}$ oz of milk are allowed daily. Since the protein is so restricted on this diet, it is believed that the body will utilize excess urea to synthesize nonessential amino acids. This diet is extremely difficult for patients to follow. (*Howard and Herbold, p. 401.*)

**38 b** Some disadvantages of the external arteriovenous shunt are the high risk of clotting and infection. However, the main disadvantage is that the connecting tube can become separated. Then fatal blood loss can occur. Venipuncture is not required to gain access to the bloodstream. (*Jones, Dunbar, and Jirovec, pp. 513–514.*)

**39 d** If the fluid passing through the cannula of the external arteriovenous shunt is straw-colored, this indicates that the blood has clotted and has separated. The physician should be notified immediately, since it may be possible to restore the patency of the shunt. (*Shafer et al., p. 476.*)

**40 d** Clotting can be caused by decreasing the blood flow through the shunt or fistula. Taking of blood pressure on the affected arm, phlebitis from withdrawing blood via a venipuncture of the involved vein, and infection of the shunt or fistula can cause clotting. Activity during hemodialysis treatment does not lead to clotting. (*Shafer et al., p. 475.*)

**41 b** Disequilibrium syndrome is a group of symptoms that occurs during hemodialysis treatment. It occurs when urea nitrogen and electrolytes are removed from the blood too rapidly in relation to their removal from the brain. (*Jones, Dunbar, and Jirovec, p. 514. Moidel, Giblin, and Wagner, p. 681. Shafer et al., p. 477.*)

**42 a** Signs and symptoms of disequilibrium syndrome are caused by fluid being pulled into the brain. The cerebral edema that results leads to confusion, restlessness, nausea and vomiting, and convulsions. (*Moidel, Giblin, and Wagner, p. 681. Shafer et al., p. 477.*)

# Bibliography

Andreoli, Kathleen G., Virginia Hunn Fowkes, Douglas P. Zipes, and Andrew G. Wallace: *Comprehensive Cardiac Care*, 3rd ed., Mosby, St. Louis, 1975.

Asperheim, Mary K., and Laurel A. Eisenhauer: *The Pharmacologic Basis of Patient Care*, 3rd ed., Saunders, Philadelphia, 1977.

Barber, Janet Miller, Lillian G. Stokes, and Diane McGovern Billings: *Adult and Child Care—A Client Approach to Nursing*, 2d ed., Mosby, St. Louis, 1977.

Beland, Irene, and Joyce Y. Passos: *Clinical Nursing: Patho-Physiological and Psychological Approach*, 3rd ed., Macmillan, New York, 1975.

Bergersen, Betty S.: *Pharmacology in Nursing*, 13th ed., Mosby, St. Louis, 1976.

Bruya, Margaret Auld, and Rose Homan Bolin: "Epilepsy: A Controllable Disease," *American Journal of Nursing*, **76**(3): 388–397, 1976.

Bushnell, Sharon S.: *Respiratory Intensive Care Nursing*, 1st ed., Beth Israel Hospital, Boston, 1973.

Byrne, Marjorie L., and Lida F. Thompson: *Key Concepts for the Study and Practice of Nursing*, Mosby, St. Louis, 1972.

Carter, Frances Monet: *Psychosocial Nursing*, 1st ed., Macmillan, New York, 1976.

Falconer, Mary A., Eleanor Sheridan, H. Robert Patterson, and Edward A. Gustafson: *The Drug, The Nurse and The Patient*, 6th ed., Saunders, Philadelphia, 1978.

Fischbach, Frances Talaska: "Easing Adjustment to Parkinson's Disease," *American Journal of Nursing*, **78**(1): 66–69, 1978.

Fox, John P., Carrie E. Hall, and Lila R. Elveback: *Epidemiology, Man, and Disease*, Macmillan, New York, 1971.

Guyton, Arthur: *A Textbook of Medical Physiology*, 4th ed., Saunders, Philadelphia, 1971.

Hamilton, Ardith: *Selected Subjects for Critical Care Nurses*, Mountain Press, Missoula, Mont., 1976.

Henderson, Virginia, and Gladys Nite: *Principles and Practice of Nursing*, 6th ed., Macmillan, New York, 1978.

Howard, Rosanne B., and Nancie Harvey Herbold: *Nutrition in Clinical Care*, McGraw-Hill, New York, 1978.

Jones, Dorothy A., Claire Ford Dunbar, and Mary Marmoll Jirovec: *Medical-Surgical Nursing*, McGraw-Hill, New York, 1978.

*Journal of the American Medical Association: Standards of Cardiopulmonary Resusitation (CPR) and Emergency Cardiac Care (ECC)*, **227**(7), February 18, 1974 (supplement).

Kübler-Ross, Elisabeth: *On Death and Dying*, Macmillan, New York, 1969.

Krause, Marie V., and Martha A. Hunscher: *Food, Nutrition and Diet Therapy*, 5th ed., Saunders, Philadelphia, 1972.

Langley, L. L., Ira R. Telford, and John B. Christensen: *Dynamic Anatomy and Physiology*, 4th ed., McGraw-Hill, New York, 1974.

Leahy, Kathleen M., M. Marguerite Cobb, and Mary C. Jones: *Community Health Nursing*, 3rd ed., McGraw-Hill, New York, 1977.

Luckmann, Joan, and Karen Creason Sorensen: *Medical-Surgical Nusing—A Psychophysiologic Approach*, Saunders, Philadelphia, 1974.

Massachusetts General Hospital: *A Manual of Nursing Procedures*, Little, Brown, Boston, 1975.

Matheney, Ruth V., and Mary Topalis: *Psychiatric Nursing*, 6th ed., Mosby, St. Louis, 1974.

Mereness, Dorothy A., and Cecelia Monat Taylor: *Essentials of Psychiatric Nursing*, 9th ed., Mosby, St. Louis, 1974.

Metheny, Norma Milligan, and W. D. Snively, Jr.: *Nurse's Handbook of Fluid Balance*, 2d ed., Lippincott, Philadelphia, 1974.

Mitchell, Pamela H.: *Concepts Basic to Nursing*, 2d ed., McGraw-Hill, New York, 1977.

Moidel, Harriet C., Elizabeth Giblin, and Bernice Wagner: *Nursing Care of the Patient with Medical-Surgical Disorders*, 2d ed., McGraw-Hill, New York, 1976.

Passman, Jerome, and Constance D. Drummond: *The EKG—Basic Techniques for Interpretation*, McGraw-Hill, New York, 1976.

Phibbs, Brendan: *The Human Heart—A Guide to Heart Disease*, 3rd ed., Mosby, St. Louis, 1975.

*Physician's Desk Reference*, 32d ed., Medical Economics Co., Oradell, N.J., 1978.

Pluckhan, Margaret: *Human Communication—The Matrix of Nursing*, McGraw-Hill, New York, 1978.

Price, Sylvia, and Lorraine Wilson: *Pathophysiology—Clinical Concepts of Disease Processes*, McGraw-Hill, New York, 1978.

Robinson, Corinne H., and Marilyn Lawler: *Normal and Therapeutic Nutrition*, 15th ed., Macmillan, New York, 1977.

Rodman, Morton J., and Dorothy W. Smith: *Clinical Pharmacology in Nursing*, Lippincott, Philadelphia, 1974.

Rossman, Maureen, Rosemary Slavin, and Edwin Taft: "Pheresis Therapy: Patient Care," *American Journal of Nursing*, **77**(7): 1135–1141, 1977.

Sanderson, Richard G.: *The Cardiac Patient—A Comprehensive Approach*, Saunders, Philadelphia, 1972.

Saxton, Dolores F., Norma H. Ercolano, and John F. Walter: *Programmed Instruction in Artithmetic, Dosages and Solutions*, 4th ed., Mosby, St. Louis, 1977.

———, and Patricia A. Hyland: *Planning and Implementing Nursing Intervention*, Mosby, St. Louis, 1975.

Seyle, Hans: *The Stress of Life*, McGraw-Hill, New York, 1956.

Shafer, Kathleen N., Janet R. Sawyer, Audrey M. McCluskey, Edna Lifgren Beck, and Wilma J. Phipps: *Medical-Surgical Nursing*, 6th ed., Mosby, St. Louis, 1975.

Sherman, Jacques L., Jr., and Sylvia Kleiman Fields: *Guide to Patient Evaluation*, Medical Examination Publishing Co., Flushing, N.Y., 1976.

Sierra-Franco, Miriam Hoglund: *Therapeutic Communication in Nursing*, McGraw-Hill, New York, 1978.

Snively, W. D., Jr., and Donna Beshear: *Textbook of Pathophysiology*, Lippincott, Philadelphia, 1972.

Stone, Brenda Hempill, "Computerized Transaxial Brain Scan," *American Journal of Nursing*, **77**(10): 1601–1604, 1977.

Stroot, Viola R., Carla Lee, and C. Ann Schaper: *Fluids and Electrolytes—A Practical Approach*, 2d ed., David Publications, Worcester, Mass., 1977.

Sweetwood, Hannelore: *Nursing in the Intensive Respiratory Care Unit*, Springer Publishing Co., New York, 1977.

Vander, Arthur J., James Sherman, and Dorothy S. Luciano: *The Mechanism of Body Function*, 2d ed., McGraw-Hill, New York, 1975.

Williams, Sue Rodwell: *Nutrition and Diet Therapy*, 3rd ed., Mosby, *St. Louis*, 1977.